Workouts in Intermediate Microeconomics

Theodore C. Bergstrom

Hal R. Varian

University of Michigan

W. W. Norton & Company • New York • London

FIRST EDITION

ISBN 0-393-95577-X

W. W. Norton & Company, Inc., 500 Fifth Avenue, New York, N.Y. 10110
W. W. Norton Ltd., 37 Great Russell Street, London WC1B 3NU

4 5 6 7 8 9 0

Contents

Preface

Persons or objects that are held in low esteem are often renamed in hopes of making them less unpopular. Undertakers are called morticians and then funeral directors. Schoolteachers are called instructors and then educators. Exercise books become workbooks and then study guides. But if the old reality doesn't change, the new name eventually becomes as disagreeable as the old, and another euphemism must be sought. This "workout book" is really an exercise book. But anyone who has endured a dozen or more years of school has been tormented by so many hopelessly insipid and boring "exercise books" as to no longer notice the apt metaphor of exercise in "exercise book." In this book we try to devise mental "workouts" that are lively stimuli for economics students who want to develop skill and agility in thinking about economics. As with physical exercise, there seems to be no way of becoming good at economics without a lot of time and hard work. But hard work, mental or physical needn't be boring. We hope this workbook is not. But if worst comes to worst, somebody could always try a new exercise book called *Economic Aerobics*.

Some readers, of sedentary inclination in matters physical, may find even metaphorical workouts exhausting. To such readers we suggest an alternative interpretation of the title. It could be a work out book as in "Work out the odd numbered problems in Chapter 11."

In these problems we occasionally make thought-voyages to other planets that feature fantastic economic customs very different from those familiar on earth. Our purpose is not to prepare you for space travel; we know of no plans to send economists into space. It turns out that in economics, as in all of science, a playful imagination is a powerful instrument for understanding. Don't worry though, we have tried to include some boring problems for those of you who plan to be bank inspectors or university administrators.

One thing you should do before you get started is to get together some colored pens or pencils. In the problems we ask you to use specific colors to draw certain lines. We ask for blue, black, and red ink. We are not just being fussy when we ask you to do this. You will find that your graphs are a lot clearer and more informative if you use different colors for the different lines. We have requested specific colors so that if somebody grades your paper, he or she will be able to tell at a glance if you have the figure right.

We've indicated the difficulty of each problem with a score from 10 to 50 and have indicated which problems involve calculus. In general the mathematics used in the problems is pretty elementary, mostly simple algebra. When we use calculus it is only very simple calculus. But despite the elementary nature of the mathematics, the problems do require some effort—like any good work out.

Acknowledgements

In writing this workout book, we have shamelessly borrowed problems from several of our colleagues, students, and friends at the University of Michigan. To us, this seems only fair, since over the years, we have also caused them many problems. Our benefactors include the following individuals: Greg Acs, Mark Bagnoli, Larry Blume, Severin Borenstein, John Cross, Roger Gordon, Debra Holt, John Miller, John Ries, Richard Porter, Ephraim Sadka, Carl Simon, Frank Stafford, Effluvia Stench, and Joe Swierzbinski. Some readers may think that they notice connections between characters in our problems and colleagues or other living persons who might happen to have similar names or characteristics. Let us assure you that any such relation is entirely accidental. The characters in our problems are all simple-minded creatures with very narrow interests.

The Market

Introduction. The problems in this chapter examine some variations on the apartment market described in the text. In most of the problems we work with the true demand curve constructed from the reservation prices of the consumers rather than the "smoothed" demand curve that we used in the text.

Remember that the reservation price of a consumer is that price where he is just indifferent between renting or not renting the apartment. At any price below the reservation price the consumer will demand one apartment, at any price above the reservation price the consumer will demand zero apartments, and exactly at the reservation price the consumer will be indifferent between having zero or one apartments.

1.1 (30) Suppose that we have 8 people who want to rent an apartment. Their reservation prices are given below. (To keep the numbers small, think of these numbers as being daily rent payments.)

Person	=	A	B	C	D	E	F	G	H
Price	=	40	25	30	35	10	18	15	5

(a) Plot the market demand curve in the following graph. Hint: when the market price is equal to some consumer i's reservation price there will be two different quantities of apartments demanded since consumer i will be indifferent between having or not having an apartment.

Price

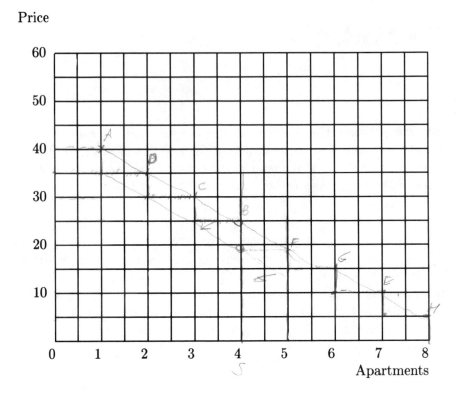

(b) Suppose the supply of apartments is fixed at 5 units. In this case there is a whole range of prices that will be equilibrium prices. What is the highest price that would make the demand for apartments equal to 5 units?_____18_____

(c) What is the lowest price that would make the market demand equal to 5 units?_____15_____

(d) With a supply of 4 apartments, which of the people A–H end up getting apartments?_____ABCD_____

(e) What if the supply of apartments increases to 6 units. What is the range of equilibrium prices?_____0–15_____

1.2 (30) Suppose that there are originally 5 units in the market, and that 1 of them is turned into a condominium.

handwritten top margin: Supply and demand are reduced / 4 units / now

(a) Suppose that person A decides to buy the condominium. What will be the highest price at which demand will equal supply? What will be the lowest price? Enter your answers in the table below under Person A. Then do the same thing for persons B, C, etc.

handwritten left margin: to low price 8/5

handwritten right margin: use a linear transformation?

Person	A	B	C	D	E	F	G	H
High price	18	18	18	18	25	25	25	25
Low price	15	15	15	15	18	15	18	18

(b) Suppose that there were two people at each reservation price and 10 apartments and that one of the apartments was turned into a condominium. What would happen to the equilibrium price? *No change*

1.3 (20) Suppose now that a monopolist owns all the apartments and that he is trying to determine which price and quantity maximize his revenues.

handwritten right margin: revenue box; monopolist seeks to maximize $p\,D(p)$ price times number of apartments demanded at that price.

(a) Fill in the box with the maximum price and revenue that the monopolist can make if he rents 1, 2, ..., 8 apartments. (Assume that he must charge one price for all apartments.)

Number	1	2	3	4	5	6	7	8
Price								
Revenue								

(b) Which of the people A–F would get apartments?_____

(c) If the monopolist were required by law to rent exactly 5 apartments, what price would he charge to maximize his revenue?_____ *18* _____

(d) Who would get apartments?_____

(e) If this landlord could charge each individual a different price, and he knew the reservation prices of all the individuals, what is the maximum revenue he could make if he rented all 5 apartments?_____

(f) If 5 apartments were rented, which individuals would get the apartments?__

1.4 (20) Suppose that there are 5 apartments to be rented and that the city rent control board sets a maximum rent of $9. Further suppose that people A, B, C, D, and E manage to get an apartment, while F, G, and H are frozen out.

(a) If subletting is legal—or, at least, practiced—who will sublet to whom

in equilibrium?_E would sublet to F oh._(Assume that people who sublet can evade
the city rent control restrictions.)

(b) What will be the maximum amount that can be charged for the sublet

payment?___$18_____

(c) If you have rent control with unlimited subletting allowed, which of

the consumers described above will end up in the 5 apartments?_____

_ABCDF_____

(d) How does this compare to the market outcome?____It's the same.____

1.5 (20) In the text we argued that a tax on landlords would not get
passed along to the renters. What would happen if instead the tax was
imposed on renters?

(a) To answer this question, consider the group of people in Problem 1.
What is the maximum that they would be willing to pay to the landlord
if they each had to pay a $5 tax on apartments to the city? Fill in the
box below with these reservation prices.

Person	A	B	C	D	E	F	G	H
Reservation Price								

(b) Using this information determine the equilibrium price if there are 5

apartments to be rented. It is _____

(c) Of course, the total price a renter pays consists of his or her rent plus

the tax. This amount is _____

(d) How does this compare to what happens if the tax is levied on the

landlords?_____

Chapter 2
The Budget Set

Introduction. The budget set represents the set of consumption bundles that the consumer can afford to purchase. The best way to construct the budget set is to first find the equation characterizing the bundles that are exactly affordable (the budget line) and draw that. If the budget line is a straight line, it is helpful to ask how much the consumer would be able to consume if she spent all of her money on one good or the other, and then connect those two points with a straight line.

2.1 (20) Draw budget lines to illustrate each of the following cases.

(a) $p_1 = 1$, $p_2 = 1$, $m = 10$.

(b) $p_1 = 2$, $p_2 = 1$, $m = 20$.

(c) $p_1 = 1$, $p_2 = 0$, $m = 10$.

(d) $p_1 = p_2$, $m = 15p_1$. (Hint: How much good 1 could you afford if you spend your entire budget on good 1?)

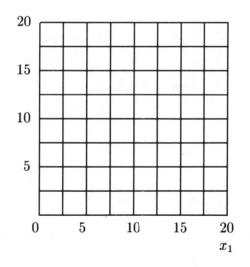

2.2 (20) You have \$40 to spend on two commodities. Commodity 1 costs \$10 per unit and commodity 2 costs \$5 per unit.

(a) Write down your budget equation._____

(b) If you spent all of your income on commodity 1, how much could you

buy?_____

(c) If you spent all of your income on commodity 2, how much could you

buy?_____

(d) Use blue ink to draw your budget line in the graph below.

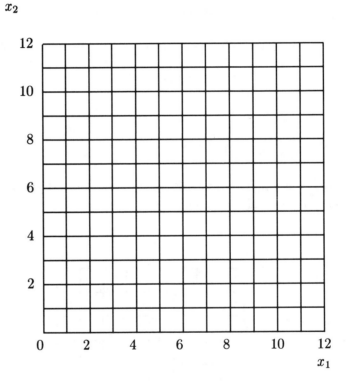

(e) Suppose that the price of commodity 1 is increased to \$20 while everything else stays the same. Write down your new budget equation.____

_____

(f) How much of commodity 1 could you now buy if you spent all of your

income on commodity 1? _____On the diagram you
drew above, use red ink to draw your new budget line.

(g) Now suppose that the amount you are allowed to spend increases to \$60 while the price of commodity 1 remains at \$20 and the price of

commodity 2 remains at \$5. Write down your budget equation._____

_____. Put this budget line on your graph in black ink.

(h) On your diagram, use black ink to shade in the area representing commodity bundles that you can afford after the increase in price and income but could not afford in part (a). Use blue ink to shade in the area representing commodity bundles that you could afford initially but can not afford after the changes.

(i) Solve algebraically for the intersection of the black and the blue budget lines. (Hint: Remember how to solve two linear equations in two

unknowns?) At the intersection of these lines, there are _____

_____units of x_1 and _____units of x_2.

2.3 (10) Illustrate in the diagram below how the budget line changes when money income and the price of bread remain fixed but the price of chocolate goes down.

chocolate

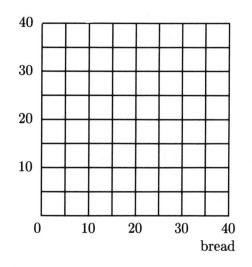

bread

2.4 (20) Your budget is such that if you spend your entire income, you could afford either 3 units of good x and 8 units of good y or 8 units of x and 3 units of y.

(j) Illustrate these two consumption bundles and draw the budget line in the graph below.

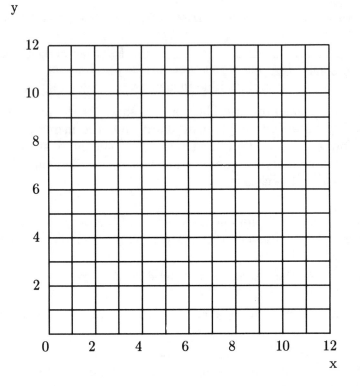

(k) What is the ratio of the price of x to the price of y?_____

(l) If you spent all of your income on x, how much x could you buy?___

_____

(m) If you like both goods and have nothing else to spend your income on, argue that you definitely would not choose to buy 5 units of x and 5 units of y at these prices and this income.

_____

_____

_____

2.5 (40) On the planet Mungo, they have two kinds of money, blue money and red money. Every commodity has two prices—a red money price and a blue money price. Every Mungoan likewise has two incomes. One is its red money income and the other is its blue money income. (There is no need for awkwardness about sex-neutral pronouns, since although Mungo has two sexes, neither of them is remotely like either of ours—but that is another story.)

In order to buy an object, one has to pay that object's red money price in red money and its blue money price in blue money. (The shops simply have two cash registers and you have to pay at both registers to buy an object.) It is forbidden to trade one kind of money for the other and this prohibition is strictly enforced by Mungo's ruthless and efficient monetary police. (Columbus, Ohio, is rumored to be a penal colony for Mungoans who have violated this restriction.)

- There are just two consumer goods on Mungo, ambrosia and bubblegum. All Mungoans prefer more of each good to less.
- The blue prices are 1 bcu (bcu stands for blue currency unit) per unit of ambrosia and 1 bcu per unit of bubble gum.
- The red prices are 2 rcus (red currency units) per unit of ambrosia and 4 rcus per unit of bubblegum.

(a) On the graph below, draw the red budget (with a red ink) and the blue budget (with blue ink) for a Mungoan named Harold whose blue income is 9 and whose red income is 24. Shade in the "budget set" containing all of the commodity bundles that Harold can afford, given his two budget constraints. Remember, Harold has to have enough blue money and enough red money to purchase a bundle of goods.

Bubblegum

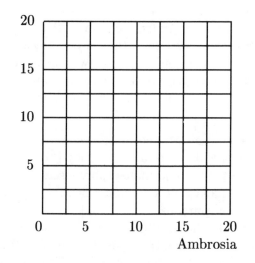

Ambrosia

(b) Another Mungoan, Gladys, faces the same prices that Harold does and has the same red income as Harold, but Gladys has a blue income of 16. Explain how it is that Gladys will not spend its entire blue income

no matter what its tastes may be. (Hint: draw a picture of Gladys's blue budget line.)

_____

_____

_____

(c) (This part is a little trickier. You may find it helpful to take some scratch paper and fiddle around with drawing some budget lines on it.) Harold's cousin, Irene, works in an ambrosia brewery. Irene is allowed a discount on the blue price of ambrosia. For Irene the blue price of ambrosia is only 1/2 bcu per unit of ambrosia, but Irene must pay the same red prices for everything and the same blue price for bubblegum that Harold and Gladys pay. Irene's red income is 24. What is the largest its blue income could be if it spends all of its blue income *and* all of its red

income? _____

(d) There is a group of radical economic reformers on Mungo who believe that the currency rules on Mungo are unfair. "Why should everyone have to pay two prices for everything," they say. They propose the following scheme. Mungo will continue to have two currencies, every good will continue to have a blue price and a red price, and every Mungoan will continue to have a blue income and a red income. But nobody needs to pay both prices.

Instead, everyone on Mungo must declare itself to be either a Blue Money Purchaser (a "Blue") or a Red Money Purchaser (a "Red") before it buys anything at all. Blue money purchasers must make all of their purchases in blue money at the blue prices, spending only their blue incomes. Red money purchasers must make all of their purchases in red money, spending only their red incomes. Suppose that Harold, whom we met above, continues to have the same income after this reform and that prices do not change. Before declaring which kind of Purchaser it will be, Harold contemplates the set of commodity bundles that it could possibly attain. Some of these it could reach by declaring itself to be a "Blue" and some it could attain by declaring itself to be a "Red". On the diagram below, shade in the entire set of commodity bundles that Harold could obtain by making one declaration or the other.

Bubblegum

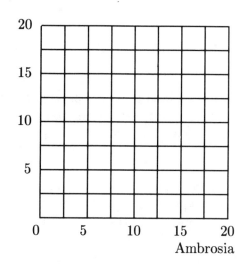

2.6 (20) Jonathan Livingstone Yuppie is a prosperous young lawyer. Although he lives in an intermediate price theory workbook, he has in his own words, "outgrown those confining two-commodity limits". Jonathan consumes three goods, unblended Scotch whiskey, designer tennis shoes, and meals in French gourmet restaurants. The price of Jonathan's brand of whiskey is $20 per bottle, the price of designer tennis shoes is $80 per pair and the price of gourmet restaurant meals is $50 per meal. After he has paid his taxes and alimony, Jonathan has $400 a week to spend.

(a) Write down a budget equation for Jonathan, where W stands for the number of bottles of whiskey, T stands for the number of pairs of tennis shoes and M for the number of gourmet restaurant meals that he

consumes._____

(b) Draw a three dimensional diagram to show his budget set. Label the intersections of the budget set with each axis.

(c) Suppose that he determines that he will buy one pair of designer tennis shoes per week. What equation must be satisfied by the combinations of restaurant meals and whiskey that he could afford?

2.7 (20) On the planet Spuddo there are only three commodities: potatoes, meatballs, and jam. Prices have been remarkably stable for the last 50 years or so. Potatoes cost 3 crowns per sack, meatballs cost 9 crowns per crock, and jam costs 6 crowns per jar.

(a) Write down a budget equation for a citizen named Gunnar who has an income of 360 crowns per year. Let P stand for the number of sacks of potatoes, M for the number of crocks of meatballs and J for the number

of jars of jam consumed by Gunnar in a year. _____

(b) The citizens of Spuddo are in general very clever people, but they are not good at multiplying by 3. This made shopping for potatoes excruciatingly difficult for many citizens. Therefore it was decided to make potatoes the numeraire while retaining the same relative prices as in the past. A new unit of currency (called the potato chip) was introduced.

What would be the price in terms of the new currency, of potatoes ____

_____, of meatballs _____, and

of jam _____? What would Gunnar's income in the new currency have to be for him to be exactly able to afford the same

commodity bundles that he could afford before the change? _____

_____Write down Gunnar's new budget equation. How can you tell that this is the same budget as he had before?

2.8 (20) Edmund Stench consumes two commodities, namely garbage and punk rock video cassettes. He doesn't actually eat the former but keeps it in his back yard where it is eaten by billy goats and assorted vermin. The reason that he accepts the garbage is that people pay him $2 per sack for taking it. He has no other source of income. Video cassettes cost him $6 each.

(a) If Edmund gets zero sacks of garbage, how many video cassettes can

he buy? _____

(b) If he gets 15 sacks of garbage, how many video cassettes can he buy?

_____

(c) Write down an equation for his budget line. _____

_____

Garbage

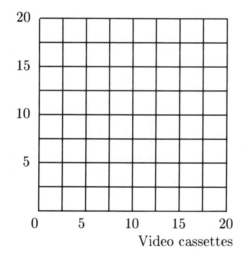

Video cassettes

(d) Draw Edmund's budget line and shade in his budget set.

2.9 (20) If you think Edmund is odd, consider his brother Emmett. Emmett consumes speeches by politicians and university administrators. He is paid $1 per hour for listening to politicians and $2 per hour for listening to university administrators. (Emmett is in great demand to help fill empty chairs in public lectures because of his distinguished appearance and his ability to refrain from making rude noises.) Emmett consumes one good for which he must pay. We have agreed not to disclose what that good is, but we can tell you that it costs $10 per unit and we shall here call it simply good X. In addition to what he is paid for consuming speeches, Emmett receives a pension of $20 per week.

(a) Write down a budget equation stating those combinations of the three commodities, good X, speeches by politicians, and speeches by university

administrators that Emmett could afford to consume per week._____

_____

(b) On the graph below, draw a two dimensional diagram showing the locus of consumptions of the two kinds of speeches that would be possible for Emmett if he consumed 10 units of X per week.

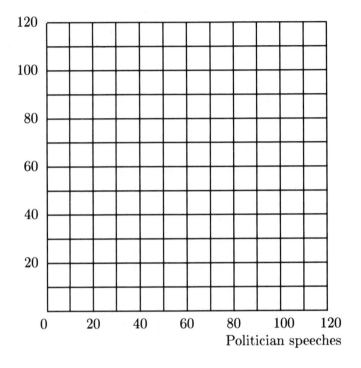

Administrator speeches

Politician speeches

2.10 (20) Harry Hype of Hollywood, California, has $5,000 to spend to advertise a new kind of dehydrated sushi. Market research shows that the people most likely to buy this new product are recent recipients of M.B.A. degrees and lawyers who own hot tubs. Harry is considering advertising in two publications, a boring business magazine and a trendy consumer publication for people who wish they lived in California.

Fact 1: Ads in the boring business magazine cost $500 each and ads in the consumer magazine costs $250 each.

Fact 2: Each ad in the business magazine will be read by 1,000 recent M.B.A.'s and 300 lawyers with hot tubs.

Fact 3: Each ad in the consumer publication will be read by 300 recent M.B.A.'s and 250 lawyers who own hot tubs.

Fact 4: Nobody who reads one magazine reads the other.

(a) If Harry spends his entire advertising budget on the business publication, explain how it is that there will be 10,000 instances of former M.B.A's reading his ads and there will be 3,000 instances of his ads being read by lawyers with hot tubs.

_____

_____

_____

(b) If he spent his entire advertising budget on the consumer publication,

how many times will an ad of his be read by a recent M.B.A.?_____

_____by a lawyer with a hot tub?_____

(c) Suppose he spent half of his advertising budget on each publication.

How many readings of his ads by recent M.B.A.'s would he get _____

_____and how many readings of his ads by lawyers with

hot tubs?_____

(d) Draw a budget line showing the combinations of number of readings by recent M.B.A's and by lawyers with hot tubs that he can obtain with his advertising budget. (Hint: You have found three points on this line already.) Does your budget extend in a straight line all the way to

the axes?_____Write an equation for this budget line?_____

_____ With a fixed advertising budget, how many instances of an ad being read by an MBA must you sacrifice to have an additional instance of an ad being read by a lawyer with a hot tub.?

_____

M.B.A.'s × 1,000

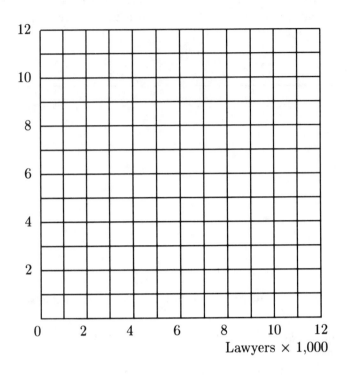

Lawyers × 1,000

Chapter 3

Preferences

Introduction. Most of the problems in this section ask you to draw indifference curves for a consumer with certain peculiar tastes. Don't be surprised or disappointed if you can not immediately see the answer when you look at the problem and don't expect that you will find the answers hiding somewhere in your textbook. You will best find the answers by thinking and doodling on scratch paper. A good way to start is to draw some axes on scratch paper and label them, then mark a point on your graph and ask yourself, "what other points on the graph would the consumer find indifferent to this point?" If it is possible, draw a line connecting such points, making sure that the shape of the line you have drawn reflect the features required by the problem. This gives you one indifference curve. Now pick another point that is preferred to the first one you drew and draw an indifference curve through it.

3.1 (30) Freddy Blodger loves money but hates to work. He has strictly convex preferences between income per week and hours of work per week.

(a) Draw some indifference curves for Freddy in the graph below.

Income per week

Hours of work per week

(b) Put your pencil on the graph at $(4, 4)$. Which directions do you have

to move to make Freddy indifferent to this point?_____

(c) Which direction do you have to move to make Freddy better off tha.

at $(4, 4)$?_____

(d) What does convexity imply about the slope of the indifference curve

as the hours of work increase?_____

3.2 (20) Randy Ratpack hates studying both economics and history. The more time he spends studying either the less happy he is. But Randy has strictly convex preferences.

(a) Sketch an indifference curve for Randy where the two commodities are hours per week spent studying economics and hours per week spent studying history. Will the slope of an indifference curve be positive or

negative? _____

Hours studying history

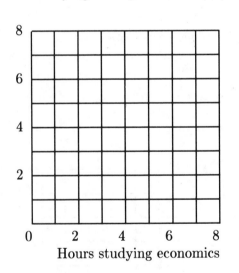

Hours studying economics

3.3 (10) Flossy Toothsome likes to spend some time studying and some time dating. In fact her indifference curves between hours per week spent studying and hours per week spent dating are concentric circles around her favorite combination which is 20 hours of studying and 15 hours of dating per week. The closer she is to her favorite combination, the happier she is.

(a) Suppose that Flossy is currently studying 25 hours a week and dating 3 hours a week. Would she prefer to be studying 30 hours a week and

dating 8 hours a week? _____(Hint: Remember the formula for the distance between two points in the plane?)

(b) On the axes below, draw a few of Flossy's indifference curves and use your diagram to illustrate which of the two time allocations discussed above Flossy would prefer.

Hours dating

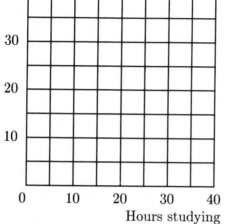

Hours studying

3.4 (20) It turns out that our friends from Mungo have three feet: two left feet and one right foot. If Mungoites always wear shoes on all feet, illustrate a typical set of indifference curves in the graph below.

Assume that if you have two left shoes and two right shoes, the extra right shoe is useless. Similarly if you have three left shoes and one right shoe, the extra left shoe is useless. Draw lines connecting the combinations of shoes that are indifferent to having 2 left shoes and 1 right shoe. Now sketch another indifference curve through the point 4 left shoes, 2 right shoes.

Left shoes

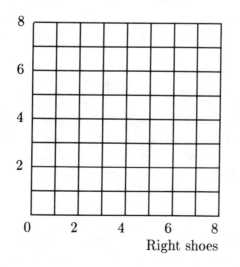

Right shoes

3.5 (20) Shirley Sixpack is in the habit of drinking three 16 ounce cans of beer each evening while watching "The Best of Bowlerama" on TV. She has a strong thumb and a big refrigerator, so that she doesn't care about the size of the cans that beer comes in, so long as she gets her 48 ounces of beer per night.

(a) On the graph below, draw some of Shirley's indifference curves between 16 ounce cans and 8 ounce cans of beer. Use blue ink to draw these indifference curves.

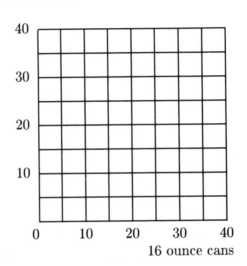

(b) Lorraine Quiche likes to have a beer while she watches Masterpiece Theatre. She only allows herself an 8 ounce glass of beer at any one time. Since her cat doesn't like beer and she hates stale beer, if there is more than 8 ounces in the can she just pours the excess into the sink. On the graph above, use red ink to draw some of Lorraine's indifference curves.

3.6 (30) Joan likes chocolate cake and ice cream, but after 10 slices of cake, she gets tired of cake and eating more cake makes her less happy. Joan always prefers more ice cream to less. Joan's parents require her to eat everything put on her plate. In the axes below use blue ink to draw a set of indifference curves that depict her preferences between plates with different amounts of cake and ice cream. Be sure to label the axes.

(a) Suppose that Joan's preferences are as before, but that her parents allow her to leave anything on her plate that she doesn't want. On the graph below, use red ink to draw some indifference curves depicting her preferences between plates with different amounts of cake and ice cream.

3.7 (20) Mary Granola consumes two goods, grapefruits and avocados. If she has more grapefruits than avocados, her marginal rate of substitution is 2: for every avocado she gives up, she has to get two more grapefruits. However, if she has fewer grapefruits than avocados, then each grapefruit she consumes is just worth 2 avocados to her; i.e., her MRS is 1/2.

(a) In the graph below, draw an indifference curve for Mary through the bundle $(10G, 10A)$. Draw another indifference curve through $(20G, 20A)$.

Grapefruits

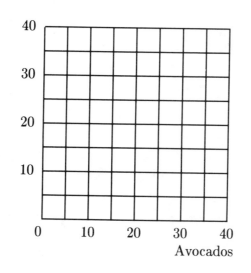

Avocados

(b) Does Mary have convex preferences?_____

3.8 (30) The Bear family is trying to decide what to have for dinner. Baby Bear says that his ranking of the possibilities is (honey, grubs, Goldilocks). Mama Bear ranks the choices (grubs, Goldilocks, honey) while Papa Bear's ranking is: (Goldilocks, honey, grubs). They decide to take each pair of alternatives and let a majority vote determine the family rankings.

(a) Papa suggests that they first consider honey vs. grubs, and then the winner of that contest vs. Goldilocks. Which alternative will be chosen?_____

_____

(b) Mama suggests instead that they consider honey vs. Goldilocks and then the winner vs. grubs. Which gets chosen?_____

(c) What order should Baby Bear suggest if he wants to get his favorite food for dinner?_____

(d) What is wrong with the Bear family's "collective preferences" as determined by voting?

_____

_____

_____

3.9 (20) Ralph Rigid likes to eat lunch at 12 noon. However, he also likes to save money so he can buy other consumption goods by attending the "early bird specials" and "late lunchers" promoted by his local diner. This means that he is willing to eat earlier or later than his preferred times if he is sufficiently compensated for it. In the graph below, draw a few of Ralph's indifference curves for money to spend on "all other goods" and dining time.

Money

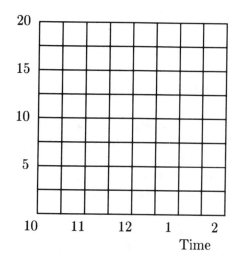

3.10 (20) Henry Hanover is currently consuming 20 cheeseburgers and 20 Cherry Cokes a week. A typical indifference curve for Henry is depicted below.

Cherry Coke

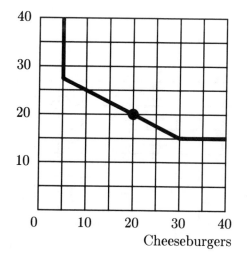

(a) If someone offered to trade Henry one extra cheeseburger for every Coke he gave up, would Henry want to do this?_____

(b) What if it were the other way around: for every cheeseburger Henry gave up, he would get an extra Coke. Would he accept this offer? _____

(c) What is the maximum number of cheeseburgers he would give up at an exchange rate of 2 cheeseburgers for 1 Coke?_____

(d) At what rate of exchange would Henry be willing to stay put at his current consumption level?_____

3.11 (20) Tommy Twit is happiest when he has 8 cookies and 4 glasses of milk per day. Whenever he has more than his favorite amount of either food, giving him still more makes him worse off. Whenever he has less than his favorite amount of either food, giving him more makes him better off. His mother makes him drink 6 glasses of milk and only allows him 4 cookies per day. One day when his mother was gone, Tommy's sadistic sister made him eat 13 cookies and only gave him 1 glass of milk, despite the fact that Tommy complained bitterly about the last 5 cookies that she made him eat and he begged for more milk. Although Tommy complained later to his mother, he had to admit that he liked the diet that his sister forced on him better than what his mother demanded.

(a) Use black ink to draw some indifference curves for Tommy that are consistent with this story.

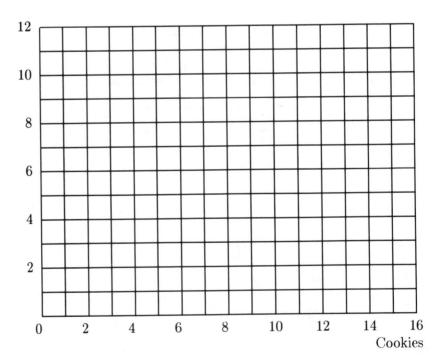

Milk

Cookies

(b) Tommy's mother believes that the optimal amount for him to consume is 6 glasses of milk and 4 cookies. She measures deviations by absolute values. If Tommy consumes some other bundle, say, (c, m), she measures his departure from the optimal bundle by $D = |6 - m| + |4 - c|$. The larger D is, the worse off she thinks Tommy is. Use blue ink in the graph above to sketch a few of Mrs. Twit's indifference curves for Tommy's consumption.

Chapter 4
Utility

Introduction. This chapter contains problems to familiarize you with various utility functions. Given a utility function $u(x,y)$, the indifference curves are determined by the equation $u(x,y) = k$ for each different value of the constant k. If you are asked to graph an indifference curve you can simply pick a value of k, solve this equation for y in terms of x, and then graph that function.

4.1 (30) Hy Perbola's utility function is $U(X,Y) = XY$.

(a) Suppose that Hy originally consumed 4 units of X and 12 units of Y. If his consumption of Y is reduced to 8, how much X must he have to be as well off as he was to begin with? _____On the graph below indicate Hy's original consumption and draw an indifference curve through this point.

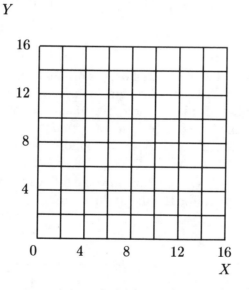

(b) Which bundle would Hy like better, 3 units of X and 10 units of Y or 4 units of X and 8 units of Y? _____

(c) As you can verify, Hy is indifferent between the two commodity bundles (4,6) and (8,3). Consider the bundles (8,12) and (16,6), each of which contains exactly twice as much of each good as the first two bundles. Is Hy also indifferent between these two bundles? _____

(d) Can you show that it is always true that if two bundles are regarded as indifferent for someone with Hy's utility function, then if you doubled the amount of each good in each bundle, the new bundles will also be regarded as indifferent?

_____

_____

_____

4.2 (20) Foster Interface has the following utility function: $U(X,Y) = 2\sqrt{X} + Y$.

(a) If Foster originally consumed 9 units of X and 10 units of Y, and if his consumption of X is reduced to 4 units, how much Y would he have to be given so that he would be exactly as well off as he was originally?

_____

(b) On the graph below, indicate Foster's original consumption and draw an indifference curve passing through this point. As you can verify, Foster is indifferent between the bundle, (9,10) and the bundle (25,6). If you doubled the amount of each good in each bundle, you would have bundles (18,20) and (50,12). Are these two bundles on the same indifference

curve?_____(Hint: How do you check whether two bundles are indifferent when you know the utility function?)

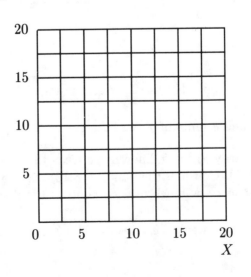

(c) Foster's utility function represents a special form of preferences described in the text. What is the name for this kind of preferences? _____

_____

4.3 (20) Recall that Mungoites have 2 left feet and 1 right foot. We want to derive a utility function for a Mungoite who has L left shoes and R right shoes. (Don't worry about fractional shoes—half a shoe is better than none.)

(a) First draw some indifference curves in the graph below.

Left shoes

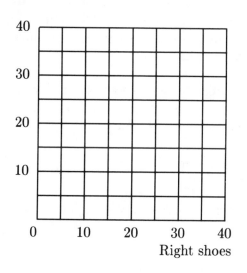

Right shoes

(b) We'll assign a utility to the bundle (L, R) that consists of the *minimum* number of left shoes the Mungoite could have, and still be as well off as it is at (L, R). Label your indifference curves with this utility function. Does this result in higher indifference curves getting labels with higher

numbers? _____

(c) If $L > 2R$, what label does an indifference curve get?_____

_____

(d) If $L < 2R$ what label does an indifference curve get?_____

(e) What is a utility function that represents Mungoite preferences for

shoes?_____

(f) If $L > 2R$, what does an extra left shoe add to utility?_____

_____

(g) If $L < 2R$ what does an extra left shoe add to utility? _____

_____

4.4 (20) Remember Shirley Sixpack and Lorraine Quiche from the last chapter? Shirley thinks a 16 ounce can of beer is just as good as two 8 ounce cans since she drinks 48 ounces at a sitting. Lorraine only drinks 8 ounces at a time and hates stale beer, so she thinks a 16 ounce can is no better or worse than an 8 ounce can.

(a) Write a utility function that represents Shirley's preferences between commodity bundles comprised of 8 ounce cans and 16 ounce cans of beer. Let X stand for the number of 8 ounce cans and Y stand for the number

of 16 ounce cans._____

(b) Now write a utility function that represents Lorraine's preferences.__

_____

(c) Write down a different utility function from the first one you wrote

that would also represent Shirley's preferences._____

(d) Give an example of two commodity bundles such that Shirley likes the first bundle better than the second bundle while Lorraine likes the second bundle better than the first bundle.

_____

4.5 (30) Which of the following are positive monotonic transformations? Circle your answers.

(a) $v = 3.141592u$

(b) $v = -17u$

(c) $v = 2u - 10,000$

(d) $v = \log u$

(e) $v = -e^{-u}$

(f) $v = 1/u$

(g) $v = -1/u$

4.6 (20) Martha Modest has preferences represented by the utility function $U(a, b) = ab/100$ where a is the number of ounces of animal crackers that she consumes and b is the number of ounces of beans that she consumes.

(a) On the graph below, sketch the locus of points that Martha finds indifferent to having 8 ounces of animal crackers and 2 ounces of beans. Also sketch the locus of points that she finds indifferent to having 6 ounces of animal crackers and 4 ounces of beans.

Beans

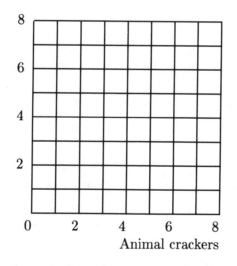

Animal crackers

(b) Bertha Brassy has preferences represented by the utility function $V(a, b) = 1,000a^2b^2$ where a is the number of ounces of animal crackers that she consumes and b is the number of ounces of beans that she consumes. On the graph below, sketch the locus of points that Bertha finds indifferent to having 8 ounces of animal crackers and 2 ounces of beans. Also sketch the locus of points that she finds indifferent to having 6 ounces of animal crackers and 4 ounces of beans.

Beans

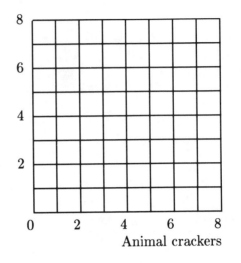

Animal crackers

(c) Are Martha's preferences convex? _____

(d) Are Bertha's?_____

(e) What can you say about the difference between the indifference curves you drew for Bertha and those you drew for Martha?_____

_____

(f) How could you tell this was going to happen without having to draw the curves?_____.

4.7 (20) Willy Wheeler has preferences represented by the utility function $U(x, y) = x_1^2 + x_2^2$.

(a) Draw a few of his indifference curves.

(b) What kind of geometric figure are they?_____

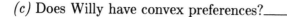

(c) Does Willy have convex preferences?_____

x_2

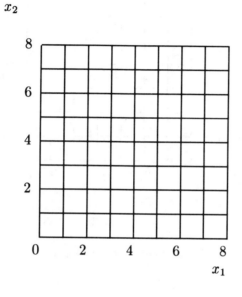

0 2 4 6 8

x_1

4.8 (20) Harry Mazzola has the utility function $u(x_1, x_2) = \min\{x_1 + 2x_2, x_2 + 2x_1\}$ where x_1 is his consumption of corn chips and x_2 is his consumption of French fries.

(a) On the graph below, use blue ink to show the locus of points for which $x_1 + 2x_2 = 12$ and also use blue ink to draw the locus of points for which $x_2 + 2x_1 = 12$. Shade in the region where both $x_1 + 2x_2 \geq 12$ and $x_2 + 2x_1 \geq 12$.

(b) What value does Harry's utility function take along the lower bound-

ary of this region?_____Use black ink to sketch in the indifference curve along which Harry's utility is 12. Also use black ink to sketch in the indifference curve along which Harry's utility is 6. Is there anything about Harry Mazzola that reminds you of Mary Granola?

x_2

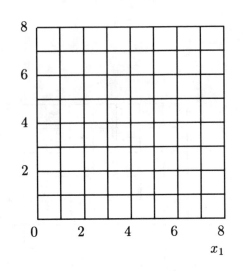

4.9 (20) Joe Bob has a utility function given by $u(x_1, x_2) = x_1^2 + 2x_1x_2 + x_2^2$.

(c) Compute Joe Bob's marginal rate of substitution of good 2 for good

1._____

(d) Joe Bob's straight cousin, Ernie, has a utility function $v(x_1, x_2) = x_2 + x_1$. Compute Ernie's marginal rate of substitution._____

_____

(e) Do $u(x_1, x_2)$ and $v(x_1, x_2)$ represent the same preferences?_____

_____

(f) Can you show that Joe Bob's utility function is a monotonic transformation of Ernie's? (Hint: Some have said that Joe Bob is square.)_____

_____

Chapter 5

Choice

Introduction. Here we use what we know about budget lines, preferences, and utility functions to determine the optimal choices of consumers. Most of the exercises here are graphical: you draw the budget lines and the indifference curves and then pick out the most preferred point on each indifference curve.

5.1 (20) Clara's utility function is $U(X, Y) = X(Y + 2)$.

(a) In the table below, fill in the quantity of Y which together with the corresponding quantity of X gives Clara a utility of 36.

X	Y
1	
2	
3	
4	
6	

(b) On the axes below mark each of these points and sketch Clara's indifference curve for $U = 36$. Suppose that the price of each good is 1 and that Clara has an income of 10. Draw in her budget line.

(c) How much X will she choose to consume? _____

(d) How much Y will she choose to consume? _____

Y

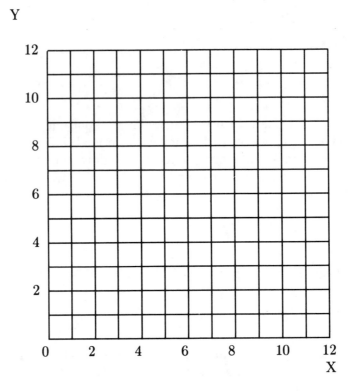

(e) Using calculus, you will find that Clara's marginal rate of substitution equals the price ratio when $(Y + 2)/X = p_X/p_Y$. Using this fact and the budget equation, solve for Clara's demand for Y as a function of prices

and her income. _____

5.2 ((20) Flem Snopes's utility function is $U(X, Y) = \sqrt{X} + Y$.

(a) On the axes below, find and label the point on the indifference curve that give Flem a utility of 10 and where he consumes 1 unit of X. Also find and label the points on this curve where he consumes 4 units of X, 9 units of X, and 16 units of X.

(b) Now label points on the indifference curve that give him a utility of 15 where he consumes respectively, 1, 4, 9, and 16 units of X. Sketch in indifference curves corresponding to utilities of 10 and 15.

(c) Suppose that the price of X is 1 and the price of Y is 2. Suppose that Flem's income is 19. Draw Flem's budget line.

(d) How much X does he choose to buy? _____How

much Y?_____

(e) Now suppose that the prices are as before, but Flem's income is 29.

Draw his new budget line. How much X will he choose? _____

_____ How much Y? _____

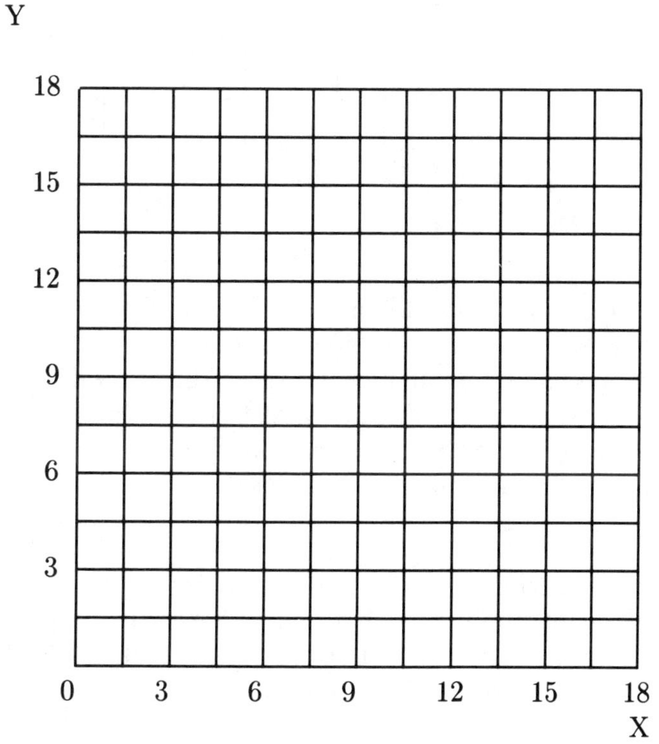

Y

5.3 (20) Remember our friend Ralph Rigid from Chapter 3? His favorite diner, Food for Thought, has adopted the following policy to reduce the crowds at lunch time: if you show up for lunch t hours before or after 12 noon, you get to deduct t dollars from your bill. (This holds for any fraction of an hour as well.)

Money

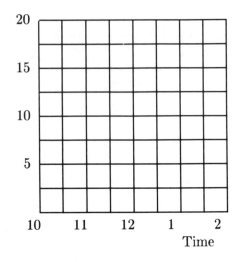

(a) Using blue ink, illustrate Ralph's budget set in the above graph, where the horizontal axis measures the time of day that he eats lunch and the vertical axis measures the amount of money that he will have to spend on things other than lunch. Assume that he has $15 total to spend and that lunch at noon costs $5. (Hint: How much money would he have left if he ate at noon? at 1 p.m.? at 11 a.m.?)

(b) Recall that Ralph's preferred lunch time is 12 noon, but that he is willing to eat at other time if the food is sufficiently cheap. Using black ink, draw in some indifference curves for Ralph that will lead to 2 P.M. as being his optimal choice of dining time.

5.4 (20) The market price for peanut butter is $2 a jar, and the market price for jam is $4 a jar.

(a) If John Laitner consumes only peanut butter, what can we say about how many jars of peanut butter John would be willing to give up to get

one jar of jam? Answer: it is (greater, less) than _____

(b) Suppose that John has an income of $80. Draw a picture that illustrates John's budget set, an indifference curve consistent with the above description, and his optimal consumption point.

(c) Is it necessary for John's indifference curve to have the same slope as his budget line at his optimal consumption point?

Jam

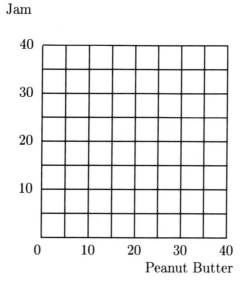

Peanut Butter

5.5 (40) Norm and Sheila consume only meat pies and beer. Meat pies used to cost $2 each and beer was $1 per can. Their income used to be $60 per week but they had to pay an income tax of $10. Use red ink to sketch their old budget line for meat pies and beer.

Beer

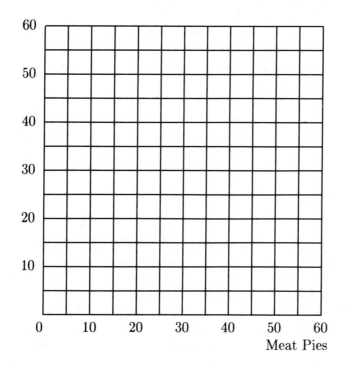

Meat Pies

(a) They used to buy 30 cans of beer per week and spent the rest of their income on meat pies. How many meat pies did they buy?_____

_____

(b) The government decided to eliminate the income tax and to put a sales tax of $1 per can on beer, raising its price to $2 per can. Assuming that Norm and Sheila's pre-tax income and the price of meat pies did not change, draw their new budget line in blue ink.

(c) The sales tax on beer induced Norm and Sheila to reduce their consumption of it to 20 cans per week. What happened to their consumption

of meat pies? _____

(d) How much revenue did this tax raise from Norm and Sheila?_____

_____

(e) Suppose that instead of just taxing beer, the government had decided to tax *both* beer and meat pies at the *same* percentage rate in such a way that it would raise the same revenue from Norm and Sheila as the tax on beer alone described above. Assuming that the price of beer and meat pies goes up by the full amount of the tax, use black ink to draw the new budget line on the graph.

(f) Are Norm and Sheila better off having just beer taxed or having both beer and meat pies taxed, if both sets of taxes raise the same revenue?

_____

5.6 (40) Joe Grad has just arrived at the big U. He has a fellowship that covers his tuition and the rent on an apartment. In order to get by, Joe has become a grader in intermediate price theory, earning $100 a month. Out of this $100 he must pay for his food and utilities in his apartment. His utilities expenses consist of heating costs when he heats his apartment and air-conditioning costs when he cools it. To raise the temperature of his apartment by a degree, it costs $2 per month (or $20 per month to raise it ten degrees). To use air-conditioning to cool his apartment by a degree, it costs $3 per month. Whatever is left over after paying the utilities, he uses to buy food at $1 per unit.

Food

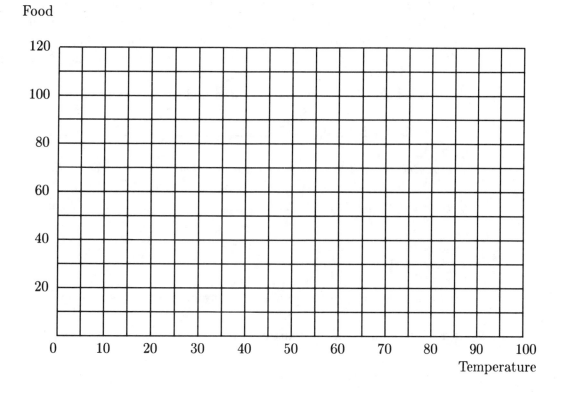

(a) When Joe first arrives in September, the temperature of his apartment is 60 degrees. Use black ink to draw Joe's budget constraint. (Hint: answering the following questions may help you to draw the graph.)

(b) What would the temperature in his room be and how much would he have left to spend on food if he spends nothing on heating or cooling?_

_____

(c) How much food could he buy if he heated the room to 70 degrees?

_____

(d) How much food could he buy if he cooled the room to 50 degrees?

_____

(e) In December, the outside temperature is 30 degrees and in August poor Joe is trying to understand macroeconomics while the temperature outside is 85 degrees. On the same graph you used above, draw Joe's budget constraints for the months of December (in blue ink) and August (in red ink.)

(f) Draw a plausible set of indifference curves for Joe in such a way that the following are true. (*i*) His favorite temperature for his apartment would be 65 degrees if it cost him nothing to heat it or cool it. (*ii*) Joe chooses to use the furnace in December, air-conditioning in August, and neither in September. (*iii*) Joe is better off in December than in August.

(g) In what months is the slope of Joe's budget constraint equal to the slope of his indifference curve?_____

(h) In December Joe's marginal rate of substitution between food and degrees Fahrenheit is _____

(i) In August it is _____

(j) In September, Joe's marginal rate of substitution between food and degrees Fahrenheit in his apartment is between _____and ___

_____

5.7 (30) The State Education Commission wants to encourage "computer literacy" in the high schools under its jurisdictions. Currently the average high school in the state devotes approximately $20,000 of its $60,000 instruction budget to this subject, and the State Education Board would like to see this amount increased. However, opinions differ on how much they would like to see it increased, and what the most effective way is to do this. The following have been proposed.

Plan A: Some members of the Commission want to see a straight grant of $10,000 to each high school in the state to spend in whatever way they see fit. These people feel that given the high importance now attached to computer literacy, most school districts would devote a significant proportion of these funds to computer education.

Plan B: Some other members of the Commission are in favor of the plan to make a $10,000 grant to each high school, but they want to *require* each school to spend at least $10,000 on computer instruction as a condition of receiving the grant.

Plan C: Another group of the Commission wants to make the $10,000 grant to high schools, but they want to require each high school receiving the grant to spend at least $10,000 *more* than they are currently spending on computer instruction.

Plan D: A fourth faction favors a matching grant program, where the State agrees to share the costs of computers with the high schools. For each dollar spent on computer education, a high school will receive a half a dollar from the state to add to its operating budget.

Plan E: The fifth group likes a modified version of the above plan: they want a matching grant, as above, but the maximum amount that each high school would get would be limited to $10,000.

We want to analyze the effect of these 5 plans on the budget possibilities of a typical high school. The graphs below have the amount of money devoted to computers on the horizontal axis, and the amount of money devoted to other instruction on the vertical axis.

(a) Show how plans A, B, C, D, and E affect the budget set of a typical high school in the graph below. Use black ink to draw the budget line without any of these plans and use colored ink for the other plans. Label the budget lines with A, B, C, and D.

Other

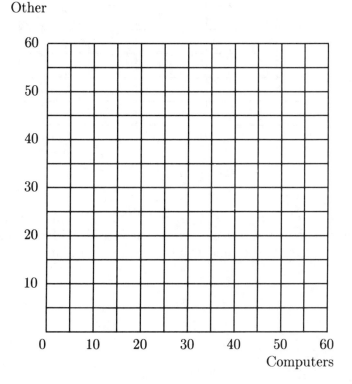

Computers

(b) Of the 5 plans, which plan would probably lead to the largest increase

in money spent on computers?_____Draw some indifference curves to illustrate your answer.

5.8 (30) The telephone company allows one to choose between two different pricing plans. For a fee of $12 per month you can make as many local phone calls as you want, at no additional charge per call. Alternatively, you can pay $8 per month and be charged 5 cents for each local phone call that you make. Suppose that you have a total of $20 per month to spend.

(a) On the graph below, use black ink to sketch a budget line for someone who chooses the first plan. Use red ink to draw a budget line for someone

who chooses the second plan. Where do the two budget lines cross?_____

_____

Other goods

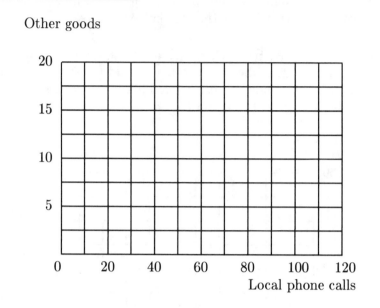

(b) On the graph above, use yellow ink to draw indifference curves for someone who prefers the second plan to the first. Use blue ink to draw an indifference curve for someone who prefers the first plan to the second.

Demand

Introduction. Many of the exercises in this chapter ask you to find a demand function for an individual when we know his preferences. In some of these problems, there is a "corner" solution where only one good is consumed. In other cases equilibrium is at a kink. (For example, this happens in the case of perfect complements.) In problems of either of these two kinds, it is usually easy to solve for the quantities demanded at given prices simply by looking at diagrams and doing a little algebra.

When the consumer is choosing positive amounts of all commodities and indifference curves have no kinks, the consumer chooses a point of tangency between his budget line and the highest indifference curve that it touches. In these cases the way to solve for the demand function is to solve two equations for two unknowns. The unknowns are the quantities of the two goods demanded. One of your two equations says the ratio of marginal utility of good 1 to the marginal utility of good 2 is equal to the ratio of the price of good 1 to the price of good 2. The other equation is just the budget constraint. Now when you have these equations, you want to solve for the quantity of good 1 demanded as a function of the prices and of income. This is the demand function for good 1. Likewise you solve for the demand for good 2 as a function of prices and income. Notice that in a demand function you should express the demand for each good only as a function of prices and income and not as a function of the quantity of the other good. Typically these problems require a little bit of calculus (to calculate the marginal utilities) and a little bit of algebra (to solve the two equations.) We have deliberately chosen examples where this calculation requires only taking very easy derivatives and solving very simple equations.

Some of the problems ask you to calculate price and or income elasticities either from demand functions that are given to you or from demand functions that you have found. These problems are especially easy if you know a little calculus. For example, if the demand function for good 1, is $x_1(p_1, p_2, m)$, and you want to calculate the income elasticity of demand when prices are (p_1, p_2) and income is m, you need only to calculate $\partial x_1(p_1, p_2, m)/\partial m$ and multiply it by $m/x_1(p_1, p_2, m)$ to find the income elasticity.

6.1 (20) Remember Shirley Sixpack, who thinks that two 8 ounce cans of beer are exactly as good as one 16 ounce can of beer. Suppose that these are the only sizes of beer available to her and that she has $20 to spend on beer. Suppose that an 8 ounce beer costs $.80 and a 16 ounce beer costs $1. On the graph below, draw Shirley's budget line in blue ink and draw some of her indifference curves in red.

8 ounce cans

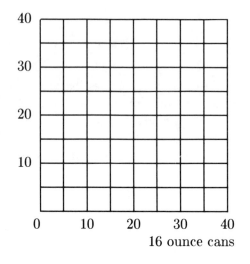

16 ounce cans

(a) At these prices, which size can will she buy, or will she buy some of each?

_____

(b) Suppose that the price of 16 ounce beers remains $1 and the price of

8 ounce beers falls to $.60. Will she buy more 8 ounce beers? _____

_____

(c) What if the price of 8 ounce beers falls to $ .40? How many 8 ounce

beers will she buy then? _____

(d) Write a general formula for Shirley's demand for 16 ounce beers as a function of prices p_8, p_{16}, and her income, m?

_____

6.2 (15) Miss Muffet always likes to have things "just so". In fact the only way she will consume her curds and whey is in the ratio of 2 units of whey per unit of curds. She has an income of $20. Whey costs $.75 per unit. Curds cost $1 per unit. She has an income of $20. On the graph below, draw Miss Muffet's budget line and plot some of her indifference curves.

(a) How much curds will Miss Muffet demand in this situation?_____

_____

(b) How much whey?_____(Hint: Have you noticed something kinky about Miss Muffet?)

whey

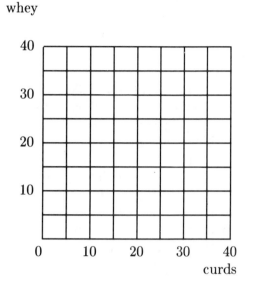

curds

6.3 (20) Linus has a demand function with the equation $q = 10 - 2p$.

(a) What is his elasticity of demand when the price is 3? _____

_____

(b) At what price is his elasticity of demand equal to -1?_____

_____

(c) Suppose that his demand function takes the general linear form, $q = a - bp$. Write down an algebraic expression for his elasticity of demand

at an arbitrary price p. _____

(d) (10) In this problem and in some of the earlier problems, we have been a bit careless in describing linear demand functions. It would have been more accurate to say that $q = \max\{0, a - bp\}$ Explain why.

_____

_____

_____

6.4 (30) Richard and Mary Stout have fallen on hard times, but remain rational consumers. They are making do on \$80 a week, spending \$40 on food and \$40 on all other goods. On the graph below, use black ink to draw a budget line. Label their consumption bundle, A.

(a) The Stouts suddenly become eligible for food stamps. This means that they can go to the agency and buy coupons that can be exchanged for \$2 worth of food, and they only have to pay \$1 for such coupons. However, the maximum number of coupons they can buy per week is 10. On the graph, draw their new budget line with red ink.

$ Worth of Other things

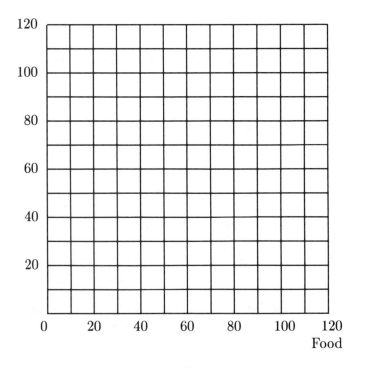

Food

(b) If the Stouts have homothetic preferences, how much more food will

they buy once they enter the food stamp program? _____

6.5 Donald Fribble is a stamp collector. The only things other than stamps that Fribble consumes are Hostess Twinkies. It turns out that Fribble's preferences are represented by the utility function $u(s, t) = s + \ln t$ where s is the number of stamps he collects and t is the number of Twinkies he consumes.

(a) Write an expression that says that the ratio of Fribble's marginal utility for Twinkies to his marginal utility for stamps is equal to the ratio

of the price of Twinkies to the price of stamps. _____

_____(Hint: The derivative of $\ln t$ with respect to t is $1/t$ and the derivative of s with respect to s is 1.)

(b) Use the budget equation and the equation that you found in the last part to solve the demand function for Twinkies when income is m, the prices are p_s for stamps and p_T for Twinkies and when $m > p_s$. The

demand function for Twinkies is _____

(c) In general, the demand for any good may depend on its own price, income, and the prices of all other goods. Which of these variables have

no effect on Donald's demand for Twinkies? _____

(d) What is Donald's price elasticity of demand for Twinkies when $m >$

p_s?_____

(e) What is his income elasticity of demand for Twinkies when $m > p_s$?

_____

(f) Donald's wife complains that whenever Donald gets an extra dollar,

he always spends it all on stamps. Is she right when $m > p_s$? _____

_____

(g) Write down Fribble's demand function for postage stamps when $m > p_s$. (Hint: Use his budget constraint and his demand function for Twinkies to find out how his demand for stamps depends on his income and the

prices of each good.)_____

(h) Suppose that the price of Twinkies is $2 and the price of stamps is $1. On the graph below, for incomes greater than $1, draw Fribble's Engel curve for Twinkies in red ink and his Engel curve for stamps in blue ink. Label the axes.

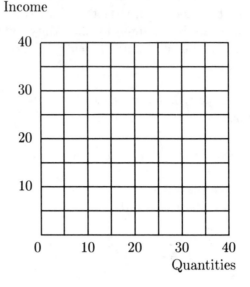

Income

Quantities

(i) If $m < p_s$, what would Fribble's demand for postage stamps be? ____

_____What would his demand for Twinkies be? (Hint: On what part of the envelope do you stick a postage stamp?)

Calculus **6.6** (20) Douglas Cornfield, of Hogsholm, Iowa has preferences which can be represented by the utility function, $u(x, y) = x^2y^3$.

(a) Write down a function expressing his marginal rate of substitution between x and y._____

(b) If Douglas is consuming 20 units of x and 10 units of y, how much x would he be willing to give up for an extra unit of y? _____

_____

(c) Suppose that Douglas has $1,000 to spend, the price of x is $5 per unit and the price of y is $20 per unit. Write down an equation that states that the slope of Doug's budget line is equal to the slope of his indifference curve at the consumption bundle (x, y)._____

(d) Write down an equation that states that the consumption bundle

(x, y) is exactly on Doug's budget line. _____

(e) Solve these two simultaneous equations to show how much of x Doug will buy and how much of y he will buy.

6.7 Following the same procedure you used in the previous problem to find Douglas Cornfield's demand at particular prices and incomes, derive general formulas for Doug's demand function for good x and good y as a function of prices and of his income. The answer is $x(p_x, p_y, m) =$

_____and $y(p_x, p_y, m) =$ _____

(a) What is the numeric value of Cornfield's income elasticity for x? ____

_____

(b) What is the numeric value of his price elasticity of demand for x?

_____

(c) In the graph below, draw Cornfield's Engel curve for x in red ink and his Engel curve for y in blue ink.

income

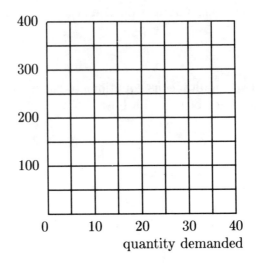

quantity demanded

(d) In the graph below, draw Cornfield's income offer curve.

y

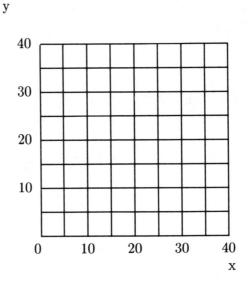

x

Calculus **6.8** (20) Douglas has a cousin named Gary Stone. Gary's preferences were just the same as Douglas's until the day he fell into a cement mixer. Gary was rescued, physically unharmed, but somehow the ordeal shifted his indifference curves. Gary's new preferences are representable by the utility function $U(x,y) = (x+1)^2(y+2)^3$.

(a) Write down an expression for Gary's marginal rate of substitution as

a function of his consumption of x and y. _____

(b) At the optimum consumption point, Gary's MRS will equal the price ratio. Use this equation and Gary's budget constraint to find Gary's demand function for x and his demand function for y. Where there is not

a corner solution, the demand functions are $x_d =$ _____

_____and $y_d =$ _____

6.9 A sharp-eyed neighbor girl, Suzy Optimum, first noticed the difference in preferences between Douglas and Gary. She observed that they responded differently to changes in income.

(a) If Douglas's income doubles will his demand for x double, more than

double, or less than double? _____

(b) If Gary's income doubles, will his demand for x double, more than

double, or less than double? _____

(c) She also noticed that for only one of the cousins is demand for x

affected by the price of y. Which cousin is that?_____

(d) After close examination, Suzy Optimum noticed that Gary's indifference curves can be found by drawing Douglas's indifference curves and then translating the graph so that its origin is moved to $(-1, -2)$. Illustrate this on the two graphs below and draw a few indifference curves. On your graphs, draw an income offer curve for each of the two cousins for the case where the price of x equals the price of y.

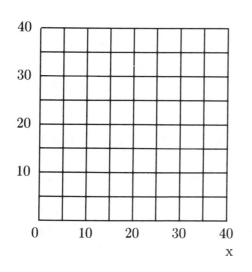

y

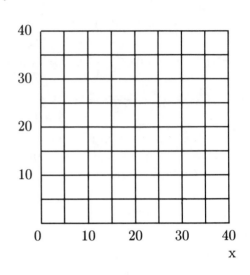

Calculus **6.10** (20) Douglas has an urbane sister, Dorothy, who lives in Cedar Rapids and has much broader interests than Douglas. She consumes 4 different commodities, a,b,c, and d. (She disdains both y and z.) Her utility function is $u(a, b, c, d) = abc^2d$.

(a) Find the ratio of Dorothy's marginal utility for b to her marginal utility for a. _____, the ratio of Dorothy's marginal utility for c to her marginal utility for a._____, the ratio of her marginal utility for d to her marginal utility for a

(b) The price of good a is 1, and the price of each of the other goods is 2. Write down equations that state the price of each of the other goods relative to the price of a equals the ratio of Dorothy's marginal utility for that good to her marginal utility for a.

(c) Use these equations and the budget constraint to solve for Dorothy's demand functions for goods a, b, c, and d._____

6.11 (40) Under current tax law certain individuals can save up to $2,000 a year in an Individual Retirement Account (IRA), a savings vehicle that has an especially favorable tax treatment. Consider an individual at a specific point in time who has income Y, which he or she wants to spend on consumption, C, I.R.A. savings, S_1, or ordinary savings S_2. Suppose that the utility function is taken to be:

$$U(C, S_1, S_2) = S_1^\alpha S_2^\beta C^\gamma.$$

The budget constraint of the consumer is given by:

$$C + S_1 + S_2 = Y$$

and the limit that he or she can contribute to the IRA is denoted by L.

(a) Derive the demand function for S_1 and S_2 for a consumer for whom the limit L *is* binding. _____(Hint: Since the consumer is at his limit I.R.A. savings, you already know the answer for how much S_1 is. Now you are left with the problem of how the consumer allocates his remaining budget between consumption and ordinary savings. But this reduces to a problem of the kind you know how to solve: a problem with two goods and a Cobb-Douglas demand function.)

(b) Derive the demand functions for S_1 and S_2 for a consumer for whom the limit L is *not* binding. _____Hint: Try the general method you used to solve for Dorothy's demand in an earlier problem.

6.12 (20) Percy consumes cakes and ale. His demand function for cakes is $q_c = m - 30p_c + 20p_a$ where m is his income, p_a is the price of ale, p_c is the price of cakes, and q_c is his consumption of cakes. Percy's income is $100 and the price of ale is $1 per unit.

(a) Is ale a substitute for cakes or a complement?_____

_____Explain. _____

(b) Write an equation for Percy's demand function for cakes where income and the price of ale are held fixed at $100 and $1. _____

_____

(c) Write an equation for Percy's inverse demand function for cakes where income and the price of ale are held fixed as above._____

_____

(d) At what price would Percy buy 30 cakes?_____

_____Use blue ink to sketch Percy's inverse demand curve for cakes on the axes below. Be sure to label the axes.

(e) Suppose that the price of ale rises to $2 per unit. On the graph you just drew, use red ink to draw in Percy's new inverse demand curve for cakes.

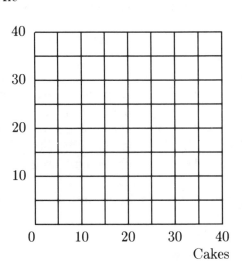

Chapter 7

NAME_____

Revealed Preference

Introduction. In the previous exercises you were given the consumer's preferences and then solved for his or her demand behavior. In this chapter we will turn this process around: you are given information about a consumer's demand behavior and want to use that information to infer something about preferences. The main tool is the principle of revealed preference: if a bundle X was purchased when Y was affordable, then X must be preferred to Y.

7.1 (20) Freddy Frolic consumes only asparagus and tomatoes, which are highly seasonal crops in Freddy's part of the world. He sells umbrellas for a living, which provides a fluctuating income depending on the weather. But Freddy doesn't mind; he never thinks of tomorrow, so each week he spends as much as he earns. One week, when the prices of asparagus and tomatoes were each $1 a pound, Freddy consumed 10 pounds of each. Use blue ink to show the budget line in the diagram below. Label Freddy's consumption bundle, with the letter A.

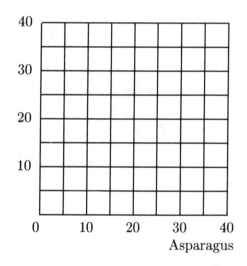

(a) What is Freddy's income?_____

(b) The next week the price of tomatoes rose to $2 a pound, but the price of asparagus remained at $1 a pound. By chance, Freddy's income had changed so that his old consumption bundle of (10,10) was just affordable at the new prices. Use red ink to draw this new budget line on the graph

above. Does your new budget line go through the point A?_____

_____

(c) What is the slope of this line?. _____

(d) How much asparagus can he afford now if he spent all of his income

on asparagus?_____

(e) What is Freddy's income now?_____

(f) Use yellow marker to highlight the bundles of goods on Freddy's new red budget line that he definitely will *not* purchase with this budget. Is it possible that he would increase his consumption of tomatoes when his budget changes from the blue line to the red one?

7.2 (10) Pierre consumes bread and wine. For Pierre, the price of bread is 4 francs per loaf and the price of wine is 4 francs per liter. Pierre has an income of 40 francs per day. Pierre consumes 6 units of wine and 4 units of bread.

Bob also consumes bread and wine. For Bob, the price of bread is 1/2 dollar per loaf and the price of wine is 2 dollars per liter. Bob has an income of \$15 per day.

(a) If Bob and Pierre have the same tastes, can you tell whether Bob is

better off than Pierre or vice versa?_____Explain

_____

_____

_____

(b) Suppose prices and incomes for Pierre and Bob are as above and that Pierre's consumption is as before. Suppose that Bob spends all of his income. Give an example of a consumption bundle of wine and bread, such that if Bob bought it, we would know that Bob's tastes are not the

same as Pierre's tastes. _____

7.3 (20) Here is a table of prices and the demands of a consumer named Ronald whose behavior was observed in 5 different price-income situations.

Obs	p_1	p_2	x_1	x_2
A	1	1	5	35
B	1	2	35	10
C	1	1	10	15
D	3	1	5	15
E	1	2	10	10

(a) Sketch each of his budget lines and label the point chosen in each case by the letters A, B, C, D, and E.

(b) Is Ronald's behavior consistent with the Weak Axiom of Revealed

Preference?_____

(c) Shade lightly in red ink, all of the points that you are certain are worse for Ronald than the bundle C.

(d) Suppose that you are told that Ronald has convex and monotonic preferences and that he obeys the strong axiom of revealed preference. Shade lightly in blue ink all of the points that you are certain are *at least as good as* the bundle C.

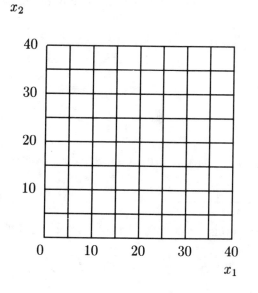

7.4 Felicia, a hard-working economics major, spent the entire term observing undergraduate behavior in the local cafeteria. She found that the typical undergraduate's demand function for weekly consumption of hamburgers and hot dogs is described by the demand functions:

$$h = \frac{m}{p_h + p_d}$$
$$d = \frac{m}{p_h + p_d}$$

In these demand functions m stands for money income, and h and d refer to hamburgers and hot dogs respectively. Felicia is interested in determining whether the behavior exhibited by the undergraduates can be viewed as utility maximization subject to a budget constraint. Having studied revealed preference theory, she decides to check these demand functions to see if they satisfy the Weak Axiom of Revealed Preference.

(a) Suppose that you have 2 different sets of prices (p_h, p_d) and (q_h, q_d) and that income is constant at 1. Write down a mathematical expression that says that the demanded bundle at the prices (p_h, p_d) is directly revealed preferred to the demanded bundle at the prices (q_h, q_d). (Use the algebraic form for the demand function given above.) Show that your expression can be simplified to $p_h + p_d \leq q_h + q_d$.

(b) Now write down a mathematical expression that says that the demand at the prices (q_h, q_d) is revealed preferred to demand at the prices (p_h, p_d).

(c) When are both of these expressions satisfied at once? _____

_____.

(d) If both expressions are satisfied at once, could different bundles be bought at the two different price situations?_____

(e) Do the demand functions given above satisfy the Weak Axiom of Revealed Preference? (Look closely at the statement of the Weak Axiom.)_

_____

7.5 (30) Here is a table that illustrates some observed prices and choices for three different goods at three different prices.

Obs	p_1	p_2	p_3	x_1	x_2	x_3
1	2	2	2	2	2	2
2	1	3	2	3	1	2
3	2	3/2	5	4	1	3/2

(a) Fill in the entry in row i and column j of the matrix below with the value of the jth bundle at the ith prices. We'll do one to get you started. The value of the bundle 1 at prices 1 is $2 \times 2 + 2 \times 2 + 2 \times 2 = 12$, so we put a 12 in row 1, column 1. The value of bundle two at prices one is $2 \times 3 + 2 \times 1 + 2 \times 2 = 12$, so we also put a 12 in row 1, column 2. Verify the entries that are already in the table, and then fill in the missing entries.

Obs	1	2	3
1	12	12	
2		10	10
3	17		

(b) Fill in the entry in row i and column j of the table below with a D if observation i is directly revealed preferred to observation j. For example, at the first observation, the consumer's expenditure is \$12; however, we have seen that it would also have cost him \$12 to buy bundle 2. Since he could have bought bundle 2, but chose instead to buy bundle 1, bundle 1 is revealed preferred to bundle 2. Thus we put a D in row 1, column 2. Formally, there is a D in row i column j if the number in the ij entry of the table in part (a) is (less than or equal to, greater than) the entry in row i, column i. Do these observation satisfy the Weak Axiom

of Revealed Preference?_____

Obs	1	2	3
1	-	D	
2		-	
3			-

(c) Now fill in row i, column j with an I if observation i is *indirectly* revealed preferred to j. Do these observations satisfy the Strong Axiom

of Revealed Preference?_____

7.6 (20) It is January and Joe Grad, whom we met in Chapter 5, is shivering in his apartment when the phone rings. It is Mandy Manana, one of the students whose price theory problems he graded last term. Mandy asks if Joe would be interested in spending the month of February in her apartment. Mandy, who has switched majors from economics to political science, plans to go to Aspen for the month and so her apartment will be empty (alas). All Mandy asks is that Joe pay the monthly service charge of $40 charged by her landlord and the heating bill for the month of February. Since her apartment is much better insulated than Joe's, it only costs $1 per month to raise the temperature by 1 degree. Joe thanks her and says he will let her know tomorrow. Joe puts his earmuffs back on and muses. If he accepts Mandy's offer, he will still have to pay rent on his current apartment but he won't have to heat it. If he moved, heating would be cheaper, but he would have the $40 service charge. The outdoor temperature averages 20 degrees Fahrenheit in February and it costs him $2 per month to raise his apartment temperature by 1 degree. Joe is still grading homework and has $100 a month left to spend on food and utilities after he has paid the rent on his apartment. The price of food is still $1 per unit.

(a) Draw Joe's budget line for February if he moves to Mandy's apartment and on the same graph, draw his budget line if he doesn't move.

(b) After drawing these lines himself, Joe decides that he would be better off not moving. From this, we can tell, using the principle of revealed preference that Joe must plan to keep his apartment at a temperature of

less than _____

Food

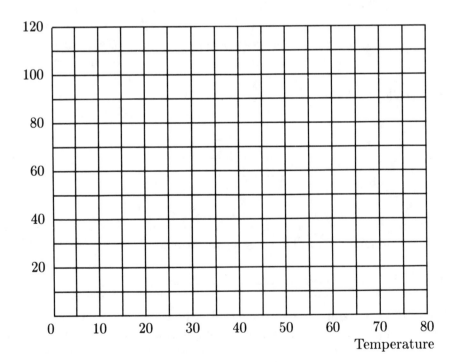

Temperature

(c) Joe calls Mandy and tells her his decision. Mandy offers to pay half the service charge. Draw Joe's budget line if he accepts Mandy's new offer. Joe now accepts Mandy's offer. From the fact that Joe accepted this offer we can tell that he plans to keep the temperature in Mandy's

apartment above _____

7.7 (20) Lord Peter Pommy is a distinguished criminologist, schooled in the latest techniques of forensic revealed preference. Lord Peter is investigating the disappearance of Sir Cedric Pinchbottom who abandoned his aging mother on a street corner in Liverpool and has not been seen since. Tireless research has revealed that Sir Cedric has left England and is living under an assumed name somewhere in the Empire. Lord Peter has three possibilities. These are R. Preston McAfee of Brass Monkey, Ontario, Canada, Richard Manning of North Shag, New Zealand, and Richard Stevenson of Gooey Shoes, Falkland Islands. Which of these is Sir Cedric? Lord Peter has obtained Sir Cedric's diary in which were recorded his consumption habits in minute detail. By careful observation, he has also been able to determine the consumption behavior of McAfee, Manning, and Stevenson. All three of these worthies, like Sir Cedric, spend their entire incomes on beer and sausage. Their dossiers reveal the following:

- **Sir Cedric Pinchbottom** — In the year before his departure, Sir Cedric consumed 10 kilograms of sausage and 20 liters of beer per week. At that time, beer cost 1 English pound per liter and sausage cost 1 English pound per kilogram.

- **R. Preston McAfee** — McAfee is known to consume 5 liters of beer and 20 kilograms of sausage. In Brass Monkey, Ontario beer costs 1 Canadian dollar per liter and sausage costs 2 Canadian dollars per kilogram.

- **Richard Manning** — Manning consumes 5 kilograms of sausage and 10 liters of beer per week. In North Shag, a liter of beer costs 2 New Zealand dollars and sausage costs 2 New Zealand dollars per kilogram.

- **Richard Stevenson** — Stevenson consumes 5 kilograms of sausage and 30 liters of beer per week. In Gooey Shoes, a liter of beer costs 10 Falkland Island pounds and sausage costs 20 Falkland Island pounds per kilogram.

(a) For each of the three fugitives, use a different color of ink to draw his budget line and label the consumption bundle he chooses. On this graph, superimpose Sir Cedric's budget line and his choice.

Sausage

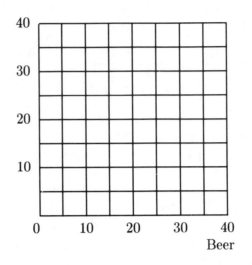

Beer

(b) After pondering the dossiers for a few moments, Lord Peter announced. "Unless Sir Cedric has changed his tastes, I can eliminate one of the suspects. Revealed preference tells me that one of the suspects is

innocent." Which one?_____

(c) After thinking a bit longer, Lord Peter announced. "If Sir Cedric left voluntarily, then he would have to be better off than he was before. Therefore if Sir Cedric left voluntarily and if he has not changed his tastes,

he must be living in _____"

7.8 The McCawber family is having a tough time making ends meet. They spend $100 a week on food and $50 on other things. A new welfare program has been introduced which gives them a choice between receiving a grant of $50 per week that they can spend any way they want, or buying any number of $2 food coupons for $1 apiece. (They naturally are not allowed to resell these coupons.) Food is a normal good for the McCawbers. As a family friend, you have been asked to help them decide on which option to choose. Drawing on your growing fund of economic knowledge, you proceed as follows.

(a) On the graph below, draw their old budget line in red ink and label their current choice C. Now use black ink to draw the budget line that they would have with the grant. If they chose the coupon option, how much

food could they buy if they spent all their money on food coupons?_____

_____How much could they spend on other things if they

bought no food?_____Use blue ink to draw their budget line if they choose the coupon option.

Other things

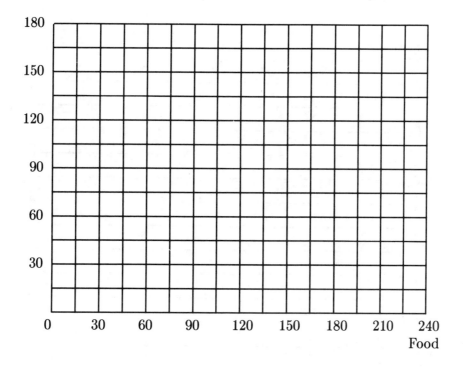

(b) Using the fact that food is a normal good for the McCawbers, and knowing what they purchased before, darken the portion of the black budget line where their consumption bundle could possibly be if they chose the lump sum grant option. Label the ends of this line segment A and B.

(c) After studying the graph you have drawn, you report to the McCawbers. "I have enough information to be able to tell you which choice to

make. You should choose the _____because

_____

_____

_____

(d) Mr. McCawber thanks you for your help and then asks, "Would you have been able to tell me what to do if you hadn't known whether food was a normal good for us? " On the axes below, draw the same budget lines you drew on the diagram above, but draw indifference curves for which food is not a normal good and for which the McCawbers would be better off with the program you advised them not to take.

Other things

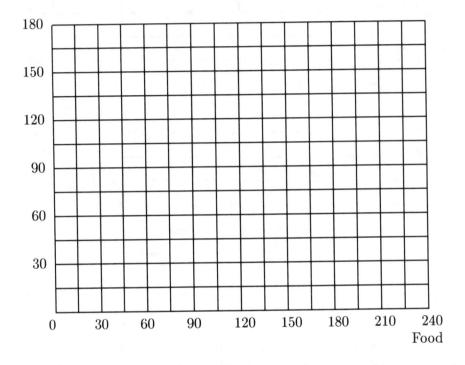

7.9 In 1984, Bruce Springsteen tried to figure out if he was making more money then than he had in 1975. In 1975, he made $2.5 million and he earned $5.4 million in 1984. The Consumer Price Index, which we will assume is a Laspeyres index with base year 1975 was 100 in 1975 and 180 in 1984. (Note: The scale of the Consumer Price Index is expressed as $100 \times I_p$ where I_p is the Laspeyres index as defined in your text.)

(a) Assuming that Bruce spent all of his income in 1975, was Bruce's 1984 income big enough to buy his 1975 bundle at 1984 prices or can't

you tell? _____

(b) What is the smallest amount of money that Bruce could have made in

1984 without changing your answer to Part a? _____

(c) How, if at all, would your answer to Part *a* change if the CPI were a Paasche index?

_____

Chapter 8
Slutsky Equation

NAME_____

Introduction. The Slutsky equation breaks down the effect of a price change into two pieces, the substitution effect and the income effect. The substitution effect measures how the consumer's demand for a good would change if its price was changed but, at the same time, income was adjusted so as to keep the original consumption bundle affordable. The income effect measures how the consumer's demand would change if the prices were kept constant and only income was allowed to change.

8.1 (20 Neville's passion is fine wine. When the prices of all other goods are fixed at current levels, Neville's demand function for high quality claret is $q = .02m - 2p$. where p is the price of claret (in British pounds) and q is the number of bottles of claret that he demands. Neville's income is 5000 pounds and the price of a bottle of suitable claret is 25 pounds.

(a) How many bottles of claret will Neville buy._____

(b) If the price of claret rose to 30 pounds, how much income would Neville have to have in order to be exactly able to afford the amount of claret and the amount of other goods that he bought before the price

change._____At this income, and a price of 30 pounds,

how many bottles would Neville buy? _____

(c) At his original income of 5000 and a price of 30, how much claret

would Neville demand?_____

(d) When the price of claret rose from 25 to 30, the number of bottles that

Neville demanded decreased by _____The substitution

effect (increased, reduced) his demand by _____bottles

and the income effect (increased, reduced) his demand by _____

_____bottles.

8.2 (10) Consider the figure below which shows the budget constraint and the indifference curves of good King Zog. Zog is in equilibrium with an income of $300, facing prices $p_x = \$4$ and $p_y = \$10$.

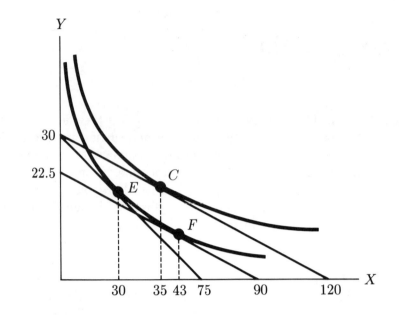

(a) How much x does Zog consume?_____

(b) If the price of x falls to \$2.50 while income and the price of y stay

constant, how much x will Zog consume?_____

(c) How much income must be taken away from Zog to isolate the Hicksian
income and substitution effects. (i.e., to make him just able to afford to

reach his old indifference curve at the new prices)?_____

_____

(d) The total effect of the price change is to change consumption from

the point _____to the point _____

(e) The income effect corresponds to the movement from the point_____

_____to the point _____while the

substitution effect corresponds to the movement from the point _____

_____to the point _____

(f) Is x a normal good or an inferior good?

(g) On the axes below, sketch an Engel curve and a demand curve that would be reasonable given the information in the figure above. Be sure to label the axes on both your graphs.

8.3 (5) Maude spends all of her income on delphiniums and hollyhocks. She thinks that delphiniums and hollyhocks are perfect substitutes. Delphiniums cost $2.00 a unit and hollyhocks cost $3.00 a unit.

(a) If the price of delphiniums decreases to $1.00 a unit, will Maud

necessarily buy more of them?_____What part of the change in consumption is due to the income effect and what part is due to the substitution effect?

_____

(b) Continue to suppose that delphiniums and hollyhocks are perfect substitutes for Maud and $p_d = \$2.00$ and $p_h = \$3.00$. If Maud has $40 to spend, draw her budget line in blue ink. Draw the highest indifference curve that she can attain in red ink, and label the point that she chooses as *A*.

delphiniums

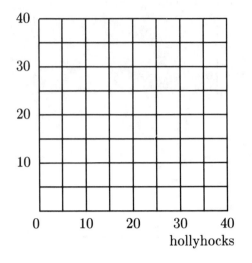

hollyhocks

(c) Now let the price of hollyhocks fall to $1.00 a unit while the price of delphiniums does not change. Draw her new budget line in black ink. Draw the highest indifference curve that she can now reach with red ink. Label the point she chooses now as *B*.

(d) How much would Maud's income have to be after the price of hollyhocks fell, so that she could just exactly afford her old commodity bundle

A?_____

(e) What part of the change in Maud's demand when the price of hollyhocks fell to $1.00 is due to the income effect and what part due to the substitution effect?

_____

8.4 (5) Suppose now that we have two goods that are perfect complements. Let the price of one good change. What part of the change in demand is due to the substitution effect and what part is due to the income effect?

_____

8.5 (20) Douglas Cornfield's demand function for good x is $x(p_x, p_y, m) = 2m/5p_x$. If his income is $1000, if the price of x is $5 and the price of y is $20, then if the price of x falls to $4, then his demand for x will change

from _____to _____

(a) If his income were to change at the same time so that he could exactly afford his old commodity bundle at $p_x = 4$, what would his new income

be?_____What would be his demand for x at this new level of

income? _____

(b) The substitution effect is a change in demand from _____

to _____The income effect of the price change is a change in

demand from _____to _____

(c) On the axes below, use blue ink to draw Douglas Cornfield's budget line before the price change. Locate the bundle he chooses at these prices on your graph and label this point A. Use black ink to draw Douglas Cornfield's budget line after the price change. Label his consumption bundle after the change by B.

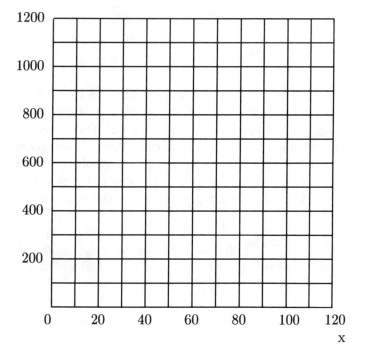

money for other goods

(d) On the graph above, use yellow ink to draw a budget line with the new prices but with an income that just allows Douglas to buy his old bundle, A. Find the bundle that he would choose with this budget line and label this bundle C.

(e) On your graph, draw a red mark over the part of the horizontal axis that represents the change in consumption of x due to the substitution effect. Draw a yellow mark over the part of the horizontal axis that represents the change in consumption of x due to the income effect.

8.6 (10) Illustrate in the diagram below indifference curves that will result in a zero substitution effect. Draw in two budget lines that illustrate this zero substitution effect.

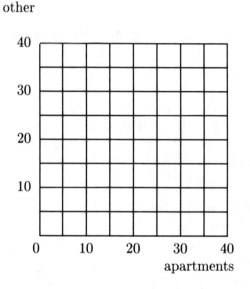

8.7 (30) Tim spends all of his income on 'Sneaky Pete' wine and 'Old Stogie' cigars. In each of the following cases, you observe an event and then try to figure out what it has told you about Tim's income elasticity of demand for each good (*i.e.*, is it a normal, inferior, or luxury good, or can you not tell anything from the event you have observed. Point it out if a good is shown to be Giffin as well. Note: these categories are not mutually exclusive). By the way, Tim has convex preferences and likes both goods.

(a) Tim finds a $10 bill on the street while looking for half-smoked cigarettes. He immediately goes out and buys $10 worth of 'Old Stogies'.

_____

_____

_____

(b) Tim loses $30 he was sure he had a moment ago. He decides to sell the rest of his bottle of wine to a 'friend' and spend the money on cigars.

_____

_____

_____

(c) The price of wine goes up and Tim decides to cut back his purchases of cigars.

_____

_____

_____

(d) The price of wine and cigars both rise by 20%. Tim cuts his expenditures on both items by the same proportion.

_____

_____

_____

(e) The price of cigars falls by 50%. Tim lowers his consumption of cigars by 5% and uses all the extra money to buy more wine.

_____

_____

_____

(f) While looking for the $30 he lost earlier, Tim finds an only slightly used bottle of Sneaky Pete. He drinks it down and does not change his purchases of wine or cigars.

_____

_____

_____

8.8 We observe that Mr. Consumer allows himself to spend $100 per month on cigarettes and ice cream. The price of cigarettes in $1 per pack while ice cream costs $2 per pint. Faced with these prices, Mr. C buys 30 pints of ice cream and 40 packs of cigarettes in January. Being from Minnesota, Mr. C's preferences for cigarettes and ice cream are unaffected by the season of the year.

(a) In February, Mr. C again has $100 for his 'vices', but now cigarettes cost $1.25 per pack. Mr. C now consumes 30 pints of ice cream and 32 packs of cigarettes. Does this tell us anything about the income elastic-

ity of demand for cigarettes?_____of demand for ice

cream?_____

(b) In March, Mr. C again has $100 to spend and ice cream is on sale for $1 per pint. Cigarettes, meanwhile, have increased to $1.50 per pack. Is he better off than in January, worse off, or can you not make such a

comparison?_____

(c) How does your answer to the last question change if cigarettes have

instead increased in March to $2 per pack?_____

(d) In April cigarettes have in fact risen to $2 per pack and ice cream is still on sale for $1 per pint. Mr. Consumer buys 34 packs of cigarettes and

32 pints of ice cream. Is he better off or worse off than in January?_____

_____Can you compare his utility to the February level?

(e) In May cigarettes stay at \$2/pack and the sale on ice cream ends, the price returns to \$2/pint. On the way to the store, however, Mr. C finds Tim's \$30. He now has \$130 to spend on 'vices.' Without knowing what he purchased, can you compare his utility to any of the previous

months?_____Which ones and how do they compare?

_____

Chapter 9

Buy and Sell

Introduction. This chapter examines demand theory when consumers receive their income from selling their endowment of goods. Remember the endowment will always be on the budget line, since the consumer always has the option of choosing not to purchase or sell anything.

9.1 (15) Abishag Appleby owns 20 quinces and 10 kumquats. She has no income from any other source, but she can buy or sell either quinces or kumquats at their market prices. The price of kumquats is two times the price of quinces. There are no other commodities of interest.

(a) How many quinces could she have if she was willing to do without

kumquats? _____

(b) Draw Abishag's budget set, using blue ink, and label the endowment bundle with the letter *E*.

Kumquats

Quinces

(c) Write down an equation for her budget line._____

_____

(d) Suppose that the price of both goods were to double, what would

happen to Abishag's budget set? _____

9.2 (15) Suppose that in the previous problem, Abishag decides to sell 10 quinces. Label her final consumption bundle in your graph with the letter C.

(a) Now suppose that the price of kumquats falls so that they cost the same as quinces. On the diagram above, draw Abishag's new budget line, using red ink.

(b) On the graph, use yellow marker to denote the portion of Abishag's new budget line where the principle of revealed preference tells us that her new demand might possibly be.

9.3 (20) Mario has a small garden where he raises eggplant and tomatoes to consume and to sell in the market. He always consumes eggplant and tomatoes together in a 1:1 ratio. One week his garden yielded 25 pounds of eggplant and 5 pounds of tomatoes. At that time the price of each vegetable was $5 per pound.

(a) What is the monetary value of Mario's endowment of vegetables?___

_____

(b) Mario ends up consuming _____pounds of tomatoes and

_____pounds of eggplant.

(c) Mario will find it optimal to sell _____pounds of _____

_____and to buy _____pounds of _____

(d) Suppose that the price of tomatoes rises to $15 a pound. What is

the value of Mario's endowment now?_____His new consump-

tion bundle consists of _____tomatoes and _____

_____eggplants.

(e) What would be Mario's consumption bundle if the price of tomatoes were \$15 and his money income were fixed at the original level given

in part *(a)*? He will consume _____pounds of tomatoes and

_____pounds of eggplant.

(f) The change in the demand for tomatoes due to the substitution ef-

fect is _____The change in the demand for tomatoes due to

the ordinary income effect is _____The change in the demand

for tomatoes due to the endowment income effect is _____The

total change in the demand for tomatoes is _____

(g) Illustrate the bundles described above and label them with the letter indicating the part they are from.

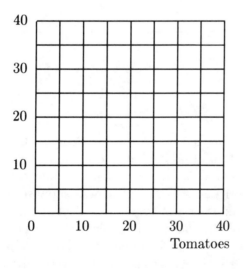

Eggplant

9.4 (20) Priscilla finds it optimal not to engage in trade at the going prices and just consumes her endowment. Draw a budget line and an indifference curve that illustrate Priscilla's situation. Use a revealed preference argument to show that when the price of good 1 falls, she must choose to consume at least as much of good 1 as before, regardless of the shape of her indifference curves.

9.5 (30) Potatoes are a Giffen good for Paddy, who has a small potato farm. The price of potatoes fell but Paddy increased his potato consumption. At first this astonished the village economist, who thought that a decrease in the price of a Giffen good was supposed to reduce demand. But then he remembered that Paddy was a net supplier of potatoes. With the help of a graph, he was able to explain Paddy's behavior. In the axes below, show how this could have happened. Put "potatoes" on the horizontal axis and "all other goods" on the vertical axis. Label the old equilibrium A and the new equilibrium B. Draw a point C so that the Slutsky substitution effect is the movement from A to C and the Slutsky income effect is the movement from C to B. On this same graph, you are also going to have to show that potatoes are a Giffen good. To do this, draw a budget line showing the effect of a fall in the price of potatoes if Paddy didn't own any potatoes, but only had money income. Label the new consumption point under these circumstances by D. (Warning: You probably will need to make a few dry runs on some scratch paper to get the whole story straight.)

9.6 Agatha must travel on the Orient Express from Istanbul to Paris. The distance is 1500 miles. You can choose to travel as many of the 1500 miles as you wish in first class coach or in second class coach. You have to pay 10 cents a mile for every mile that you travel second class and 20 cents a mile for every mile that you travel first class. Agatha much prefers first class to second class travel, but because of a misadventure in an Istanbul bazaar, Agatha has only $200 left with which to buy her tickets. Luckily, she still has her toothbrush and a suitcase full of provisions which she plans to eat on the way. Agatha therefore plans to spend her entire $200 on her tickets for her trip. She will travel as far as she can afford to on first class with her $200 but she must travel all the way to Paris.

(a) On the graph below, use red ink to show the locus of combinations of first and second class tickets that Agatha can just afford to purchase with her $200. Use blue ink to show the locus of combinations of first and second class tickets that are sufficient to carry her the entire distance from Istanbul to Paris. Locate the combination of first and second class miles that Agatha will choose on your graph and label it *A*.

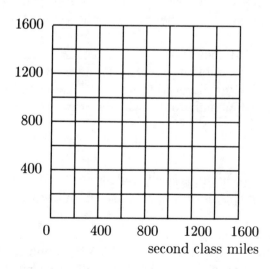

first class miles

(b) Let m_1 be the number of miles she travels by first class coach and m_2 be the number of miles she travels by second class coach. Write down two equations that you can solve to find the number of miles she chooses to travel by first class coach and the number of miles she chooses to travel by second class coach.

_____

(c) The number of miles that she travels by second class coach is _____

_____

(d) Suppose that just before she was ready to buy her tickets, the price of second class tickets fell to $.05 while the price of first class tickets remained at $.20. On the graph that you drew above, use pencil to show the combinations of first and second class tickets that she can afford with her $200 at these prices. On your graph, locate the combination of first and second class tickets that she would now choose. (Remember, she is going to travel as much first class as she can afford to and still make the 1,500 mile trip on $200). Label this point C. How many miles does she travel by second class now?_____(Hint: For an exact solution you will have to solve two linear equations in two unknowns.) Is second class travel a normal good for Agatha?_____Is it a Giffen good for her?_____

(e) Suppose that just after the price change, Agatha misplaced her handbag. Although she kept most of her money in her sock, the money she lost was just enough so that she could exactly afford the combination of first and second class tickets that she bought before the price change.

How much money did she lose? _____Use black ink to draw the locus of combinations of first and second class tickets that she can just afford after discovering her loss. Label the point that she chooses with a B. How many miles will she travel by second class now?

_____

(f) Suppose that Agatha finds her handbag again. How many miles will she travel by second class now (assuming she didn't buy any tickets before she found her lost handbag)? _____When the price of second class tickets fell from $.10 to $.05, how much of a change in Agatha's demand for second class tickets was due to a substitution effect?

_____How much of a change was due to an income

effect? _____

9.7 Suppose that Agatha from the previous problem had spent her $200 to buy first and second class tickets on the Orient Express when the price of first class tickets was $.20 and the price of second class tickets was $.10. After she boarded the train, she discovered to her amazement that the price of second hand tickets has fallen to $.05 while the price of first class tickets remains at $.20. She also learned that it is possible when you are on the train to buy or sell first class tickets for $.20 a mile and to buy or sell second class tickets for $.05 a mile. Agatha has no money left to buy either kind of ticket, but she does have the tickets that she has already bought.

(a) On the graph below, use pencil to show the combinations of tickets that she could afford at the old prices. Use blue ink to show the combinations of tickets that will take her exactly 1500 miles. Mark the point that she chooses with the letter *A*.

first class miles

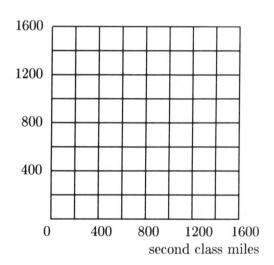

second class miles

(b) Use red ink to draw a line showing all of the combinations of first class and second class travel that she can afford by trading her endowment of first and second class tickets at the new prices on board the train.

(c) On your graph, show the point that she chooses after finding out about the price change. Does she choose more less or the same amount

of second class tickets?_____

Labor Supply

Introduction. Here we examine some labor supply functions. It is convenient to consider the demand for leisure, and to let labor supply be the difference between the endowment of leisure and the demand for leisure.

10.1 (30) Fred has just arrived at college and is trying to figure out how to supplement the meager checks that he gets from home. "How can anyone live on $50 a week for spending money?" he asks. But he asks to no avail. "If you want more money, get a job," say his parents.

So Fred glumly investigates the possibilities. The amount of leisure time that he has left after allowing for necessary activities like sleeping, brushing teeth, and studying for his economics classes is 50 hours a week. He can get a part-time job at a local fast food establishment cleaning tables at $5.00 an hour. Given that Fred's utility function for leisure and money to spend on consumption is $U(C, L) = CL$, we want to determine how many hours he will end up working per week.

Let's try to solve Fred's problem algebraically. A utility function of the form $u(x_1, x_2) = x_1 x_2$ is a special case of a Cobb–Douglas utility function. It turns out that the demand functions for this utility have the form:

$$x_1 = \frac{m}{2p_1}$$
$$x_2 = \frac{m}{2p_2}$$

(a) The two goods that Fred is concerned with are money to spend on consumption, which has a price of 1, and leisure which has a price of

_____

(b) Fred has an endowment that consists of $50 of money to spend on

consumption and _____ hours of leisure, some of which he might "sell" for money.

(c) The money value of his endowment bundle, including both his money

allowance and the market value of his leisure time is therefore _____

_____ The amount of money that he will find optimal to spend on consumption is given by the Cobb–Douglas demand function. It is

_____

(d) The amount of leisure that Fred will choose to consume is _____

_____hours. This means that his optimal labor supply will be

_____hours.

(e) Illustrate Fred's optimal consumption and labor supply in the graph below and draw a few indifference curves. The indifference curves should be consistent with the utility function given above.

Consumption

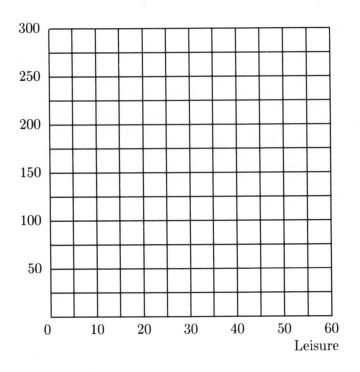

(f) Can you write down the algebraic formula for Fred's demand for leisure, where the price of other goods is 1, the wage rate is w, where $\bar{C}$ is his income sent from home and where $\bar{L} = 50$ is his total endowment of leisure time? To give you a clue, lets find his demand function for consumption. The total value of Fred's endowment is $m = \bar{C} + 50w$. Using the Cobb-Douglas demand function for consumption demand and recalling that the price of consumption goods is 1, we have

$$C = m/2$$
$$= \frac{(\bar{C} + 50w)}{2} = \bar{C}/2 + 25w$$

Now to find the supply function for labor, you need to find his demand function for leisure and subtract his leisure demand from his endowment

of leisure. The answer is _____

(g) Given that Fred's parents send him $50 a week, what is Fred's supply

function of labor as a function of the wage rate? _____

_____ hours. What would his supply function of labor be if his parents

didn't send him any money? _____ hours.

10.2 (20 Fred's cousin Norman is in the same situation. He has the same
tastes for consumption and leisure, the same job opportunities, and the
same amount of free time. But there are two differences between Fred
and Norman. The first one is that Norman's parents send him a $100
check each week. The second one is that Norman lives across town and
would have to take a taxi cab to the fast food place, which he estimates
would cost him $50 a week. He doesn't mind riding the cab, since he can
study on it, but the $50 fare seems a bit steep. How much money would
Norman have left to spend on consumption if he took the cab to work

each week? _____ On the graph below, draw Norman's budget
set and illustrate his optimal consumption and labor supply if he decides
to work. (Use the information from the last problem.)

(a) What utility does he get from this choice? _____

(b) What if Norman decided not to work at all? What utility would he

get? _____

(c) What is Norman's utility maximizing supply of labor? _____

_____ hours.

(d) Illustrate Norman's budget set and indifference curves in the graph
below, along with his optimal supply of labor.

Consumption

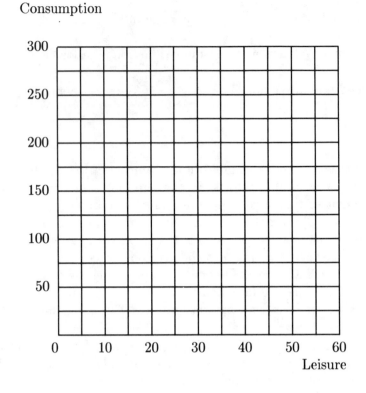

10.3 (5) If leisure is an inferior good, must the slope of the labor supply function necessarily be positive? Explain.

_____

_____

_____

10.4 (20) Wally Piper is a plumber. He charges $10 per hour for his work and he can work as many hours as he likes. Wally has no source of income other than his labor. On the graph below, draw Wally's budget set, showing the various combinations of weekly leisure and income that Wally can afford.

Income

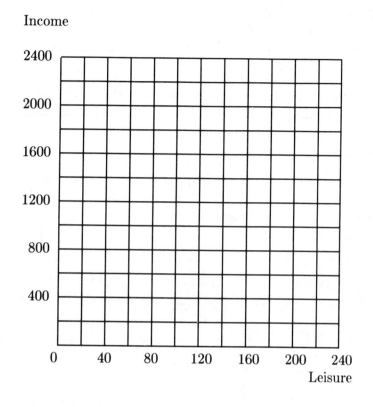

(a) Write down an equation that describes Wally's budget constraint.

_____

(b) While self employed, Wally chose to work 40 hours per week. The construction firm, Glitz and Drywall, had a rush job to complete. They offered Wally $20 an hour and said that he could work as many hours as he liked. Wally still chose to work only 40 hours per week. On the graph you drew above, draw in Wally's new budget line and draw indifference curves that are consistent with his choice of working hours when he was self–employed and when he worked for Glitz and Drywall.

(c) Glitz and Drywall were in a great hurry to complete their project and wanted Wally to work more than 40 hours. They decided that instead of paying him $20 per hour, they would pay him only $10 an hour for the first 40 hours that he worked per week and $20 an hour for every hour of "overtime" that he worked beyond 40 hours per week. On the graph that you drew above, use red ink to sketch in Wally's budget line with this pay schedule. Draw the indifference curve through the point that Wally chooses with this pay schedule. Will Wally work more than 40 hours or

less than 40 hours per week with this pay schedule? _____

_____

10.5 Mr. I. M. Cog works in a machine factory. In each of the following situations write down Mr. Cog's budget constraint. Let C be the number of consumer goods he consumes and let R be the number of hours of leisure that he chooses.

(a) Mr. Cog earns $5.00 an hour, has 18 hours to devote to labor or leisure, and consumer goods cost $1.00 each. He has no non-labor income.

_____.

(b) Mr. Cog faces the identical circumstances as above, but he also re-

ceives $10.00 in interest from his meager savings._____

_____.

(c) Mr. Cog faces the same conditions as in part (a), but decides that he can live on only 4 hours of sleep per night, and therefore devotes 20 hours

a day to either labor of leisure._____.

(d) After vehemently complaining to the management that he "just feels like a Cog in a machine factory," Mr. Cog gets a raise from $5.00 an hour to $10.00 an hour. He continues to devote 20 hours a day to either labor

or leisure._____.

10.6 (20) George Johnson earns $5 per hour in his job as a truffle sniffer. After allowing time for all of the activities necessary for bodily upkeep, George has 80 hours per week to allocate between leisure and labor. Sketch the budget constraints for George resulting from the following government programs.

(a) There is no government subsidy or taxation of labor income.

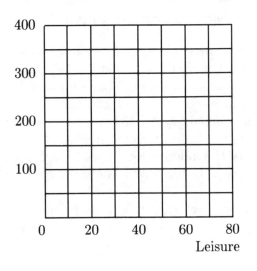

Consumption

Leisure

(b) All individuals receive a lump sum payment of $100 per week from the government. There is no tax on the first $100 per week of labor income. But all labor income above $100 per week is subject to a 50% income tax.

Consumption

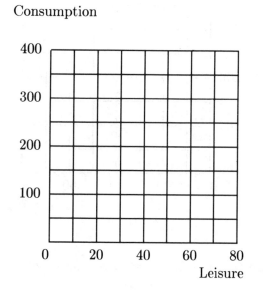

(c) If an individual is not working, he receives a payment of $100. If he works he does not receive the $100 and all wages are subject to a 50% income tax.

Consumption

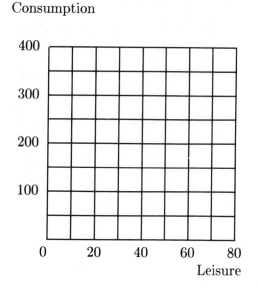

(d) The same conditions as in part (c) apply, with the exception that the first 20 hours of labor are exempt from the tax.

Consumption

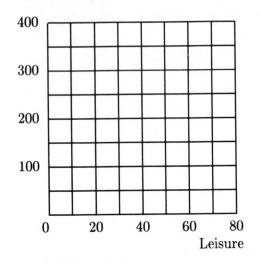

(e) All wages are taxed at 50%, but as an incentive to encourage work, the government gives a payment of $100 to anyone who works more than 20 hours a week.

Consumption

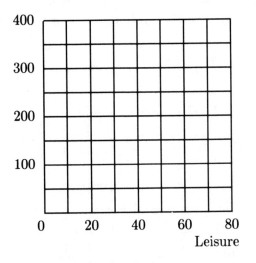

Intertemporal Choice

Introduction. Here we examine some applications of present value. Remember: the present value of a stream of payments indicates the value of the endowment. Thus a stream of payments that has a higher present value than another stream must be preferred to one with a lower present value.

11.1 (30) Chillingsworth owns a large, poorly insulated home. His annual fuel bill for home heating averages $500 per year. An insulation contractor suggests to him the following options.

Plan A. Insulate just the attic. If he does this, he will permanently reduce his fuel consumption by 15%. Total cost of insulating the attic is $500.

Plan B. Insulate the attic and the walls. If he does this, he will permanently reduce his fuel consumption by 20%. Total cost of insulating the attic and the walls is $900.

Plan C. Insulate the attic and the walls and install a solar heating unit. If he does this, he will permanently reduce his fuel costs to zero. Total cost of this option is $10,000 for the solar heater and $900 for the insulating.

(a) Assume for simplicity of calculations that the house and the insulation will last forever. Calculate the present value of the dollars saved on fuel from each of the three options if the interest rate is 10%. The present

values are: Plan A?_____Plan B?_____Plan C?___

_____

(b) Each plan requires an expenditure of money to undertake. The difference between the present value and the present cost of each plan is: Plan

A?_____Plan B?_____Plan C?_____

(c) If the price of fuel is expected to remain constant which option should he choose if he can borrow and lend at an annual interest rate of 10%?

_____

(d) Which option should he choose if he can borrow and lend at an annual

rate of 5%?_____

(e) Suppose that the government offers to pay half of the cost of any insulation or solar heating device. Which option would he now choose at

interest rates 10%? _____ 5%? _____

(f) Suppose that there is no government subsidy but suppose that fuel prices are expected to rise by 5% per year. What is the present value of fuel savings from each of the three proposals if interest rates are 10%. (Hint: If a stream of income is growing at x% and being discounted at y%, its present value should be the same as that of a constant stream of income discounted at what percent? You may use an approximation.)

Plan A? _____ Plan B? _____ Plan C? _____

_____ Which proposal should Chillingsworth choose if interest rates

are 10%? _____ 5%? _____

11.2 (10) You are considering investing in a project with the following features. If you undertake the project, then right now you would have to buy a machine that costs $100. One year from now you would have to spend $55 more to maintain the machine. There are no other costs or expenses. Two years from now the machine would produce output that is worth $x and then the machine would fall apart and have no resale value.

(a) If the interest rate is 10%, write an equation that can be solved for the

smallest amount that $x could be for this to be a worthwhile investment. __

_____

11.3 (10) Peregrine Pickle purchases (c_1, c_2) and earns (m_1, m_2) in periods 1 and 2 respectively. Suppose the interest rate is r.

(a) Write down Peregrine's intertemporal budget constraint in present

value terms _____.

(b) If Peregrine does not consume anything in period 1, what is the most

he can consume in period 2? _____.
This is the (future value, present value) of his endowment.

(c) If Peregrine does not consume anything in period 2, what is the most

he can consume in period 1? _____.
This is the (future value, present value) of his endowment.

(d) What is the slope of his intertemporal budget constraint?_____

_____.

11.4 (20) Becky Sharp has a utility function $U(c_1, c_2) = c_1^a c_2^{1-a}$ where $0 < a < 1$ and where c_1 and c_2 are her consumptions in periods 1 and 2 respectively.

Recall that preferences of this type are known as Cobb–Douglas preferences. We saw earlier that if utility has the form $u(x_1, x_2) = x_1^a x_2^{1-a}$ and the budget constraint has the standard form, then the demand functions for the goods have the form $x_1 = am/p_1$ and $x_2 = (1-a)m/p_2$.

(a) Suppose that Becky's income is m_1 in period 1 and m_2 in period 2. Write down her budget constraint in terms of present values.

(b) We want to compare this budget constraint to one of the "standard"

form. In terms of Becky's budget constraint, what is p_1?_____

_____What is p_2?_____What is m?_____

(c) Suppose that $a = .2$. Solve for Becky's demand functions for consumption in each period as a function of m_1, m_2, and r. Her demand function for consumption in period 1 is:

(d) Her demand function for consumption in period 2 is:

(e) An increase in the interest rate will (increase) (decrease) her period 1 consumption. It will (increase) (decrease) her period 2 consumption and (increase) (decrease) her savings in period 1.

11.5 (20) Decide whether each of the following statements is True or False. Then explain why your answer is correct. Draw a graph to illustrate your argument concerning each of the statements. (Hint: You need to use the Slutsky decomposition into income and substitution effects.)

(a) "If both current and future consumption are normal goods, an increase in the interest rate will necessarily make a saver save more."

_____

_____

_____

(b) "If both current and future consumption are normal goods, an increase in the interest rate will necessarily make a saver choose more consumption in the second period."

_____

_____

_____

11.6 (20) Suppose that a consumer has an endowment of $20 each period.

He can borrow money at an interest rate of 200%, and he can lend money at a rate of 0%.

(a) Use blue ink to illustrate his budget set in the graph below. (Hint: The boundary of the budget set is not a single straight line.)

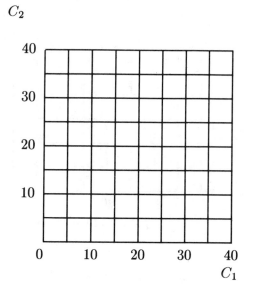

C_2

(b) The consumer is offered an investment that will change his endowment to $m_1 = 30$ and $m_2 = 15$. Would the consumer be (better off) (worse off) or (can't tell) by taking this new endowment? Use red ink to draw the new budget set in the graph above.

(c) Now use pencil or black ink to draw the budget set for $m_1 = 15$, $m_2 = 30$. Is the consumer (better off) (worse off) or (can't tell) with this endowment than with the original endowment?

11.7 (40) Nickleby has an income of $2,000 this year and he expects an income of $1,100 next year. He can borrow and lend money at an interest rate of 10%. Consumption goods cost $1 per unit this year and there is no inflation.

(a) What is the present value of Nickleby's endowment? _____

(b) What is the future value of Nickleby's endowment? _____

(c) With blue ink, show the combinations of consumption this year and consumption next year that he can afford. Label Nickelby's endowment with the letter E.

Consumption next year

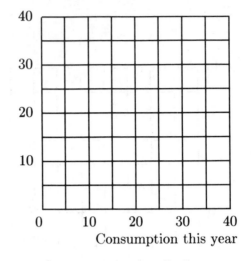

Consumption this year

(d) Suppose that Nickleby has the utility function $U(C_1, C_2) = C_1 C_2$. Write down Nickleby's marginal rate of substitution between consumption this year and consumption next year. (Your answer will be a function of the variables C_1, C_2.)

(e) What is the slope of Nickleby's budget line? _____

(f) Write down an equation that states that the slope of Nickleby's indifference curve between consumption in the two years is equal to the slope

of his budget line when the interest rate is 10%. _____

(g) What is the second equation that one must solve to find the optimal

C_1 and C_2?_____

(h) Solve these two equations. Nickleby will consume _____

_____units in period 1 and _____units in period 2. Label this point A on your diagram.

(i) Will he borrow or save in the first period?_____How much?__

_____

(j) On your graph use red ink to show what Nickleby's budget line would be if the interest rate rose to 20%. Knowing that Nickleby chose the point *A* at a 10% interest rate, even without knowing his utility function, you can determine that his new choice can not be on certain parts of his new budget line. Use yellow marker to darken the part of his new budget line where that choice can not be.

(k) What are the two equations that one must solve to find Nickleby's

optimal choice when the interest rate is 20%. _____

(l) Solve for Nickleby's optimal choice when the interest rate is 20%.

Nickleby will consume _____units in period 1 and _____

_____units in period 2.

(m) Will he borrow or save in the first period?_____How much?__

_____

11.8 (20) We return to the planet Mungo. On Mungo, macroeconomists and bankers are jolly, clever creatures, and there are two kinds of money, yellow money and blue money. Recall that to buy something in Mungo you have to pay for it twice, once with blue money and once with yellow money. Everything has a blue money price and a yellow money price and nobody is ever allowed to trade one kind of money for the other. There is a blue money bank where you can borrow and lend blue money at a 50% annual interest rate. There is a yellow money bank where you can borrow and lend yellow money at a 25% annual interest rate.

A Mungoan named Jane consumes only one commodity, ambrosia, but it must decide how to allocate its consumption between this year and next year. Jane's income this year is 100 blue currency units and no yellow currency units. Next year, its income will be 100 yellow currency units and no blue currency units. The blue currency price of ambrosia is one b.c.u. per flagon this year and will be two b.c.u.'s per flagon next year. The yellow currency price of ambrosia is one b.c.u. per flagon this year and will be the same next year.

(a) If Jane spent all of its blue income in the first period, it would be

enough to pay the blue price for _____flagons of ambrosia. If
Jane saved all of this year's blue income at the blue money bank, it would

have _____b.c.u.'s next year. This would give it enough blue

currency to pay the blue price for _____flagons of ambrosia.
On the graph below, draw Jane's blue budget line, depicting all of those
combinations of current and next period's consumption that it has enough
blue income to buy.

Ambrosia next period

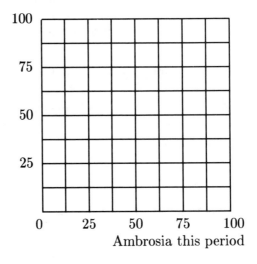

Ambrosia this period

(b) If Jane planned to spend no yellow income in the next period and
to borrow as much yellow currency as it can pay back with interest with
next period's yellow income, how much yellow currency could it borrow?

_____

(c) The (exact) real rate of interest on blue money is _____The

real rate of interest on yellow money is _____

(d) On the axes below, draw Jane's blue budget line and its yellow budget
line. Shade in all of those combinations of current and future ambrosia
that Jane can afford given that she has to pay with both currencies.

Ambrosia next period

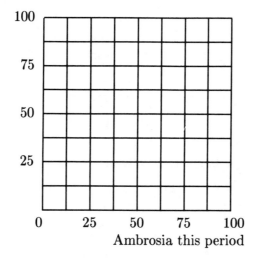

(e) It turns out that Jane finds it optimal to operate *on* its blue budget line and *beneath* its yellow budget line. Find such a point on your graph and mark it with a C.

(f) On the following graph, show what happens to Jane's original budget set if the blue interest rate rises and the yellow interest rate does not change. On your graph shade in the part of the new budget line where Jane's new demand could possibly be. (Hint: Apply the principle of revealed preference. Think about what bundles were available but rejected when Jane chose to consume at C before the change in blue interest rates.)

Ambrosia next period

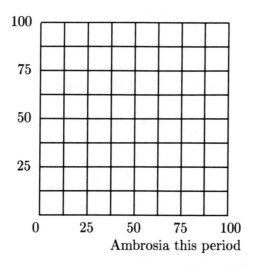

11.9 (20) Dr. No owns a bond, serial number 007, issued by the James Company. The bond pays $100 for each of the next three years, at which time the bond is retired and pays its face value of $1000.

(a) How much is the James bond 007 worth to Dr. No at an interest rate of 10%? _____.

(b) How valuable is James bond 007 at an interest rate of 5%? _____

_____

(c) Ms. Yes offers Dr. No $1,100 for the James bond 007. Should Dr. No say yes or no to Ms. Yes if the interest rate is 10%? _____.

What if the interest rate is 5%? _____

(d) In order to destroy the world, Dr. No hires Professor Know to develop a nasty zap beam. In order to lure Professor Know from his cushy-soft university position, Dr. No will have to pay the professor $100 a year. The nasty zap beam will take three years to develop, at the end of which it can be built for $1000. If the interest rate is 5% how much money will

Dr. No need today to finance this dastardly program? _____

_____If the interest rate was at 10% would the world be in more

or less danger from Dr. No? _____

11.10 (10) If a consumer is a borrower and the interest rate falls will

she remain a borrower or become a lender? _____

_____. Will she be better or worse off after the change?

_____

11.11 (10) Illustrate preferences for which the consumer is neither a borrower nor a lender regardless of the interest rate. Label the endowment with the letter E and draw a couple of budget lines.

C_2

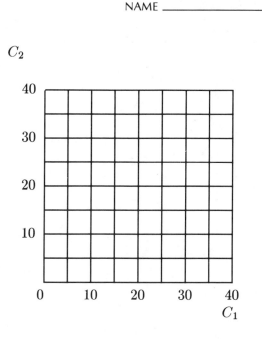

11.12 (40) Consider a two period model where the consumer has income (m_1, m_2) and consumption (c_1, c_2). He has to pay income tax at rate t in each period, and the interest rate is constant at r.

(a) Suppose that the interest income is tax exempt. Write down the

intertemporal budget constraint. _____

(b) Suppose that the consumer now has to pay income tax on his interest income, and gets to deduct his interest expenses. What is the form of his

budget constraint? _____

Now suppose that the consumer can invest some amount X in a pension plan in period 1. He does not have to pay taxes on the amount put in the pension plan in period 1. The money in the pension plan will earn interest at rate r, and the consumer does not have to pay tax on this interest income. However, when the consumer withdraws his money, $X(1 + r)$, in period 2, he has to pay tax on it as income.

(c) If the consumer consumes c_1 in period 1, how much will he be able to

save in the pension plan? _____

(d) What is the consumer's intertemporal budget constraint?

Asset Markets

Introduction. The fundamental equilibrium condition for asset markets is that in equilibrium the rate of return on all assets must be the same. This simple condition has many important implications that we will investigate in this chapter.

12.1 (10) You are thinking about buying two plots of land. The first one is a plot in a good neighborhood. You are certain you can sell this land in a year's time for $121,000. The second plot is in a slightly shabby neighborhood, but you are sure that this plot will be worth $110,000 in a year. (Both of these amounts are net of sales costs, etc.) Because of other obligations, you can only hold each property for a year, and due to strict zoning regulations no one can use the property for any purpose during that year. The market interest rate is 10% per year.

(a) At what price would you just be willing to purchase the first plot?__

_____

(b) At what price would you just be willing to purchase the second plot?__

_____

(c) What will be the rate of appreciation of value on the lot in the

good neighborhood? _____What about the lot in the

shabby neighborhood? _____

12.2 (30) Publicity agents for the Detroit Felines announce the signing of a phenomenal new quarterback, Archie Parabola. They say that the contract is worth $1,000,000 and will be paid in installments of $50,000 per year for the next 20 years. The contract contains a clause that guarantees he will get all of the money even if he is injured and can not play a single game. Sports writers declare that Archie has become an "instant millionaire".

(a) Archie's brother, Fenwick, who majored in economics, explains to Archie that he is not a millionaire. In fact, his contract is worth less than half a million dollars. Explain in words why this is so.

_____

_____

_____

Archie wasn't too good at math; in fact, he thought that the next number after 50 was "Hike!" So his brother tried to reason out the calculation for him. Here is how it goes:

(b) Suppose that the interest rate is 10% and is expected to remain at 10% forever. How much would it cost the team to buy Archie a perpetuity that would pay him and his heirs $1 per year *forever*?_____

(c) How much would it cost to buy a perpetuity that paid $50,000 a year for ever? _____

(d) If the interest rate is 10%, what is the present value of $1 to be received in 20 years?_____(Use a calculator or the table in the text to find a numerical answer.)

(e) If the interest rate is and will remain at 10%, how much is the present value of a stream of income of $1 per year starting 20 years from now and going on forever? _____(Hint: Since the interest rate is assumed never to change, in 20 years perpetuities will cost the same in the money of that time as they cost now in current dollars. But the cost of buying that perpetuity is deferred for 20 years.)

(f) What is the present value of a stream of $1 per year for 20 years?_____

_____(Hint:All you have to do is subtract the value of a perpetuity paying $1 per year, starting in 20 years from the value of such a perpetuity starting now.)

(g) Use the answer to the above question to calculate the present value

of Archie's contract? _____

Calculus **12.3** (20) You are the business manager of P. Bunyan Forests, Inc. and are trying to decide when you should cut your trees. The market value of the lumber that you will get if you let your trees reach the age of t years is given by the function $W(t) = e^{.20t - .001t^2}$. Mr. Bunyan can earn an interest rate of 5% per year on money in the bank. (Hint: It follows from elementary calculus that if $F(t) = e^{g(t)}$, then $F'(t)/F(t) = g'(t)$.)

(a) How old should Mr. Bunyan let the trees get?_____

_____

(b) At what age do the trees have the greatest market value?_____

_____

12.4 (20) You expect the price of a certain painting to rise by 8% per year forever. The market interest rate for borrowing and lending is 10%. Assume there are no brokerage costs in purchasing or selling.

(a) If you pay $\$x$ for the painting now and sell it in a year, how much has it cost you to hold the painting rather than to have loaned the $\$x$ at the

market interest rate? _____

(b) You would be willing to pay $100 a year to have the painting on your walls. Write an equation that you can solve for the price at which you

would be just willing to buy the painting _____

(c) How much should you be willing to pay to buy the painting? _____

_____.

(d) Does the amount you would be willing to pay to buy the painting now depend on whether you would get tired of the painting after a while and

decide to sell it? _____

12.5 (20) J. Cousteau owns a catfish farm, and has calculated that if he buys $10 of catfish he can expect the amounts of money given in the following table from harvesting the fish at various times in the future. If Mr. Cousteau puts money in the bank he can receive 10% interest.

Harvest Time	1	2	3	4	5
Value of Fish	12	13.8	15.18	16.4	17.37
Rate of Return					
Total Value					

(a) Fill in the third line of the table with the rate of return that M. Cousteau earned in the previous period.

(b) When should he harvest those "little suckers"?_____

_____

(c) Fill in the last line of the table with the value of M. Cousteau's initial $10 investment if he follows the optimal harvesting rule.

12.6 (20) Fisher Brown is taxed at 40% on his income from ordinary bonds. Ordinary bonds pay 10% interest. Interest on municipal bonds is not taxed at all.

(a) If the interest rate on municipal bonds is 7%, should he buy municipal

bonds or ordinary bonds?_____

(b) Hunter Black makes less money than Fisher Brown and is taxed at only 25% on his income from ordinary bonds. Which kind of bonds should

he buy? _____

(c) If Fisher has $1,000,000 in bonds and Hunter has $10,000 in bonds,

how much taxes does Fisher pay on his interest from bonds?_____

_____How much taxes does Hunter pay on his interest

from bonds?_____

(d) The government is considering a new tax plan under which no interest income will be taxed. If the interest rates on the two types of bonds do not change, and Fisher and Hunter are allowed to adjust their portfolios,

how much will Fisher's after-tax income be increased?_____

_____How much will Hunter's after-tax income be increased?__

_____

(e) What would the change in the tax law do to the demand for municipal

bonds if the interest rates did not change?_____

(f) What interest rate will new issues of municipal bonds have to pay in

order to attract purchasers?_____

(g) What do you think will happen to the market price of the old municipal bonds, which had a 7% yield originally?

_____

12.7 (20) In the text we discussed the market for oil assuming zero production costs, but now suppose that it is costly to get the oil out of the ground. Suppose that it costs $5 dollars per barrel to extract oil from the ground. Let the price in period t be denoted by p_t and let r be the interest rate.

(a) If a firm extracts a barrel of oil in period t, how much profit does it

make in period t? _____

(b) If a firm extracts a barrel of oil in period $t + 1$, how much profit does

it make in period $t + 1$? _____

(c) What is the present value of the profits from extracting a barrel of

oil in period $t + 1$?_____What is the present value of

profit from extracting a barrel of oil in period t? _____

(d) If the firm is willing to supply oil in each of the two periods, what must be true about the relation between the present value of profits from

sale of a barrel of oil in the two periods? _____

_____Express this relation as an equation _____

_____

(e) Solve the equation in the above part for p_{t+1} as a function of p_t and

r._____

(f) Is the percentage rate of price increase between periods larger or smaller than the interest rate? _____

12.8 (20) On the planet Stinko, the principle industry is turnip growing. The turnips are processed in Ole Factories to produce food and drink for the residents. For centuries the turnip fields have been fertilized by guano which was deposited by the now-extinct giant scissor-billed kiki-bird. It costs $5 per ton to mine kiki-bird guano and deliver it to the fields. Unfortunately, the country's stock of kiki-bird guano is about to be exhausted. Fortunately the scientists on Stinko have devised a way of synthesizing kiki-guano from political science textbooks and swamp water. This method of production makes it possible to produce a product indistinguishable from kiki-guano and to deliver it to the turnip fields at a cost of $30 per ton. The interest rate on Stinko is 10%. There are perfectly competitive markets for all commodities.

(a) Given the current price and the demand function for kiki guano, the last of the deposits on Stinko will be exhausted exactly one year from now. What is the current price of kiki-guano delivered to the turnip fields?_____

(Hint: In equilibrium, sellers must be indifferent between selling their kiki guano right now or at any other time before the total supply is exhausted. But we know that they must be willing to sell it right up until the day, one year from now, when the supply will be exhausted and the price will be $30, the cost of synthetic guano.)

(b) Suppose that everything is as we have said previously except that the deposits of kiki-guano will be exhausted 10 years from now. What must be the current price of kiki-guano? _____(Hint: $1.1^{10} = 2.59$.)

12.9 (30) In the text we considered a competitive market for oil. Here let us consider what would happen if there were one firm that owned all the oil and charged a price that would maximize the present value of its stream of profits. (That is, the single firm behaved as a monopolist.) Suppose that the demand for oil is constant at D barrels per year, the total supply of oil is S barrels, and there is an alternative technology widely available that will provide synthetic oil at C dollars per barrel.

(a) What price would the monopoly set for its oil?_____

_____

(b) Would the price rise at the rate of interest?_____

Chapter 13

Uncertainty

13.1 (20) Clarence Bunsen is an expected utility maximizer. His preferences among contingent commodity bundles are represented by the expected utility function

$$u(c_1, c_2, \pi_1, \pi_2) = \pi_1\sqrt{c_1} + \pi_2\sqrt{c_2}.$$

Clarence's friend, Hjalmer Ingqvist, has offered to bet him $1,000 on the outcome of the toss of a coin. That is, if the coin comes up heads, Clarence must pay Hjalmer $1,000 and if the coin comes up tails, Hjalmer must pay Clarence $1,000. The coin is a fair coin, so that the probability of heads and the probability of tails are both 1/2. If he doesn't accept the bet, Clarence will have $10,000 with certainty. In the privacy of his car dealership office over at Bunsen Motors, Clarence is making his decision. (Clarence uses the pocket calculator that his son, Elmer, gave him last Christmas. You will find that it will be helpful for you to use a calculator too.) Let Event 1 be "coin comes up heads" and let Event 2 be "coin comes up tails".

(a) If Clarence accepts the bet, then in Event 1, he will have _____

_____dollars and in Event 2, he will have _____

_____dollars.

(b) Since the probability of each event is 1/2, Clarence's expected utility for a gamble in which he gets c_1 in Event 1 and c_2 in Event 2 can be

described by the formula _____

(c) Therefore, Clarence's expected utility if he accepts the bet with Hjalmer

will be _____(Use that calculator.)

(d) If Clarence decides not to bet, then in Event 1, he will have _____

_____dollars and in Event 2, he will have _____

_____dollars.

(e) If Clarence decides not to bet, his expected utility will be _____

_____

(f) Having calculated his expected utility if he bets and if he does not bet, Clarence determines which is higher and makes his decision accordingly.

Does Clarence take the bet?_____

13.2 (30) It is a slow day at Bunsen Motors, so since he has his calculator warmed up, Clarence Bunsen (whose preferences toward risk were described in the last problem) decides to study his expected utility function more closely.

(a) Clarence first thinks about really *big* gambles. What if he bet his entire $10,000 on the toss of a coin, where he loses if heads and wins if

tails? Then if the coin came up heads, he would have _____

_____dollars and if it came up tails, he would have _____

_____dollars. His expected utility if he took the bet

would be _____while his expected utility if he didn't

take the bet would be _____Therefore, he concludes that he would not take such a bet.

(b) Clarence then thinks "Well, of course I wouldn't want to take a chance on losing all of my money on just an ordinary bet. But, what if somebody offered me a really good deal. Suppose I had a chance to bet where if a fair coin came up heads, I lost my $10,000, but if it came up tails, I would win $50,000. Would I take the bet? If I took the bet, my expected

utility would be _____while if I didn't take the bet, my

expected utility would be _____Therefore, I should _

_____the bet."

(c) Clarence later asks himself, "If I make a bet where I lose my $10,000 if the coin comes up heads, what is the smallest amount that I would have to win in the event of tails in order to make the bet a good one for me to take?" After some trial and error, Clarence finds that the answer is

_____

You might want to find the answer by trial and error too, but it is easier to find the answer by solving down an equation. On the left side of your equation you would write down Clarence's utility if he doesn't bet. On the right side of the equation, you write down an expression for Clarence's utility if he makes a bet so that his consumption will be zero in Event 1 and x in Event 2. Then you can solve this equation for x, which will allow you to easily compute the answer to Clarence's question. The

equation that you write when you do this is _____

_____. The solution for x is _____

(d) Your answer to the last part gives you two points on Clarence's indifference curve between the contingent commodities, money in Event 1 and money in Event 2. (Poor Clarence has never heard of indifference curves or of contingent commodities, so you will have to work this part for him, while he heads down to the Chatterbox Cafe for morning coffee.) One of these points is where money in both events is $10,000. On the graph below, label this point, A. The other is where money in Event 1 is zero

and money in Event 2 is _____On the graph below, label this point B.

Money in Event 2 ($\times 1,000$)

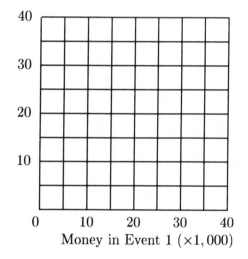

Money in Event 1 ($\times 1,000$)

(e) You can very quickly find a third point on this indifference curve. The coin is a fair coin and the only reason that Clarence cares whether heads or tails turn up, is because that determines his prize. Therefore Clarence will be indifferent between two gambles that are the same except that the assignment of prizes to outcomes are reversed. In this example, Clarence will be indifferent between point B on the graph and a point in which

he gets zero if Event 2 happens and _____if Event 1 happens. Find this point on the Figure above and label it C.

(f) Another gamble that is on the same indifference curve for Clarence as not gambling at all is the gamble where he loses $5,000 if heads turn up

and where he wins _____dollars if tails turn up. (Hint: To solve this problem, put the utility of not betting on the left side of an equation and on the right side of the equation, put the utility of having $10,000 - $5,000$ in Event 1 and $10,000 + x$ in Event 2. Then solve the resulting equation for x. On the axes above, plot this point and label it D. Now sketch in the entire indifference curve through the points that you have labelled.)

13.3 (30) Hjalmer Ingkvist's son-in-law, Earl, has not worked out very well. It turns out that Earl likes to gamble. His preferences over contingent commodity bundles are represented by the expected utility function

$$u(c_1, c_2, \pi_1, \pi_2) = \pi_1 c_1^2 + \pi_2 c_2^2.$$

(a) Just the other day, some of the boys were down at Skoog's tavern when Earl stopped in. They got to talking about just how bad a bet they could get him to take. At the time, Earl had $100. Kenny Olson shuffled a deck of cards and offered to bet Earl $20 that Earl would not cut a spade from the deck. Assuming that Earl believed that Kenny wouldn't cheat, the probability that Earl would win the bet was 1/4 and the probability that Earl would lose the bet was 3/4. If he won the bet,

Earl would have _____dollars and if he lost the bet, he

would have _____dollars. Earl's expected utility if he

took the bet would be _____and his expected utility

if he did not take the bet would be _____Therefore he refused the bet.

(b) Just when they started to think Earl might have changed his ways, Kenny offered to make the same bet with Earl except that they would bet $100 instead of $20. What is Earl's expected utility if he takes that

bet? _____Would Earl be willing to take this bet?

_____

(c) Let Event 1 be the event that a card drawn from a fair deck of cards is a spade. Let Event 2 be the event that the card is not a spade. Earl's preferences between income contingent on Event 1, c_1, and income contingent

on Event 2, c_2, can be represented by the equation._____

_____. Use blue ink on the graph below to sketch Earl's indifference curve passing through the point $(100, 100)$.

Money in Event 2

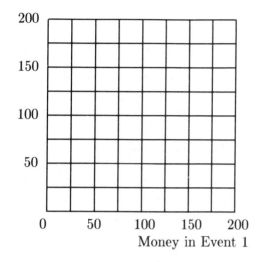

0   50   100   150   200
Money in Event 1

(d) On the same graph, let us draw Hjalmer's son-in-law Earl's indifference curves between contingent commodities where the probabilities are different. Suppose that a card is drawn from a fair deck of cards. Let Event 1 be the event that the card is black. Let event 2 be the event that the card drawn is red. Suppose each event has probability 1/2. Then Earl's preferences between income contingent on event 1 and

income contingent on event 2 are represented by the formula _____

_____On the graph, use red ink to show two of Earl's indifference curves, including the one that passes through $(100, 100)$.

13.4 (20) Sidewalk Sam makes his living selling sunglasses at the boardwalk in Atlantic City. If the sun shines, Sam makes $30 and if it rains Sam only makes $10. For simplicity, we will suppose that there are only two kinds of days, sunny ones and rainy ones.

(a) One of the casinos in Atlantic City has a new gimmick. They are accepting bets on whether or not it will be sunny or rainy the next day. The way it works is, the casino sells dated "rain coupons" for $1 each. If it rains the next day, the casino will give you $2 for every rain coupon you bought on the previous day. If it doesn't rain, your rain coupon is worthless. Sam buys these coupons on credit from the casino. At the end of any day, he takes his earnings from sunglasses sales and the coupons that he bought the previous day. He first goes to the credit window at the casino and pays $1 for each of the coupons that he bought the day before. If it was a rainy day, he then walks over to the pay out window and gets $2 for each of the rain coupons he bought the day before. If it has not been rainy, he just throws away his rain coupons. In the graph

below, mark Sam's "endowment" of contingent consumption if he makes no bets with the casino, and label it E.

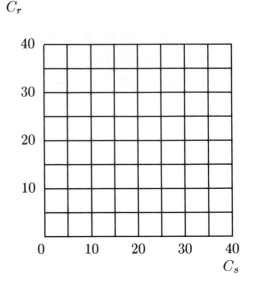

C_r

C_s

(b) On the same graph, mark the combination of consumption contingent on rain and consumption contingent on sun that he could achieve by buying 10 rain coupons from the casino. Label it A.

(c) On the same graph, use blue ink to draw the budget line representing all of the other patterns of consumption that Sam can achieve by buying rain coupons. (Assume that he can buy fractional coupons, but not negative amounts of them.) What is the slope of Sam's budget line at points

above and to the left of his initial endowment?_____

(d) Suppose that the casino also sells sunshine coupons. These tickets cost \$2. With these tickets, the casino gives you \$1 if it doesn't rain and nothing if it does. Sam can get the same credit arrangement as for rain coupons. On the graph above, use red ink to sketch in the budget line of contingent consumption bundles that Sam can achieve by buying sunshine tickets.

(e) If the price of a dollar's worth of consumption when it rains is set equal to 1, what is the price of a dollar's worth of consumption if it

shines? _____

13.5 (30) Suppose that Sidewalk Sam from the previous problem has the following utility function for consumption in the two states of nature:

$$u(c_s, c_r, \pi) = c_s^{1-\pi} c_r^{\pi},$$

where c_s is the dollar value of his consumption if it shines, c_r is the dollar value of his consumption if it rains, and π is the probability that it will rain.

(a) Suppose now that the probability that it will rain is $\pi = .5$. Recall that if a utility function has the form Cobb–Douglas form, $u(x_1, x_2) = x_1^a x_2^{1-a}$, then demand functions take the form $x_1 = am/p_1$ and $x_2 = (1-a)m/p_2$, where m is the monetary value of the endowment. Using the prices derived

above, the value of Sam's endowment is _____

(b) Using this fact, what is Sam's optimal amount of consumption when

it rains? _____

(c) How many rain coupons will Sam buy? _____How

many sunshine coupons will he buy?_____

13.6 (20) Sidewalk Sam's brother Morgan von Neumanstern is an expected utility maximizer. His von Neumann–Morgenstern utility function for wealth is $u(c) = \ln c$. Sam's brother also sells sunglasses on another beach in Atlantic City and makes exactly the same income that Sam does. He can make exactly the same deal with the casino that Sam can. If Morgan believes that there is a 50% chance of rain and a 50% chance of sun every day, what would his expected utility of consuming (c_r, c_s)

be? _____.

(a) How does Morgan's utility function compare to Sam's? Is one a

monotonic transformation of the other? _____

(b) What will Morgan's optimal pattern of consumption be? Answer:

Morgan will consume _____on the sunny days and _____

_____on the rainy days. How does this compare to Sam's con-

sumption? _____

13.7 (20) Billy John Pigskin, of Mule Shoe, Texas has a von Neumann-Morgenstern utility function of the form $u(c) = \sqrt{c}$. Billy John also weighs about 300 pounds and can outrun jackrabbits and pizza delivery trucks. Billy John is beginning his senior year of college football. If he is not seriously injured, he will receive a \$1,000,000 contract for playing professional football. If an injury ends his football career, he will receive a \$40,000 contract as a refuse removal facilitator in his home town. There is a 10% chance that Billy John will be injured badly enough to end his career.

(a) What is Billy John's expected utility? _____

(b) If Billy John pays $\$p$ for an insurance policy that would give him $1,000,000 if he suffered a career ending injury while in college, then he would be sure to have an income of $\$1,000,000 - p$ no matter what happened to him. Write an equation that can be solved to find the largest price that Billy John would be willing to pay for such an insurance policy.

_____.

(c) Solve this equation for p. _____

13.8 (30) You have $200 and are thinking about betting on the Big Game next Saturday. Your team, the Golden Boars, are scheduled to play their traditional rivals the Robber Barons. It appears that the going odds are 2 to 1 against the Golden Boars. That is to say if you want to bet $10 on the Boars you can find someone who will agree to pay you $20 if the Boars win in return for your promise to pay him $10 if the Robber Barons win. Similarly if you want to bet $10 on the Robber Barons, you can find someone who will pay you $10 if the Robber Barons win, in return for your promise to pay him $20 if the Robber Barons lose. Suppose that you are able to make as large a bet as you like, either on the Boars or on the Robber Barons so long as your gambling losses do not exceed $200. (To avoid tedium, let us ignore the possibility of ties.)

(a) If you do not bet at all, you will have $200 whether or not the Boars win. If you bet $50 on the Boars then after all gambling obligations

are settled, you will have a total of _____dollars if the

Boars win and _____dollars if they lose. On the graph below, use blue ink to draw a line that represents all of the combinations of "money if the Boars win" and "money if the Robber Barons win" that you could have by betting from your initial $200 at these odds.

Money if the Boars Lose

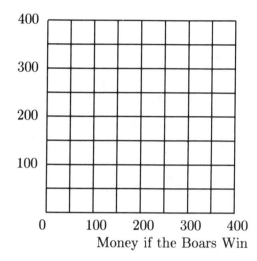

Money if the Boars Win

(b) Label the point on this graph where you would be if you did not bet at all with an *E*.

(c) After careful thought you decide to bet $50 on the Boars. Label the point you have chosen on the graph with a *C*. Suppose that after you have made this bet, it is announced that the star Robber Baron quarterback suffered a sprained thumb during a tough economics midterm examination and will miss the game. The market odds shift from 2 to 1 against the Boars to "even money" or 1 to 1. That is, you can now bet on either team and the amount you would win if you bet on the winning team is the same as the amount that you would lose if you bet on the losing team. You can not cancel your original bet, but you can make new bets at the new odds. Suppose that you keep your first bet, but you now also bet $50 on the Robber Barons at the new odds. If the Boars win, then after you collect your winnings from one bet and your losses from the other, how much

money will you have left? _____If the Robber Barons win, how much money will you have left after collecting your winnings

and paying off your losses? _____

(d) Use red ink to draw a line on the diagram you made above, showing the combinations of "money if the Boars win" and "money if the Robber Barons win" that you could arrange for yourself by adding possible bets at the new odds to the bet you made before the news of the quarterback's misfortune. On this graph, label the point *D* that you reached by making the two bets discussed above.

Chapter 14

NAME_____

Asset Markets with Uncertainty

14.1 (30) Ms. Lynch has a choice of two assets: the first is a risk free asset which offers a rate of return of r_f, and the second is a risky asset (a china shop which caters to large mammals) which has an expected rate of return of r_m and a standard deviation of σ_m.

(a) If x is the percent of wealth Ms. Lynch invests in the risky asset

what is the equation for the expected rate of return on the portfolio?___

_____What is the equation for

the standard deviation of the portfolio?_____

_____

(b) By solving the second equation above for x and substituting the result into the first equation, derive an expression for the rate of return on the

portfolio in terms of the portfolio's riskiness. _____

_____

(c) Suppose that Ms. Lynch can borrow money at the interest rate r_f and invest it in the risky asset. If $r_m = 20$, $r_f = 10$ and $\sigma_m = 10$, what will be Ms. Lynch's expected return if she borrows an amount equal to

100% of her initial wealth and invests it in the risky asset? _____

_____(Hint: This is just like investing 200% of her wealth
in the risky asset.)

(d) Suppose that Ms. Lynch can borrow or lend at the risk free rate. If r_f is 10%, r_m is 20%, and σ_m is 10% what is the formula for the "budget

line" Ms. Lynch faces? _____Plot this
budget line in the graph below.

Expected Return

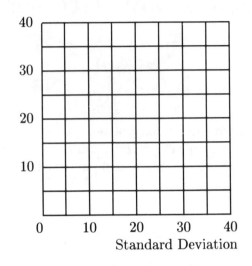

Standard Deviation

(e) Which of the following risky assets would Ms. Lynch prefer to her present risky asset, assuming she can only invest in one risky asset at a time, and that she can invest a fraction of her wealth in whichever risky asset she chooses. Write the words "better", "worse", or "same" after each of the assets.

Asset A with $r_a = 17\%$, and $\sigma_a = 5\%$ _____,

Asset B with $r_b = 30\%$, and $\sigma_b = 25\%$ _____,

Asset C with $r_c = 11\%$, and $\sigma_c = 1\%$ _____,

Asset D with $r_d = 25\%$, and $\sigma_d = 14\%$ _____

(f) Suppose Ms. Lynch's utility function has the form $u(r_x, \sigma_x) = r_x - 2\sigma_x$.

How much of her portfolio will she invest in the original risky asset? __

_____(You might want to graph a few of Ms. Lynch's indifference curves before answering, e.g., graph the combinations of r_x and σ_x which imply $u(r_x, \sigma_x) = 0, 1 \ldots$, etc.)

14.2 (30) Fenner Smith is contemplating dividing his portfolio between two assets, a risky asset that has an expected return of 30% and a standard deviation of 10%, and a safe asset that has an expected return of 10% and a standard deviation of 0%.

(a) If Mr. Smith invests x percent of his wealth in the risky asset, what

will be his expected return? _____

(b) If Mr. Smith invests x percent of his wealth in the risky asset what

will be the standard deviation of his wealth? _____

(c) Solve the above two equations for the expected return on Mr. Smith's

wealth as a function of the standard deviation he accepts._____

_____

(d) Plot this "budget line" on the graph below.

Expected Return

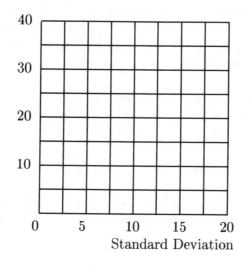

Standard Deviation

(e) If Mr. Smith's utility function is $u(r_x, \sigma_x) = \min\{r_x, 30 - 2\sigma_x\}$, then

Mr. Smith's optimal value of r_x is _____, and his op-

timal value of σ_x is _____(Hint: you will need to solve
two equations in two unknowns. One of the equations is the budget constraint.)

(f) Plot Mr. Smith's optimal choice and an indifference curve through it
in the graph.

(g) What fraction of his wealth should Mr. Smith invest in the risky

asset?_____

14.3 (20) Assuming that the Capital Asset Pricing Model is valid complete the following table. In this table p_0 is the current price of asset i
and Ep_1 is expected price of asset i next period.

r_f	r_m	r_i	β_i	p_0	Ep_1
10	20	10		100	
10	20		1.5		125
10		20	2	200	
0	30		2/3	40	48
10	22		0	80	

14.4 (20) Farmer Alf Alpha has a pasture located on a sandy hill. The return to him from this pasture is a random variable depending on how much rain there is. In rainy years the yield is good, in dry years the yield is poor. The market value of this pasture is $5,000. The expected return from this pasture is $500 with a standard deviation of $100. Every inch of rain above average means an extra $100 in profit and every inch of rain below average means another $100 less profit than average. Farmer Alf has another $5,000 that he wants to invest in a second pasture. There are two possible pastures that he could buy.

(a) One is located on low land that never floods. This pasture yields an expected return of $500 per year no matter what the weather is like. What is Alf Alpha's expected rate of return on his *total* investment if he buys this pasture for his second pasture?_____What is the standard deviation of his rate of return in this case?_____

_____

(b) Another pasture that he could buy is located on the very edge of the river. This gives very good yields in dry years but in wet years it floods. This pasture also costs $5,000. The expected return from this pasture is $500 and the standard deviation is $100. Every inch of rain *below* average means an extra $100 in profit and every inch of rain above average means another $100 less profit than average. If Alf buys this pasture and keeps his original pasture on the sandy hill, what is his expected rate of return on his total investment. _____What is the standard deviation of the rate of return on his total investment in this case?_____

_____

(c) If Alf is a risk averter, which of these two pastures should he buy and why?

_____

Chapter 15

Consumer's Surplus

15.1 (20) In the graph below, you see a representation of Sarah Gamp's indifference curves between cucumbers and other goods. Suppose that the references prices of cucumbers and the reference price of "other goods" are both 1.

Other goods

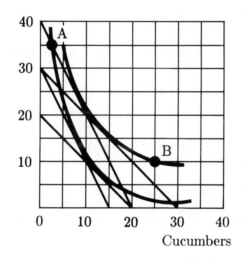

Cucumbers

(a) What is the money metric utility for the bundle *A*?_____

(b) What is the money metric utility for the bundle *B*?_____

(c) Suppose now that the reference price for cucumbers is 2 and the reference price for other goods is 1. Now what is the money metric utility

of bundle *A*? _____

(d) What is the money metric utility of bundle *B* using these new reference

prices? _____

(e) No matter what the reference prices, the money metric utility of bundle A must be (higher, lower) than the money metric utility for bundle B.

15.2 (20) Suppose a consumer considers goods x and y to be perfect complements, that is $u(x, y) = \min\{x, y\}$.

(a) What level of utility does the consumer achieve with the bundle

$(4, 4)$?_____

(b) If the prices are \$2 and \$2 per unit of x and y respectively, what is

the money metric utility level for this bundle?_____

(c) What is the level of money metric utility if the prices are $(2, 3)$? ___

_____

(d) What level of utility does the consumer obtain with the bundle $(5, 8)$?__

_____

(e) What are the levels of money metric utility for this bundle with prices

$(2, 2)$ and $(2, 3)$ respectively?_____, and _____

_____

15.3 (20) The Consumer was in the store the other day in order to pick up some more x's and y's (of which, as you know, The Consumer is peculiarly fond). The Consumer's utility function is: $u(x, y) = x^{1/2}y^{1/2}$. Her income is \$20.

(a) When the prices of goods x and y are \$2 and \$.50 respectively, her

demand for x is _____and for y is _____

(b) What level of utility would The Consumer's money metric utility

function assign to the x, y bundle $(5, 20)$, if the prices are (\$2, \$.50)._____

_____

(c) What level of money metric utility would be assigned to the bundle $(20, 5)$ when prices are ($2, $.50)?_____What about the bundle $(4, 25)$?_____

15.4 (20) F. Flintstone has quasilinear preferences and his inverse demand function for Brontosaurus Burgers is $P(b) = 30 - 2b$. Mr. Flintstone is currently consuming 10 burgers at a price of 10 dollars.

(a) How much money would he be willing to pay to have this amount rather than no Burgers at all?_____What is his level of (net) consumer's surplus?_____

(b) The town of Bedrock, the only supplier of Brontosaurus Burgers, decides to raise the price from $10 a burger to $14 a burger. What is Mr. Flintstone's change in consumer's surplus?_____

15.5 (10) Karl Kapitalist is willing to produce $p/2 - 5$ widgets at every price, p. If the price of widgets is $100, what is Karl's producer's surplus if he is producing 45 widgets?_____

15.6 (20) Ms. Q. Moto loves to ring the church bells for up to 10 hours a day. Where m is income, and x is hours of bell ringing, her utility function is: $u(m, x) = m + 3x$ so long as $x \leq 10$. If $x > 10$ she develops painful blisters and is worse off than if she didn't ring the bells. Her income, m, is equal to $100 and the sexton allows her to ring the bell for 10 hours.

(a) Due to complaints from the villagers, the sexton has decided to restrict Ms. Moto to 5 hours of bell ringing per day. This is bad news for Ms. Moto. In fact she regards it as just as bad as losing _____ _____dollars of income.

(b) The sexton relents and offers to let her ring the bells as much as she likes so long as she pays $2 per hour for the privilege. How much ringing does she do now? _____This tax on her activities is as bad as a loss of how much income?_____

(c) The villagers continue to complain. The sexton raises the price of bell

ringing to $4 an hour. How much ringing does she do now?_____

_____This tax, as compared to the situation in which she could ring

the bells for free is as bad as a loss of how much income?_____

15.7 (30) A clever and charming economics graduate student named John, is interested in only two things (besides economics), dating beautiful and intelligent women and eating chocolate chip cookies. His utility function is $u(x, y) = x_1^{1/2} x_2^{1/2}$ where x_1 is the number of hours per week spent dating beautiful women and x_2 is the number of bags of chocolate chip cookies that he consumes. He finds that he spends $1 an hour on dates and $1 per bag on chocolate chip cookies. He has only $20 per month to spend.

(a) What is John's optimal level of consumption at these prices and in-

come? _____

(b) Write an expression for $m(1, 1, x_1, x_2)$, the minimum cost at prices

(1,1) of purchasing a bundle that John likes as well as (x_1, x_2). _____

_____(Hint: Note that the formula for the money metric utility function for the Cobb-Douglas case in your textbook simplifies greatly for this special case.)

(c) One day, John was shocked to discover that the government had put a tax of $1 per bag on chocolate chip cookies so that the price was now

$2. How much of each good did John buy then? $x_1 =$_____,

$x_2 =$ _____

(d) How much revenue did the government collect from John by means

of its tax on cookies? _____

(e) How much income would John have needed at the pre-tax prices to be

as well off as he was after the tax was imposed? _____

(f) How much would John have been willing to pay to avoid the tax?___

_____This amount is known as the _____

_____variation.

(g) Which is larger, this amount or the amount of revenue collected from John by the tax?

(h) Write an expression for $m(1, 2, x_1, x_2)$, the minimum cost at prices

$(1, 2)$ of purchasing a bundle that John likes as well as (x_1, x_2). _____

_____After the tax was imposed, how much would you

have to pay John to make him as well off as he was before the tax?_____

_____This amount is known as the _____

_____variation.

(i) Which is bigger, the compensating or the equivalent variation, or are

they the same?_____

15.8 (30) At time t the prices are (p_1^t, p_2^t) and The Consumer optimally chooses (x_1^t, x_2^t). At time s the prices are (p_1^s, p_2^s) and The Consumer optimally chooses (x_1^s, x_2^s). The total expenditures in periods s and t are therefore $e^t = p_1^t x_1^t + p_2^t x_2^t$ and $e^s = p_1^s x_1^s + p_2^s x_2^s$.

(a) Using the money metric utility function $m(p_1, p_2, x_1, x_2)$ write an expression for how much money The Consumer would need at time t to

be as well off as he was at time s. _____

(b) The true cost of living index, I, is the amount of money The Consumer would need at time t to be as well off as he was at time s divided by his expenditure at time s. Using the answer to the above question, write

down an expression for I. _____

(c) One way that The Consumer could be as well off at time t as he was at time s is by consuming the *same* bundle at time t as he consumed at

time s. How much would this cost him? _____

(d) This means that $m(p_1^t, p_2^t, x_1^s, x_2^s)$ must be (greater than or equal to, exactly equal to, less than or equal to) $p_1^t x_1^s + p_2^t x_2^s$.

(e) The Laspeyres price index is defined by:

$$L_P = \frac{p_1^t x_1^s + p_2^t x_2^s}{e^s}.$$

The Laspeyres price index must be (greater than or equal to, exactly equal to, less than or equal to) the true cost of living index I.

15.9 (30) Suppose The Consumer's preferences can be represented by the utility function $u(x_1, x_2) = \min\{x_1, x_2\}$.

(a) What is the form of his money metric utility function? _____

_____Write an expression for his true cost of living index, using the simplification gained from the fact that he would have bought

the same amount of both goods in period s. ?_____

(b) If The Consumer's preferences can be represented by the utility function $u(x_1, x_2) = x_1 + x_2$ what is the form of his money metric utility

function? _____His true cost of living index?_____

_____

Calculus **15.10** (40) Lolita, an intelligent and charming Holstein cow, consumes only two goods, cow feed (made of ground corn and oats) and hay. Her preferences are represented by the utility function $U(x, y) = x - x^2/2 + y$ where x is her consumption of cow feed and y is her consumption of hay. Lolita has been instructed in the mysteries of budgets and optimization and always maximizes her utility subject to her budget constraint. Lolita has an income of m which she is allowed to spend as she wishes on cow feed and hay. The price of hay is always $1, and the price of cow feed will be denoted by p where $0 < p \le 1$.

(a) Write Lolita's inverse demand function for cow feed._____

_____(Hint: Lolita's utility function is quasilinear. When y is the numeraire and the price of x is p, the inverse demand function for someone with quasilinear utility $f(x) + y$ is found by simply by setting

$p = f'(x)$.) Write Lolita's demand function for cow feed. _____

_____

(b) If the price of cow feed is p and her income is m, how much cow feed does Lolita choose?_____How much hay does she choose?_____(Hint: The money that she doesn't spend on feed is used to buy hay.)

(c) Plug these numbers into her utility function to find out the utility level that she enjoys at this price and this income._____

(d) Recall that the money metric utility, $m(1, p, x, y)$ is defined to be the amount of income one would need when the price of hay is \$1, and the price of feed is p, to be as well off as she was with the bundle (x, y). Write an equation that says that Lolita is exactly as well off with income m and price p as she would be with bundle (x, y) _____

_____.

(e) Use the above expression to derive the result that $m(1, p, x, y) = x - x^2/2 + y - (1 - p)^2/2$. Write a sentence explaining what you did.

_____

(f) Suppose that Lolita's daily income is \$3 and that the price of feed is \$.50. What bundle does she buy?_____What bundle would she buy if the price of cow feed rose to \$1? _____

_____

(g) How much money would Lolita be willing to pay to avoid having the price of hay rise to \$1?_____This amount is known as the _____variation.

(h) Suppose that the price of cow feed rose to \$1. How much extra money would you have to pay Lolita to make her as well off as she was at the old prices? _____This amount is known as the _____ _____variation. Which is bigger, the compensating or the equivalent variation, or are they the same? _____

(i) At the price \$.50 and income \$3, how much (net) consumer's surplus

is Lolita getting?_____

Market

16.1 (30) In Gas Pump, South Dakota, there are two kinds of consumers, Buick owners and Dodge owners. Every Buick owner has a demand function for gasoline: $D_B(p) = 20 - 5p$ for $p \leq 4$ and $D_B(p) = 0$ if $p > 4$. Every Dodge owner has a demand function $D_D(p) = 15 - 3p$ for $p \leq 5$ and $D_D(p) = 0$ for $p > 5$. (Quantities are measured in gallons per week and price is measured in dollars.) Suppose that Gas Pump has 150 consumers, 100 Buick owners and 50 Dodge owners.

(a) If the price is \$3, what is the total amount demanded by each individual Buick Owner? _____and by each individual Dodge owner?_____

(b) What is the total amount demanded by all Buick owners?_____

_____What is the total amount demanded by all Dodge owners?_____

(c) What is the total amount demanded by all consumers in Gas Pump at a price of 3? _____

(d) On the graph below, use blue ink to draw the demand curve representing the total demand by Buick owners. Use black ink to draw the demand curve representing total demand by Dodge owners. Use red ink to draw the market demand curve for the whole town.

(e) What is the slope of the market demand curve for the whole town when the price of gasoline is \$1 per gallon? _____

(f) What is the slope of the market demand curve for the town when the price of gasoline is \$4.50 per gallon?_____

(g) What is the slope of the market demand curve when the price of gasoline is \$10 per gallon_____ *(h)* At what prices does the market demand curve have kinks? _____

_____

Dollars per gallon

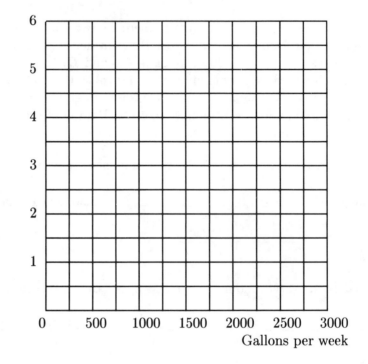

Gallons per week

16.2 (20) For each of the following demand curves, compute the inverse demand curve.

(a) $D(p) = \max\{10 - 2p, 0\}$ _____

(b) $D(p) = 100p^{-.5}$ _____

(c) $\ln D(p) = \ln 20 - 2\ln p$ _____

(d) $\ln D(p) = 10 - 4p$ _____

16.3 (20) Ms. Child is considering purchasing a nice bottle of wine. Her utility function for bottles of wine, b, and money to be spent on other things, y, is given by $u(b, y) = 75b^2 + y^2/100$. Wine comes only in discrete units of bottles and costs p dollars per bottle, and she has exactly \$100 to spend.

(a) Does Ms. Child have convex preferences?

(b) If Ms. Child pays $20 for one bottle of wine, how much will she have

to spend on other goods?_____What will be her utility

level? _____

(c) Write down an equation that determines Ms. Child's reservation price

for a bottle of wine. _____

(d) What is Ms. Child's reservation price for a bottle of wine? _____

_____

16.4 (20) Ken's utility function is $u_K(x_1, x_2) = x_1 + x_2$ and Barbie's utility function is $u_B(x_1, x_2) = (x_1 + 1)(x_2 + 1)$. Good 1 can only be provided in discrete amounts: we will always have either $x_1 = 0$ or $x_1 = 1$. The price of the two goods are $p_1 = 1$ and $p_2 = 1$, and Ken and Barbie each have wealth $\$m > 1$.

(a) What is Ken's reservation price for good 1? _____

(b) Write an equation that can be solved to find Barbie's reservation price

for good 1. _____What is Barbie's reservation price for

good 1? _____

(c) If Ken and Barbie each have a wealth of 3, plot the market demand curve for good 1.

Quantity

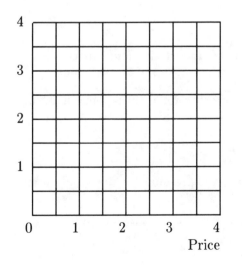

Price

16.5 (20) The demand function for yo-yos is $D(p) = 4 - 2p + \frac{1}{100}M$ where p is the price of yo-yos and M is income. If M is 100 and p is 1:

(a) What is the income elasticity of demand for yo-yos?_____

_____

(b) What is the price elasticity of demand for yo-yos?_____

_____

16.6 (10) If the demand function for zarfs is $P = 10 - Q$.

(a) At what price will total revenue realized from their sale be at a maximum? _____

(b) How many widgets will be sold at that price? _____

_____

16.7 (30) The demand function for football tickets for a typical game at a large midwestern university is $D(p) = 200,000 - 10,000p$. The university has a clever and avaricious athletic director who sets his ticket prices so as to maximize revenue. The university's football stadium holds 110,000 spectators.

(a) Write down the inverse demand function _____

(b) Write an expression for total revenue as a function of the number of tickets sold._____

(c) Write down an expression for marginal revenue as a function of the number of tickets sold._____

(d) On the graph below, use blue ink to draw the inverse demand function and use red ink to draw the marginal revenue function. On your graph, also draw a vertical blue line representing the capacity of the stadium.

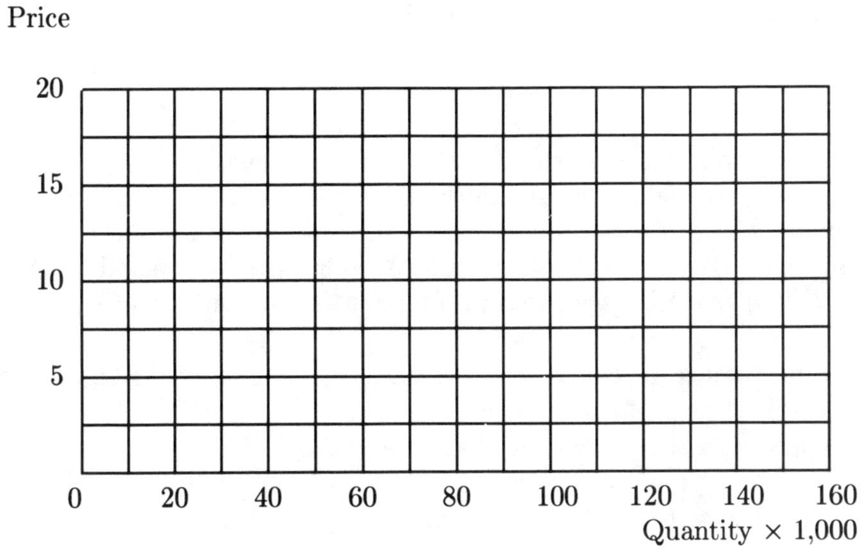

Price

(e) What price will generate the maximum revenue? _____

_____What quantity will be sold at this price?_____

_____

(f) At this quantity, what is marginal revenue?_____At

this quantity, what is the price elasticity of demand?_____

_____Will the stadium be full?_____

(g) A series of winning seasons caused the demand curve function for football tickets to shift upwards. The new demand function is $q(p) =$

$300,000 - 10,000p$. What is the new inverse demand function?_____

_____

(h) Write an expression for marginal revenue as a function of output._____

_____Use red ink to draw the new demand function and use black ink to draw the new marginal revenue function.

(i) Ignoring stadium capacity, what price would generate maximum revenue? _____What quantity would be sold at this price?_

_____Does the stadium hold this many people?_

_____

(j) As you noticed above, the quantity that would maximize total revenue given the new higher demand curve is greater than the capacity of the stadium. Clever though the athletic director is, he can not sell seats he hasn't got. He notices that if he moves along his new demand function, his total revenue is an increasing function of the number of seats sold

until the number of seats is _____which is bigger than

his stadium capacity. Therefore he should sell _____

_____tickets at a price of _____

(k) When he does this, his marginal revenue from selling an extra seat is

_____The elasticity of demand for tickets at this price

quantity combination is _____

(l) How much could the athletic director increase the revenue per game by adding 1,000 new seats to his stadium's capacity and adjusting the

ticket price to maximize his revenue?_____

(m) How much could he increase the revenue per game by adding 40,000

new seats?_____60,000 new seats?_____

_____

(n) Why is the extra revenue gained from adding 40,000 seats not given by 40 times the extra revenue gained from adding 1,000 seats?

_____

_____

_____

Calculus **16.8** (30) The demand function for drangles is $q(p) = (p+1)^{-2}$.

(a) What is the price elasticity of demand at price p? _____

(b) At what price is the price elasticity of demand for drangles equal to

minus one?_____

(c) Write an expression for total revenue from the sale of drangles as a

function of their price._____Use calculus to find the
revenue maximizing price. Don't forget to check the second order condition.

_____

_____

_____

(d) Suppose that the demand function for drangles takes the more general
form $q(p) = (p+a)^b$ where $a > 0$ and $b < -1$. Calculate an expression

for the price elasticity of demand at price p. _____At

what price is the price elasticity of demand equal to -1?_____

_____

Chapter 17

Supply and Demand

Introduction. Supply and demand problems are bread and butter for economists. In the problems below, you will typically want to solve for equilibrium prices and quantities by writing an equation that sets supply equal to demand. Where the price received by suppliers is the same as the price paid by demanders, one writes supply and demand as functions of the same price variable, p, and solves for the price that equalizes supply and demand. But if, as happens with taxes and subsidies, suppliers face different prices from demanders, it is a good idea to denote these two prices by separate variables, p_s and p_d. Then one can solve for equilibrium by solving a system of two equations in the two unknowns p_s and p_d. The two equations are the equation that sets supply equal to demand and the equation that relates the price paid by demanders to the net price received by suppliers. For example if demanders must pay a tax or $\$t$ for every unit they purchase, then $p_d = p_s + t$.

17.1 (30) The demand for yak butter is $q = 120 - 4p$ and the supply is $2p - 30$ where p is the price measured in dollars per hundred pounds and q is the quantity measured in hundred pound units.

(a) On the axes below, use blue ink to draw the demand curve and the supply curve for yak butter.

Price

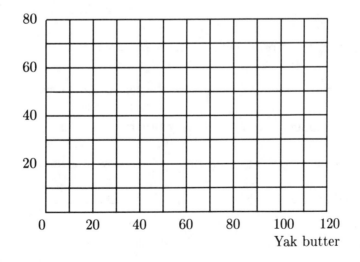

(b) Write down the equation that you would solve to find the equilibrium

price._____

(c) What is the equilibrium price of yak butter? _____

_____What is the equilibrium quantity? _____

_____Locate the equilibrium price and quantity on the graph and label them p_1 and q_1.

(d) A terrible drouth strikes the central Ohio steppes, traditional homeland of the yaks. The supply schedule shifts to $2p - 60$. The demand schedule remains as before. Draw the new supply schedule. Write down the equation that you would solve to find the new equilibrium price of

yak butter._____

(e) The new equilibrium price is _____and the quantity is _

_____Locate the new equilibrium price and quantity on the graph and label them p_2 and q_2.

(f) The government decides to relieve stricken yak butter consumers and producers by paying a subsidy of \$5 per hundred pounds of yak butter to producers. If p is the price paid by consumers for yak butter, what is

the total amount received by producers for each unit they produce?_____

_____When the price paid by consumers is p, how

much yak butter is produced? _____

(g) Write down an equation that can be solved for the equilibrium price

paid by consumers, given the subsidy program. _____

_____What are the equilibrium price paid by consumers and quantity

of yak butter now?_____

(h) Suppose the government had paid the subsidy to consumers rather

than producers. What would be the equilibrium net price paid by consumers?_

_____The equilibrium quantity would be ____

_____

17.2 (20) Here are the supply and demand equations for throstles, where p is the price in dollars:

$$D(p) = 200 - p$$
$$S(p) = 150 + p.$$

On the axes below, draw the demand and supply curves for throstles, using blue ink.

Price

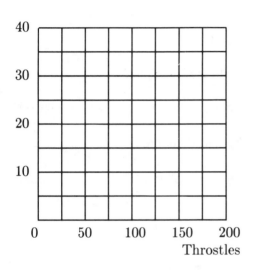

Throstles

(a) What is the equilibrium price _____and quantity _____

_____of throstles.

(b) Suppose that the government decides to restrict the industry to selling only 160 throstles. What will be the equilibrium demand price for 160

units? _____How many throstles would suppliers supply at

that price?_____What price would the suppliers need

to get in order to supply just 160 units?_____

(c) The government wants to make sure that only 160 throstles are bought, but it doesn't want the firms in the industry to receive more than the minimum price that it would take to have them supply 160 units of the good. One way to do this is for the government to issue 160 ration coupons. Then in order to buy a throstle, a consumer would need to present a ration coupon along with the necessary amount of money to pay for the good. If the ration coupons were freely bought and sold on the open market, what would be the equilibrium price of these coupons.?

_____

(d) On the graph above, shade in the area that represents the deadweight loss from restricting the supply of throstles to 160. How much is this

expressed in dollars?_____(Hint: What is the formula for the area of a triangle?)

17.3 (20) The demand curve for salted codfish is $D(P) = 100 - 5P$ and the supply curve $S(P) = 5P$.

(a) The equilibrium market price is _____and the equi-

librium quantity sold is _____

(b) A quantity tax of \$2 per unit sold is placed on salted codfish. The

new price paid by the demanders will be _____and the new

price received by the suppliers will be _____The equilibrium

quantity sold will be _____

(c) The deadweight loss due to this tax will be _____

17.4 (20) The demand function for merino ewes is $D(P) = 100/P$ and the supply function is $S(P) = P$.

(a) What is the equilibrium price? _____

(b) What is the equilibrium quantity?_____

(c) An ad valorem tax of 300% is imposed on merino ewes so that the price paid by demanders is four times the price received by suppliers. What is the equilibrium price paid by the demanders for merino ewes

now?_____What is the equilibrium price received by

the suppliers for merino ewes? _____What is the equilibrium

quantity?_____

17.5 (20) King Kanuta rules over a small tropical island, Nutting Atoll, whose primary crop is coconuts. The main currency of Nutting Atoll is dollars. The demand function, expressing total demand for coconuts per week by King Kanuta's subjects is given by $D(P) = 1,200 - 100P$ and the supply curve for coconuts per week is given by $S(p) = 100P$.

(a) What will be the equilibrium price of coconuts and the equilibrium quantity sold?_____

(b) One day the King decided to impose a tax on his subjects in order to collect coconuts for the Royal Larder. The King required that every consumer who consumed a coconut would have to pay a coconut to the King as a tax. Thus, if a consumer wanted 5 coconuts for himself, he would have to purchase 10 coconuts in order to give 5 to the King. If the price paid to suppliers is p_S and the cost to a consumer of getting an extra coconut is p_D, write an expression that relates p_D to p_S.

(c) When the price paid to suppliers is p_S, how many coconuts will be demanded as a function of p_S for purposes of consumption? (Hint: Express p_D in terms of p_S and substitute into the demand function.)_____

_____

(d) Recalling that for every coconut demanded by the King's subjects, the King gets a coconut, write an equation relating the demand function $D(p_D)$ and the supply function $S(p_S)$ that must hold in equilibrium.____

_____

(e) Solve this equation for the equilibrium value of p_S and the equilibrium total number of coconuts produced._____

(f) King Kanuta's subjects resented paying the extra coconuts to the King, and whispers of revolution started spreading throughout the palace. Worried by the hostile atmosphere, the King changed the coconut tax. Now, the shopkeepers who sold the coconuts would be responsible for paying the tax. For every coconut sold to a consumer, the shopkeeper would have to pay one coconut to the King. This plan resulted in _____

_____coconuts being sold to the consumers. The shopkeepers got _____per coconut after paying their tax to the King, and

the consumers paid a price of _____per coconut.

17.6 (20) Schrecklich and LaMerde are two justifiably obscure 19th century impressionist painters. The world's total stock of paintings by Schrecklich is 100 and the world's stock of paintings by LaMerde is 150. The two painters are regarded by connoisseurs as being very similar in style. Therefore the demand for either painter's work depends both on its own price and the price of the other painter's work. The demand function for Schrecklich is $D_S(P) = 200 - 4P_S - 2P_L$ and the demand function for LaMerdes is $D_L(P) = 200 - 3P_L - P_S$, where P_S and P_L are respectively the price in dollars of a Schrecklich painting and a LaMerde painting.

(a) Write down two simultaneous equations that state the equilibrium condition that the demand for each painter's work equals supply.

(b) Solving these two equations, one finds that the equilibrium price

of Schrecklichs is _____and the equilibrium price of

LaMerdes is _____

(c) On the diagram below draw a line that represents all of combinations of prices for Schrecklichs and LaMerdes such that the supply of Schrecklichs equals the demand for Schrecklichs. Draw a second line that represents those price combinations at which the demand for LaMerdes equals the supply of LaMerdes. Label the unique price combination at which both markets clear with the letter E.

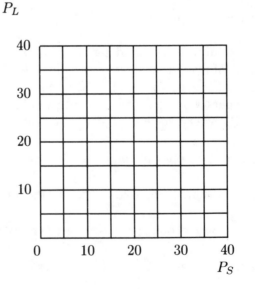

(d) A fire in a bowling alley in Hamtramck, Michigan, destroyed one of the world's largest collections of works by Schrecklich. The fire destroyed a total of 10 Schrecklichs. After the fire the equilibrium price of Schrecklichs was _____and the equilibrium price of LaMerdes was

_____

(e) On the diagram you drew above, use red ink to draw a line that shows the locus of price combinations at which the demand for Schrecklichs equals the supply of Schrecklichs after the fire. On your diagram, label the new equilibrium combination of prices E'.

17.7 (20) The demand function for a commodity has a constant price elasticity equal to -1. When the price of the good is \$10 per unit, the total amount demanded is 6,000 units.

(a) Write down an equation for the demand function._____

_____Graph this demand function below with blue ink. (Hint: If the demand curve has a constant price elasticity equal to ϵ, then $D(p) = ap^\epsilon$ for some constant a. You have to use the data of the problem to solve for the constants a and ϵ that apply in this particular case.)

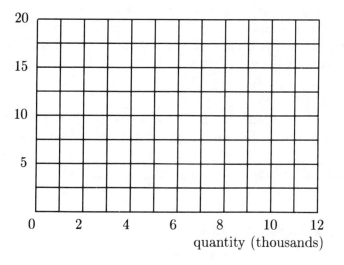

(b) If the supply is perfectly inelastic at 5,000 units, what is the equilib-

rium price? _____Show the supply curve on your graph and label the equilibrium with an E.

(c) Suppose that the demand curve shifts outward by 10%. Write down

the new equation for the demand function._____Suppose
that the supply curve remains vertical but shifts to the right by 5%. Solve

for the new equilibrium price_____and quantity ____

_____

(d) By what percentage approximately did the equilibrium price rise? __

_____Use red ink to draw the new demand curve and
the new supply curve on your graph.

(e) Suppose that in the above problem the demand curve shifts outward
by x% and the supply curve shifts right by y%. By approximately what

percentage will the equilibrium price rise?_____

17.8 (30) An economic historian* reports that econometric studies indicate for the pre-civil war period, 1820–1860, the price elasticity of demand for cotton from the American South was approximately one. Due
to the rapid expansion of the British textile industry, the demand curve
for American cotton is estimated to have shifted outwards by about 5%
per year during this entire period.

(a) If during this period, cotton production in the U.S. grew by 3% per
year, what (approximately) must be the rate of change of the price of

cotton during this period. _____

(b) Graph the demand for cotton through the point where the price is 20

and the quantity is 20. What is the total revenue when the price is 20? __

_____What is the total revenue when the price is 10?

_____

_____

* Gavin Wright, *The Political Economy of the Cotton South,* W. W.
Norton, 1978.

price of cotton

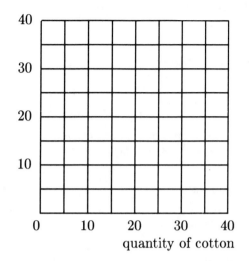

quantity of cotton

(c) If the change in the quantity of cotton supplied by the U.S. is to be interpreted as a movement along an upward sloping long run supply

curve, what would the elasticity of supply have to be? _____

_____(Hint: From 1820 to 1860 quantity rose by about 3% per

year and price rose by _____per cent per year. [See your earlier answer.] If the quantity change is a movement along the long run supply curve, then the long run price elasticity must be what?)

(d) The American Civil War, beginning in 1861, had a devastating effect on cotton production in the American South. Production fell by about 50% and remained at that level throughout the war. What would you

predict would be the effect on the price of cotton? _____

_____

(e) What would be the effect on total revenue of cotton farmers in the

American South? _____

(f) The expansion of the British textile industry ended in the 1860's and for the remainder of the 19th century the demand curve for American cotton remained approximately unchanged. By about 1900, the American South approximately regained its prewar output level. What do you think

happened to cotton prices then? _____

17.9 (10) The number of bottles of chardonnay demanded per year is $1,000,000 - 90,000P$, where P is the price per bottle (in U.S. dollars). The number of bottles supplied is $10,000P$.

(a) What is the equilibrium price? _____What is the

equilibrium quantity? _____

(b) Suppose that the government introduces a new tax such that the wine maker must pay a tax of $5 per bottle for every bottle that he produces.

What is the new equilibrium price paid by consumers?_____

_____What is the new price received by suppliers? _____

_____What is the new equilibrium quantity? _____

17.10 (20) The inverse demand function for bananas is $P_d = 18 - 3Q_d$ and the inverse supply function is $P_s = 6 + Q_s$ where prices are measured in cents. In equilibrium it must be that the quantity demanded equals the quantity supplied, so that $Q_s = Q_d$. If there are no taxes or subsidies, it must also be that in equilibrium, the demand price equals the supply price, $P_s = P_d$. Therefore you can solve for the equilibrium quantity by setting $6 + Q = 18 - 3Q$ where $Q = Q_s = Q_d$.

(a) If there are no taxes or subsidies, what is the equilibrium quantity?

_____What is the equilibrium market price? _____

_____

(b) If a subsidy of 2 cents per pound is paid to banana growers, then in equilibrium it still must be that the quantity demanded equals the quantity supplied, but now the price received by sellers is 2 cents higher than the price paid by consumers. What equation involving the inverse demand and supply curves can we solve to find the new equilibrium quan-

tity? _____.

(c) What is the new equilibrium quantity? _____

(d) What is the new equilibrium price received by suppliers? _____

_____

(e) What is the new equilibrium price paid by demanders? _____

_____

(f) What is the change in the price paid by the demanders caused by the

subsidy, expressed as a percentage of the old price?_____

_____

(g) If the cross-elasticity of demand between bananas and apples is +.5, what will happen to the quantity of apples demanded as a consequence of the banana subsidy, if the price of apples stays constant? (State your

answer in terms of percentage change.) _____

_____.

17.11 (20) The demand curve for ski lessons is given by $D(p_D) = 100 - 2p_D$ and the supply curve is given by $S(p_S) = 2p_S$.

(a) What is the equilibrium price? _____

(b) What is the equilibrium quantity? _____

(c) A tax of $10 per ski lesson is imposed on consumers. Write down an equation that relates the price paid by demanders to the price received by

suppliers. _____Write down an equation that states that supply equals demand. _____

_____.

(d) Solve these two equations for the two unknowns p_S and p_D. What is

the equilibrium price p_D facing demanders of the good? _____

_____

(e) How much of the good will be supplied if the $10 tax is imposed?

_____

(f) A senator from a mountainous state suggests that although ski lesson consumers are rich and deserve to be taxed, ski instructors are poor and deserve a subsidy. He proposes a $6 subsidy on production while maintaining the $10 tax on consumption of ski lessons. This policy would be equivalent to

_____

17.12 (20) Suppose that in Ham Harbor there are two kinds of renters: short-term and long-term. The demand of the long-term renters for apartments is given by $D_L = 100 - 4p$ and the demand of the short-term renters is given by $D_S = 200 - 6p$. The total supply of apartments in Ann Arbor is 100.

(a) What is the market clearing price? _____

(b) What is the equilibrium demand by the long-term people? _____

_____the short-term people? _____

(c) Now suppose that all of the apartments rented by the long-term people are converted to condominiums and bought by their current residents.

Write the equation for the new supply of *rental* housing._____

_____

(d) Write the equation that determines the new equilibrium price for

rental housing. _____What will the

new equilibrium rental price for apartments be? _____

(e) In nearby Yipsilanti there are similar short-term and long-term renters but with different demand curves and different tastes than the Ann Arbor renters. The current price of apartments in Yipsilanti is $30. Then the same sort of condo conversion occurs. What will happen to the equilib-

rium price of apartments? _____.

Chapter 18

Technology

18.1 (20) Prunella raises peaches. Her production function is $f(L,T) = L^{\frac{1}{2}}T^{\frac{1}{2}}$, where L is the amount of labor she uses and T is the amount of land she uses.

(a) This production function exhibits (constant, increasing, decreasing) returns to scale.

On the graph below, use blue ink to draw a curve showing Prunella's output as a function of labor input if she has 1 unit of land. Locate the points on your graph at which the amount of labor is 0, 1, 4, 9, and 16 and label them.

output

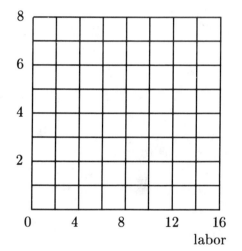

(b) Assuming she has 1 unit of land, how much extra output does she get from adding an extra unit of labor when she uses 1 unit of labor?

_____, 4 units of labor?_____If you know calculus, compute the marginal product of labor at these input levels and compare it with the result from the unit increase in labor output found above.

(c) Suppose that Prunella increases the size of her orchard to 4 units of land. Use red ink to draw a new curve on the graph above showing output as a function of labor input. Also use red ink to draw a curve showing marginal product of labor as a function of labor input when the amount of land is fixed at 4.

18.2 (20) Suppose that the production function is given by $f(x_1, x_2) = x_1 + x_2$.

(a) The marginal product for x_1 is _____, and (increases, remains constant, decreases) as x_1 increases. The marginal product of x_2 is _____, and (increases, remains constant, decreases) as x_1 increases. The technical rate of substitution between x_2 and x_1 is _____This technology demonstrates (increasing, constant, decreasing) returns to scale.

(b) Suppose that the production function is given by $f(x_1, x_2) = x_1 + 3x_2$.

The marginal product for x_1 is _____, and (increases, remains constant, decreases) as x_1 increases. The marginal product of x_2 is _____, and (increases, remains constant, decreases) as x_2 increases. The technical rate of substitution between x_2 and x_1 is _____This technology demonstrates (increasing, constant, decreasing) returns to scale.

18.3 (20) Suppose x_1 and x_2 are used in fixed proportions and $f(x_1, x_2) = \min\{x_1, x_2\}$.

(a) Suppose that $x_1 < x_2$. The marginal product for x_1 is _____, and (increases, remains constant, decreases) for small increases in x_1. For x_2 the marginal product is _____, and (increases, remains constant, decreases) for small increases in x_2. The technical rate of substitution between x_2 and x_1 is _____This technology demonstrates (increasing, constant, decreasing) returns to scale.

(b) Suppose that $f(x_1, x_2) = \min\{x_1, x_2\}$ and $x_1 = x_2 = 10$. What

is the marginal product of a small increase in x_1? _____

_____What is the marginal product of a small increase in x_2?

_____What is the effect of a small increase in x_1 on

the marginal product of a small increase in x_2. _____

_____

Calculus **18.4** (20) Suppose the production function is Cobb-Douglas and $f(x_1, x_2) = x_1^{1/2} x_2^{3/2}$.

(a) Write an expression for the marginal product of x_1 at the point (x_1, x_2).

(b) The marginal product of x_1 (increases, decreases, remains constant)

_____for small increases in x_1, holding x_2 fixed.

(c) The marginal product of good 2 is _____, and it (increases, remains constant, decreases) for small increases in x_2.

(d) An increase in the amount of x_2, (increases, leaves unchanged, increases) the marginal product of x_1. _____

(e) The technical rate of substitution between x_2 and x_1 is _____

_____

(f) This technology demonstrates (increasing, constant, decreasing) returns to scale.

18.5 (20) You manage a crew of 100 workers who could be assigned to make either of two products. Product A requires 2 workers per unit of output. Product B requires 8 workers per unit of output.

(a) Write down an equation to express the combinations of products A

and B that could be produced using exactly 100 workers. _____

_____On the diagram below, shade in the area depicting
the combinations of A and B that could be produced with 100 workers.
(Assume that it is possible for some workers to do nothing at all and that
there are no other limitations on production possibilities.)

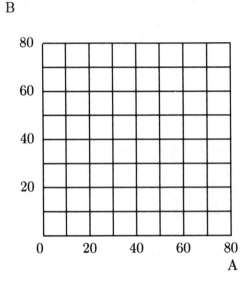

(b) Suppose now that every unit of product A that is produced requires
the use of 2 shovels as well as 2 workers and that every unit of product B
produced requires 4 shovels and 8 workers. On the graph you have just
drawn, use a different color ink to shade in the area depicting combinations of A and B that could be produced with 60 shovels if there were
no worries about the labor supply. Write down an equation for the set of

combinations of A and B that require exactly 60 shovels._____

_____

(c) On the diagram you have just drawn, show the area that represents
possible output combinations when one takes into account both the limited supply of labor and the limited supply of shovels.

(d) On your diagram locate the feasible combinations of inputs that use
up all of the labor and all of the shovels. If you didn't have the graph,
what equations would you solve to determine this point?

18.6 (20) Timothy Alsike of Baraboo, Wisconsin, has just purchased 80 acres of pasture land. He is thinking about what kind of cows to put on his new pasture. Holsteins (the black and white ones) are bigger than Guernseys (the sweet–looking reddish brown ones) and produce more milk than Guernseys, but this milk has a lower percentage butterfat content than Guernsey milk.

(a) The pasture will support 1 Guernsey cow for every 4 acres or 1 Holstein cow for every 5 acres. Timothy plans to have a mixed herd, some Guernseys some Holsteins. Write an expression to describe the set of combinations of Guernseys and Holsteins that he could support on his pasture. Illustrate this set on the graph below. (Don't worry about the anatomical implausibility of fractional cows. Having a cow for half the

time is for this example the equivalent of having half of a cow.) _____

_____

Holsteins

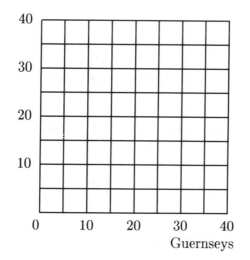

Guernseys

(b) Suppose that Holsteins each produce 60 pounds of milk and 2 pounds of butterfat per day and Guernseys produce 40 pounds of milk and 2 pounds of butterfat per day. Show on a graph the various combinations of milk and butterfat that could be produced on the pasture. (Hint: What combination of milk and butterfat would he produce if all of his cows were Holsteins? What if they were all Guernseys? What if they were half and half?)

Butterfat

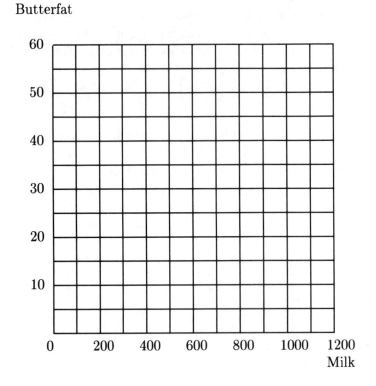

Calculus **18.7** (10) Give an example of a Cobb-Douglas production function that has increasing returns to scale but diminishing marginal returns to each factor.

_____

18.8 (30) Suppose the production function has the form:

$$f(x_1, x_2, x_3) = Ax_1^a x_2^b x_3^c$$

where $a+b+c > 1$. Prove that this production function exhibits increasing returns to scale.

_____

_____

_____

(a) For what values of a, b, and c, would this production function exhibit

decreasing returns to scale?_____constant returns to

scale?_____

18.9 (20) The production function for fragles is $f(K, L) = L/2 + \sqrt{K}$, where L is the amount of labor used and K the amount of capital used.

(a) There are (constant, increasing, decreasing) returns to scale. The marginal product of labor is (constant, increasing, decreasing).

(b) In the short run, capital is fixed at 4 units. Labor is variable. On the graph below, use blue ink to draw output as a function of labor input in the short run. Use red ink to draw the marginal product of labor as a function of labor input in the short run and use black ink to draw the average product of labor as a function of labor input in the short run.

Fragles

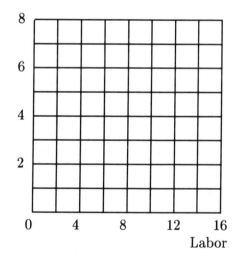

Profit Maximization

19.1 (20) Brother Jed takes heathens and reforms them into righteous individuals. There are two inputs needed in this process: heathens (which are widely available), and preaching. The production function has the following form: $r_p = \min\{h, p\}$, where r_p is the number of righteous persons produced, h is the number of heathens who attend Jed's sermons, and p is the number of hours of preaching. For every person converted, Jed receives a payment of s from the grateful convert. Sad to say, heathens do not flock to Jed's sermons of their own accord. Jed must offer heathens a payment of w to attract them to his sermons. Suppose the amount of preaching is fixed at $\bar{p}$ and that Jed operates as a prophet maximizer ... that is, a *profit* maximizer.

(a) Sketch the shape of this production function in the graph below. Label the axes and indicate the amount of the input where $h = \bar{p}$.

(b) If $h < \bar{p}$, what is the marginal product of heathens?_____

_____What is the value marginal product of an additional

heathen?_____

(c) If $h > \bar{p}$, what is the marginal product of heathens?_____

_____What is the value marginal product in this case? _____

_____

(d) If $w < s$, how many heathens will be converted?_____

_____If $w > s$, how many heathens will be converted? _____

_____

19.2 (10) Is it possible for a competitive profit maximizing firm in long-run equilibrium to be earning positive profits *and* have a production function which exhibits increasing returns to scale? Why or why not?

_____

_____

_____

19.3 (20) A profit maximizing firm produces one output, y, and uses one input, x, to produce it. The price per unit of the factor is denoted by w and the price of the output is denoted by p. You observe the firm's behavior over three periods and find the following:

Period	y	x	w	p
1	1	1	1	1
2	2.5	3	.5	1
3	4	8	.25	1

Table 1. Observations on a profit maximizing firm.

(a) Write down an equation which gives the firm's profits, π, as a function of the amount of input x it uses, the amount of output y it uses, and the

per unit cost of the input w. _____

(b) Rearrange this expression so that it expresses the level of output, $f(x)$,

in terms of profits, inputs, and factor price. _____

_____.

(c) In the diagram below, draw the appropriate isoprofit line for each of the three periods. Utilizing the theory of revealed profitability, shade in a possible technology for the observed production behavior.

Output

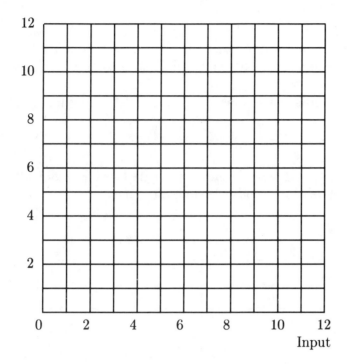

Input

19.4 (20) Allie's Apples, Inc. purchases apples in bulk and sells two products, boxes of apples and jugs of cider. Allie's has capacity limitations of three kinds: warehouse space, pressing facilities, and crating facilities. A box of apples requires 6 units of warehouse space, 2 units of crating facilities, and no pressing facilities. A jug of cider requires 3 units of warehouse space, 2 units of crating facilities, and 1 unit of pressing facilities. The total amounts available each day are: 1200 units of warehouse space, 600 units of crating facilities, and 250 units of pressing facilities.

(a) If the only capacity limitations were on warehouse facilities, and if all warehouse space were used for the production of apples, how many

boxes of apples could be produced in one day? _____

_____How many jugs of cider could be produced each day if, instead, all warehouse space were used in the production of cider and there were

no other capacity constraints? _____Draw a blue line in the following graph to represent the warehouse space constraint on production combinations.

(b) Following the same reasoning, draw a red line to represent the constraints on output to limitations on crating capacity. How many boxes of apples could Allie produce if he only had to worry about crating capacity?

_____How many jugs of cider? _____

(c) Finally draw a black line to represent constraints on output combinations due to limitations on pressing facilities. How many boxes of apples could Allie produce if he only had to worry about the pressing capac-

ity and no other constraints? _____How many jugs of cider?

_____

(d) Now shade the area which represents feasible combinations of daily production of apples and cider for Allie's Apples.

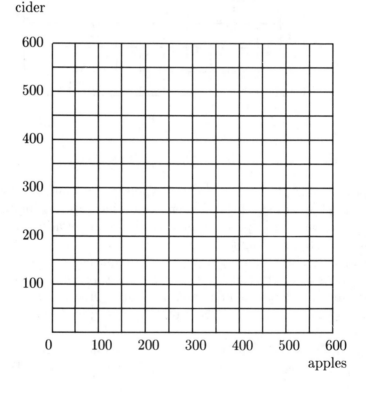

cider

(e) Allie's can sell apples for $5.00 per box of apples and cider for $2.00 per jug. Draw a black line to show the combinations of sales of apples and cider that would generate a revenue of $1000 per day. Draw a black isoprofit line for $5,000 per day. Draw a black isoprofit line that maximizes

profits. At the profit maximizing production plan, Allie's is producing _

_____boxes of apples and _____

_____jugs of cider and total revenues are _____

Calculus **19.5** (20) The short-run production function of a competitive firm is given by $f(L) = 6L^{2/3}$. If $w = 6$ and $p = 3$, how many units of labor will the

firm hire? _____How much output will it produce?

_____

Calculus **19.6** (20) A Los Angeles firm uses a single input to produce a recreational commodity according to a production function $f(x) = 4\sqrt{x}$, where x is the number of units of input. The commodity sells for $100 per unit. The input costs $50 per unit.

(a) Write down a function that states the firm's profit as a function of

the amount of input._____

(b) What is the profit maximizing amount of input?_____

_____of output?_____

(c) Suppose that the firm is taxed $20 per unit of its output and the price of its input is subsidized by $10. What is its new output level?

_____What is its new input level? _____

_____

(d) Suppose that instead of these taxes and subsidies, the firm is taxed at 50% of its profits. Write down its after-tax profits as a function of the

amount of input. _____What is the

profit maximizing amount of output?_____

19.7 (30) T-bone Pickens is a corporate raider. This means that he looks for companies that are not maximizing profits, buys them, and then tries to operate them at higher profits. T-bone claims that he learned his methods from studying agricultural economics in the School of Animal Husbandry where they taught him to "buy sheep and sell deer."

In any event T-bone is examining the records for a couple of refineries that he might buy, the Shill Oil Company, and the Golf Oil Company. Each of these companies buys oil and produces gasoline. During the time period that T-bone is examining, the price of gasoline fluctuated significantly, while the cost of oil remained constant at $10 a barrel. For simplicity, we assume that oil is the only input to gasoline production.

Shill Oil produced 1 million barrels of gasoline using 1 million barrels of oil when the price of gasoline was $10 a barrel. When the price of gasoline was $20 a barrel, Shill produced 3 million barrels of gasoline using 4 million barrels of oil. Finally, when the price of gasoline was $40 a barrel, Shill used 10 million barrels of oil to produce 5 million barrels of gasoline.

Golf Oil (which is managed by Martin E. Lunch III) did exactly the same when the price of gasoline was $10 and $20, but when the price of gasoline hit $40, Golf produced 3.5 million barrels of gasoline using 8 million barrels of oil.

(a) Using black ink plot Shill Oil's isoprofit lines and choices for the three different periods. Label them 10, 20, and 40. Using red ink draw Golf Oil's isoprofit line and production choice. Label it with a 40 in red ink.

Million barrels of gasoline

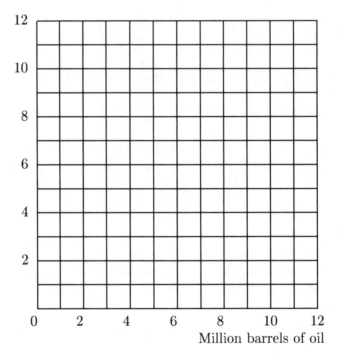

Million barrels of oil

(b) Is there any evidence that Shill Oil is not maximizing profits? Explain?

_____

_____

_____

(c) Is there any evidence that Golf Oil is not maximizing profits? Explain?

_____

_____

_____

(d) How much profits could Golf Oil have made when the price of gasoline was $40 a barrel if they had chosen to produce the same amount that they

did when the price was $20 a barrel? _____What profits did

Golf actually make when the price of gasoline was $40?_____

19.8 (10) After carefully studying Shill Oil, T-bone Pickens decides that it has probably been maximizing its profits. But he still is very interested in buying Shill Oil. He wants to use the gasoline they produce to fuel his delivery fleet for his chicken farms, Capon Truckin'. In order to do this Shill Oil would have to be able to produce 5 million barrels of gasoline from 8 million barrels of oil. Mark this point on your graph. Assuming that Shill always maximizes profits, would it be technologically feasible for it to produce this input-output combination? Why or why not?

_____

_____

_____

19.9 Suppose that firms operate in a competitive market, attempt to maximize profits, and only use one factor of production. Then we know that for any changes in the input and output price, the input choice and the output choice must obey the Weak Axiom of Profit Maximization, $\Delta p \Delta y - \Delta w \Delta x \geq 0$.

Which of the following propositions can be proven by the Weak Axiom of Profit Maximizing Behavior (WAPM)? Respond yes or no and give a short argument.

(a) If the price of the input does not change, then a decrease in the price of the output will imply that the firm will produce the same amount or less output.

_____

(b) If the price of the output remains constant, then a decrease in the input price will imply that the firm will use the same amount or more of the input.

_____

(c) If both the price of the output and the input increase and the firm uses more of the input, then the firm will produce more output.

_____

(d) If both the price of the output and the input increase and the firm produces less output, then the firm will use more of the input.

_____

Cost Functions

20.1 (20) Nadine sells user-friendly software. Her firm's production function is: $f(x_1, x_2) = x_1 + 2x_2$, where x_1 is the amount of unskilled labor and x_2 is the amount of skilled labor that she employs.

(a) In the graph below, draw a production isoquant representing input combinations that will produce 20 units of output. Draw another isoquant representing input combinations that will produce 40 units of output.

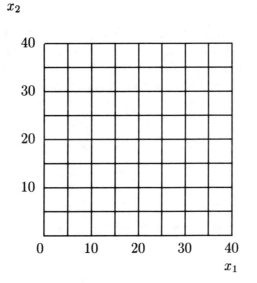

(b) Does this production function exhibit increasing, decreasing or constant returns to scale?_____

(c) If Nadine uses only unskilled labor, how much unskilled labor would she need in order to produce y units of output? _____

(d) If Nadine uses only skilled labor to produce output, how much skilled labor would she need in order to produce y units of output? _____

_____

(e) If Nadine faces factor prices $(1, 1)$ what is the cheapest way for her to produce 20 units of output? $x_1 =$_____, $x_2 =$_____

(f) If Nadine faces factor prices $(1, 3)$, what is the cheapest way for her to produce 20 units of output? $x_1 =$_____, $x_2 =$_____

(g) If Nadine faces factor prices (w_1, w_2), what will be the minimal cost of producing 20 units of output? _____

(h) If Nadine faces factor prices (w_1, w_2), what will be the minimal cost of producing y units of output? _____

20.2 (20) The Ontario Brassworks produces brazen effronteries. As you know brass is an alloy of copper and zinc, used in fixed proportions. The production function is given by: $f(x_1, x_2) = \min\{x_1, 2x_2\}$, where x_1 is the amount of copper it uses and x_2 is the amount of zinc that it uses in production.

(a) Illustrate a typical isoquant for this production function in the graph below.

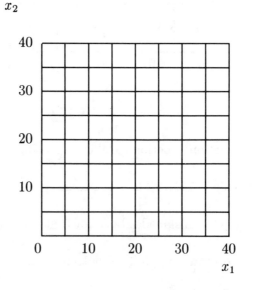

(b) Does this production function exhibit increasing, decreasing or constant returns to scale?_____

(c) If the firm wanted to produce 10 effronteries, how much copper would

it need? _____How much zinc would it need?_____

_____

(d) If the firm faces factor prices $(1,1)$ what is the cheapest way for it

to produce 10 effronteries? _____How much will this

cost?_____

(e) If the firm faces factor prices (w_1, w_2), what is the cheapest cost to

produce 10 effronteries? _____

(f) If the firm faces factor prices (w_1, w_2), what will be the minimal cost

of producing y effronteries? _____

20.3 (20) Joe Grow, an avid indoor gardener, has found that the number
of happy plants, h, depends on the amount of light, l, and water, w.
In fact, Joe noticed that plants require two parts light for every one
part water, and any more or less will be wasted. Thus, Joe's production
function is as follows: $h = \min\{l, 2w\}$.

(a) Suppose Joe is using 1 unit of light, what is the least amount of water

he can use and still produce a happy plant?_____

(b) Suppose Joe wants to produce 2 happy plants, what are the minimum

amounts of light and water required?_____

(c) If each unit of light costs w_1 and each unit of water costs w_2, what

does Joe's cost function look like as a function of w_1, w_2, and h?_____

_____.

(d) What is Joe's conditional factor demand for light? $l(w_1, w_2, h) =$

_____

(e) What about for water? $w(w_1, w_2, h) =$ _____

20.4 (20) Joe's sister, Flo Grow, is a university administrator. She uses an alternative method of gardening. Flo has found that happy plants only need fertilizer, and talk. (*Warning:* Any frivolous observations about university administrators' talk being a perfect substitute for fertilizer is regarded by the authors of this workbook as being in extremely poor taste.) Where f is the number of bags of fertilizer used and t is the number of hours she talks to her plants, the number of happy plants produced is exactly $h = t + 2f$. Suppose fertilizer costs w_1 per bag and talk costs w_2 per hour.

(a) If Flo uses no fertilizer, how many hours of talk must she devote if she wants one happy plant?_____

(b) If she doesn't talk to her plants at all, how many bags will she need for one happy plant?_____

(c) If $w_2 < w_1/2$, would it be cheaper for Flo to use fertilizer or talk to raise one happy plant?_____

(d) Write down an expression for Flo's cost function.

(e) What is Flo's conditional factor demand for talk?

_____

_____

_____

(f) What is her conditional factor demand for fertilizer?

_____

_____

_____

20.5 (30) Remember T-bone Pickens, the corporate raider? Now he's concerned about his chicken farms, Pickens' Chickens. He feeds his chickens on a mixture of soybeans and corn, depending on the prices of each. According to the data submitted by his managers, when the price of soybeans was $10 a bushel and the price of corn was $10 a bushel, they used 50 bushels of corn and 150 bushels of soybeans for each coop of chickens. When the price of soybeans was $20 a bushel and the price of corn was $10 a bushel, they used 300 bushels of corn and no soybeans. When the price of corn was $20 a bushel and the price of soybeans was $10 a bushel, they used 250 bushels of soybeans and no corn. During each of these periods, the number of chickens produced was the same.

(a) Graph these three input combinations and isocost lines in the following diagram.

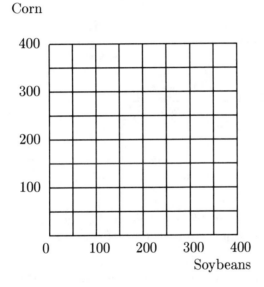

(b) How much money did Pickens' managers spend when the prices were

$(10, 10)$? _____When the prices were $(10, 20)$? _____

_____When the prices were $(20, 10)$? _____

(c) Is there any evidence that Picken's managers were not minimizing costs? Why or why not?

_____

_____

_____

(d) Pickens wonders whether there are any prices of corn and soybeans at which his managers will use 50 bushels of soybeans and 150 bushels of corn to produce the same number of chickens. How much would this production plan cost when the prices were $p_s = 10$ and $p_c = 10$? _____

_____When the prices were $p_s = 10, p_c = 20$? _____When the prices were $p_s = 20$, $p_c = 10$? _____

(e) If Pickens' managers were always minimizing costs, could 50 bushels of soybeans and 150 bushels of corn ever be a cost minimizing bundle at any prices which produced the same level of output as the other input choices? Why?

_____

_____

_____

20.6 (10) A geneological firm called Roots produces its output using only one input. Its production function is $f(x) = \sqrt{x}$.

(a) Does the firm have increasing, constant, or decreasing returns to scale?_____

(b) How many units of input does it take to produce 10 units of output?___ _____If the input costs w per unit, what does it cost to produce 10 units of output? _____

(c) How many units of input does it take to produce y units of output? __ _____. If the input costs w per unit, what does it cost to produce y units of output? _____

(d) If the input costs w per unit, what is the average cost of producing y

units? $AC(w, y) = $ _____

20.7 (10) A university cafeteria produces square meals, using only one input and a rather remarkable production process. We are not allowed to say what that ingredient is, but an authoritative kitchen source says that "fungus is involved". The cafeteria's production function is $f(x) = x^2$, where x is the amount of input and $f(x)$ is the number of square meals produced.

(a) Does the cafeteria have increasing, constant, or decreasing returns to

scale?_____

(b) How many units of input does it take to produce 100 square meals?__

_____If the input costs w per unit, what does

it cost to produce 100 square meals? _____

(c) How many units of input does it take to produce y square meals? _

_____If the input costs w per unit, what does it cost to

produce y square meals? _____

(d) If the input costs w per unit, what is the average cost of producing y

square meals? $AC(w, y) = $ _____

20.8 (10) A cost-minimizing firm finds that its marginal product of capital is 6 and its marginal product of labor is 2. It must be that w/r equals

_____

Calculus **20.9** (10) If the production function is given by $f(K, L) = 2 \ln K + 3 \ln L$ and the wage rate of labor and the rental rate of capital are both 1, then

the cost minimizing ratio K/L must be _____

20.10 (20) Irma's Handicrafts produces plastic deer for lawn ornaments. "It's hard work", says Irma, "but anything to make a buck." Her production function is given by: $f(x_1, x_2) = (\min\{x_1, 2x_2\})^{1/2}$, where x_1 is the amount of plastic used, x_2 is the amount of labor used, and $f(x_1, x_2)$ is the number of deer produced.

(a) In the graph below, draw a production isoquant representing input combinations that will produce 4 deer. Draw another production isoquant representing input combinations that will produce 5 deer.

x_2

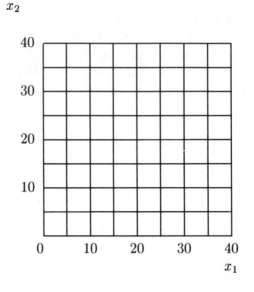

(b) Does this production function exhibit increasing, decreasing, or constant returns to scale?_____

(c) If Irma faces factor prices $(1, 1)$, what is the cheapest way for her to produce 4 deer? _____. How much does this cost?_____

(d) At the factor prices $(1, 1)$, what is the cheapest way to produce 5 deer? _____How much does this cost?_____

_____

(e) At the factor prices $(1, 1)$, the cost of producing y deer with this technology is $c(1, 1, y) =$_____

(f) At the factor prices, (w_1, w_2), the cost of producing y deer with this technology is $c(w_1, w_2, y) =$_____

20.11 (20) Al Deardwarf is another lawn ornament manufacturer. Al has found a way to automate the production of lawn ornaments completely. He doesn't use any labor, only wood and plastic. Al says he likes the business "because I needs the dough." Al's production function is given by: $f(x_1, x_2) = (x_1 + 2x_2)^{1/2}$, where x_1 is the amount of plastic used, x_2 is the amount of wood used, and $f(x_1, x_2)$ is the number of deer produced.

(a) In the graph below, draw a production isoquant representing input combinations that will produce 4 deer. Draw another production isoquant representing input combinations that will produce 5 deer.

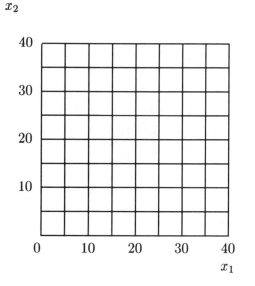

(b) Does this production function exhibit increasing, decreasing, or constant returns to scale?_____

(c) If Al faces factor prices $(1, 1)$, what is the cheapest way for him to produce 4 deer? _____How much does this cost?____

_____

(d) At the factor prices $(1, 1)$, what is the cheapest way to produce 6 deer? _____How much does this cost?_____

_____

(e) At the factor prices $(1, 1)$, the cost of producing y deer with this technology is $c(1, 1, y) =$_____

(f) At the factor prices, $(1,3)$, the cost of producing y deer with this technology is $c(1,3,y) = $ _____

20.12 (10) Suppose that Al Deardwarf from the last problem can not vary the amount of wood that he uses in the short run and is stuck with using 20 units of wood. Suppose also that he can change the amount of plastic that he uses even in the short run.

(a) If the cost of plastic is \$1 per unit and the cost of wood is \$1 per unit, how much would it cost Al to make 100 deer? _____

(b) Write down Al's short run cost function at these factor prices. _____

_____

Chapter 21

Cost Curves

21.1 (20) Mr. Otto Carr, owner of Otto's Autos, sells cars. Otto buys autos for $c each and has no other costs.

(a) What is his total cost if he sells 5 cars?_____What if he sells 10 cars?_____Write down the equation for Otto's total costs assuming he sells y cars: $TC(y) =$ _____

_____

(b) What is Otto's average cost function? $AC(y) =$_____For every additional auto Otto sells his costs increase by? _____

_____Write down Otto's marginal cost function $MC(y) =$_____

_____

(c) In the graph below draw Otto's average and marginal cost curves if $c = 20$.

AC, MC

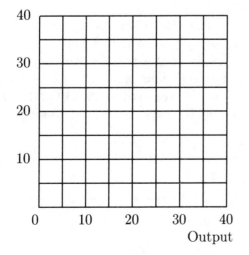

Output

(d) Suppose Otto has to pay $b a year to produce obnoxious television commercials. Otto's total cost curve is now: $TC(y) =$ _____ _____, his average cost curve is now: $AC(y) =$ _____ _____, and his marginal cost curve is: $MC(y) =$ _____

_____

(e) If $b = \$100$, use red ink to draw Otto's average cost curve on the graph above.

21.2 (10) Otto's brother, Dent Carr, is in the auto repair business. Dent recently had little else to do, and decided to calculate his cost conditions. He found that the total cost of repairing s cars is $TC(s) = 2s^2 + 10$. But Dent's attention was diverted to other things ... and that's where you come in. Please complete the following:

Dent's Total Variable Costs: _____,

Total Fixed Costs: _____,

Average Variable Costs: _____,

Average Fixed Costs: _____,

Average Total Costs: _____,

Marginal Costs: _____

21.3 (20) A third brother, Rex Carr, owns a junk yard. Rex can use one of two methods to destroy cars. The first involves purchasing a hydraulic car smasher which costs $200 a year to own and then spending $1 for every car smashed into oblivion; the second method involves purchasing a shovel that will last one year and costs $10 and paying the last Carr brother, Scoop, to bury the cars at a cost of $5 each.

(a) Write down the total cost functions for the two methods where y is output per year: $TC_1(y) =$ _____, $TC_2(y) =$ _____

_____

(b) The first method has an average cost function _____

_____and a marginal cost function _____

_____. For the second method these costs

are _____and _____

_____.

(c) If Rex wrecks 40 cars per year, which method should he use? _____

_____If Rex wrecks 50 cars per year, which method

should he use? _____What is the smallest number of cars per

year for which it would pay him to buy the hydraulic smasher?_____

_____

21.4 (20) Mary Magnolia wants to open a flower shop, the Petal Pusher, in a new mall. She has her choice of three different floor sizes, 200 square feet, 500 square feet, or 1,000 square feet. The monthly rent will be $1 a square foot. Mary estimates that if she has F square feet of floor space and sells y bouquets a month, her variable costs will be $c_v(y) = y^2/F$ per month.

(a) If she has 200 square feet of floor space, write down her marginal

cost function: _____and her average cost function: _

_____At what amount of output is average cost

minimized?_____At this level of output, how much is

average cost?_____

(b) If she has 500 square feet, write down her marginal cost function: _

_____and her average cost function: _____

_____. At what amount of output is average cost min-

imized? _____At this level of output, how much is

average cost?_____

(c) If she has 1,000 square feet of floor space, write down her marginal

cost function: _____and her average cost function: __

_____At what amount of output is average cost

minimized?_____At this level of output, how much is

average cost?_____

(d) Use red ink to show Mary's average cost curve and her marginal cost curves if she has 200 square feet. Use blue ink to show her average cost curve and her marginal cost curve if she has 500 square feet. Use black ink to show her average cost curve and her marginal cost curve if she has 1,000 square feet. Label the average cost curves AC and the marginal cost curves MC.

Dollars

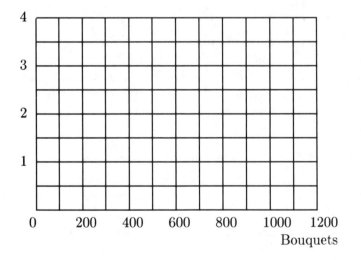

(e) Use yellow marker to show Mary's long run average cost curve and her long run marginal cost curve in your graph. Label them LRAC and LRMC.

Calculus **21.5** (20) Touchie MacFeelie publishes comic books. The only inputs he needs are old jokes and cartoonists. His production function is

$$Q = .1 J^{\frac{1}{2}} L^{\frac{3}{4}}$$

where J is the number of old jokes used, L the number of hours of cartoonists' labor used as inputs, and Q is the number of comic books produced.

(a) Does this production process exhibit increasing, decreasing, or constant returns to scale? _____Explain your answer.

_____

(b) If the number of old jokes used is 100, write an expression for the marginal product of cartoonists' labor as a function of L. _____

_____Is the marginal product of labor decreasing or increasing as the amount of labor increases? _____

Calculus **21.6 (20)** Touchie MacFeelie's irascible business manager, Gander Mac-Grope, announces that old jokes can be purchased for $1 each and that the wage rate of cartoonists' labor is $2.

(a) Suppose that in the short run, Touchie is stuck with exactly 100 old jokes (for which he paid $1 each) but is able to hire as much labor as he wishes. How much labor would he have to hire in order produce Q comic

books? _____

(b) Write down Touchie's short run total cost as a function of his output

_____

(c) His short run marginal cost function is _____

(d) His short run average cost function is _____

Calculus **21.7 (40)** Touchie asks his brother, Sir Francis MacFeelie, to study the long run picture. Sir Francis, who has carefully studied the appendix to Chapter 20 in your text, prepared the following report.

(a) If all inputs are variable, and if old jokes cost $1 each and cartoonist labor costs $2 per hour, the cheapest way to produce exactly one comic

book is to use _____jokes and _____hours of labor. (Fractional jokes are certainly allowable.)

(b) This would cost _____dollars.

(c) Given our production function, the cheapest proportions in which to use jokes and labor are the same no matter how many comic books we print. But when we double the amount of both inputs, the number of comic books produced is multiplied by _____.

Calculus **21.8** If the cost function of a firm is $c(y) = 4y^2 + 16$, then the output level that minimizes average cost is _____.

(a) For the above cost function, average variable cost is minimized when output is equal to _____.

Calculus **21.9** Consider the cost function $c(y) = y^2 + 4$.

(a) The average cost function is _____.

(b) The marginal cost function is _____.

(c) The level of output that yields the minimum average cost of production is _____.

(d) The average variable cost function is _____.

(e) At what level of output does average variable cost equal marginal cost? _____.

21.10 (10) A competitive firm has a production function of the form: $Y = 2L + 5K$. If $w = \$2$ and $r = \$3$, what will be the minimum cost of producing 10 units of output? _____.

Firm Supply

22.1 (5) A profit maximizing perfectly competitive firm will always oper-

ate where market price is equal to _____Furthermore, it must be true that at the given output level marginal cost is (rising, falling) and that the price is (greater than, less than) the firm's average variable costs.

Calculus **22.2** (20) A competitive firm has the following short run cost function: $c(y) = y^3 - 8y^2 + 30y + 5$. The firm will operate in the short run if and

only if the price is greater than or equal to _____.

22.3 (20) Remember Otto's brother, Dent Carr, who is in the auto repair business? Dent found that the total cost of repairing s cars is $c(s) = 2s^2 + 100$.

(a) This implies that Dent's average cost is equal to _____

_____average variable cost is equal to _____and

his marginal cost is equal to _____On the graph below plot the above curves, and also plot Dent's supply curve.

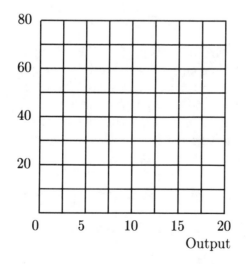

(b) If the market price is $20, how many cars will Dent be willing to repair?_____If the market price is $40, how many cars will Dent repair?_____

(c) Suppose the market price is $40 and Dent maximizes his profits. On the above graph, shade in and label the following areas: total costs, total revenue, and total profits.

22.4 (20) Suppose that a firm produces with a constant returns to scale technology, and that the minimum cost of producing one unit of output is $\bar{c}$ dollars.

(a) What is the minimum cost of producing y units of output? _____

_____If this firm operates in a competitive market and the market price is greater than $\bar{c}$, how many units of output will the firm be willing to produce? _____What if the market price is less than $\bar{c}$? _____What if the market price is equal to $\bar{c}$? _____

(b) If a large number of the above firms operate in a given market, what do you think the equilibrium market price will be? _____

_____Can you tell how much each of the firms will produce in equilibrium?_____

Calculus **22.5** (20) Mr. McGregor owns a 5-acre cabbage patch. He forces his wife, Flopsy, and his son, Peter, to work in the cabbage patch without wages. Assume for the time being that the land can be used for nothing other than cabbages and that Flopsy and Peter can find no alternative employment. The only input that Mr. McGregor pays for is fertilizer. If he uses x sacks of fertilizer, the amount of cabbages that he gets is $10\sqrt{x}$. Fertilizer costs $1 per sack.

(a) What is the total cost of the fertilizer needed to produce 100 cabbages? _____What is the total cost of the amount of fertilizer needed to produce y cabbages? _____

(b) If the only way that Mr. McGregor can vary his output is by varying the amount of fertilizer applied to his cabbage patch, write an expression

for his marginal cost curve. _____

(c) If the price of a cabbage is \$2 per cabbage, how many cabbages will

Mr. McGregor produce? _____How many sacks of fer-

tilizer will he buy?_____

(d) The price of fertilizer and of cabbages remain as before, but Mr. McGregor learns that he could find summer jobs for Flopsy and Peter in a local sweatshop. Flopsy and Peter would together earn \$300 for the summer, which Mr. McGregor could pocket, but they would have no time to work in the cabbage patch. Without their labor, he would get no cabbages. Now what is Mr. McGregor's total cost of producing y cabbages?

_____

(e) Should he continue to grow cabbages or should he put Flopsy and

Peter to work in the sweatshop?_____How high would the total wages that Flopsy and Peter could earn in the sweatshop have to be before it would pay him to send them to the sweatshop rather than the cabbage

patch? _____

22.6 (30) Severin, the herbalist, is famous for his hepatica. His total cost function is $c(y) = y^2 + 10$ for $y > 0$ and $c(0) = 0$. (That is, his cost of producing zero units of output is zero.)

(a) What is his marginal cost function? _____What is

his average cost function?_____

(b) At what quantity is his marginal cost equal to his average cost?_____

_____At what quantity is his average cost minimized?_

_____

(c) In a competitive market, what is the lowest price at which he will

supply a positive quantity? _____How much would he

supply at that price?_____

22.7 (30) Stanley Ford makes mountains out of molehills. He can do this with almost no effort, so for the purposes of this problem, let us assume that molehills are the only input used in the production of mountains. Suppose mountains are produced at constant returns to scale and that it takes 100 molehills to make 1 mountain. The current market price of molehills is $20 each. A few years ago, Stan bought an "option" that permits him to buy up to 2,000 molehills at $10 each. His option contract explicitly says that he can buy fewer than 2,000 molehills if he wishes, but he can not resell the molehills that he buys under this contract. In order to get governmental permission to produce mountains from molehills, Stanley would have to pay $10,000 for a molehill-masher's license.

(a) The marginal cost of producing a mountain for Stanley is _____

_____if he produces fewer than 20 mountains. The marginal cost

of producing a mountain is _____if he produces more than 20 mountains.

(b) On the graph below, show Stanley Ford's marginal cost curve (in blue ink) and his average cost curve (in red ink).

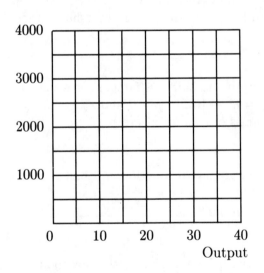

(c) If the price of mountains is $1,600, how many mountains will Stanley

produce? _____

(d) The government is considering raising the price of a molehill masher's license to $11,000. Stanley claims that if it does so he will have to go out

of business. Is Stanley telling the truth? _____What

is the highest fee for a license that the government could charge without

driving him out of business? _____

(e) Stanley's lawyer, Eliot Sleaze, has discovered a clause in Stanley's option contract that allows him to resell the molehills that he purchased under the option contract at the market price. On the graph above, use a pencil to draw Stanley's new marginal cost curve. If the price of mountains remains $1,600, how many mountains will Stanley produce

now? _____

22.8 (30) Lady Wellesleigh makes silk purses out of sows' ears. She is the only person in the world who knows how to do so. It takes one sow's ear and 1 hour of her labor to make a silk purse. She can buy as many sows' ears as she likes for $1 each. Lady Wellesleigh has no other source of income than her labor. Her utility function is a Cobb-Douglas function $U(c,r) = c^{1/3}r^{2/3}$, where c is the amount of money per day that she has to spend on consumption goods and r is the amount of leisure that she has. Lady Wellesleigh has 24 hours a day that she can devote either to leisure or to working.

(a) Lady Wellesleigh can either make silk purses or she can earn $5 an hour as a seamstress in a sweat shop. If she worked in the sweat shop, how

many hours would she work?_____(Hint: To solve for this amount, write down Lady Wellesleigh's budget constraint and recall how to find the demand function for someone with a Cobb-Douglas utility function.)

(b) If she could earn a wage of w an hour as a seamstress, how much

would she work?_____

(c) If the price of silk purses is p, how much money will Lady Wellesleigh earn per purse after she pays for the sows' ears that she uses as inputs.

_____

(d) If she can earn $5 an hour as a seamstress, what is the lowest price

at which she will make any silk purses? _____

(e) What is the supply function for silk purses?_____

_____(Hint: The price of silk purses determines the "wage rate" that Lady W. can earn by making silk purses. This determines the number of hours she will choose to work and hence the supply of silk purses.)

Chapter 23

Industry Supply

23.1 (30) Al Deardwarf's cousin, Zwerg, makes plaster garden gnomes. The technology in the garden gnome business is as follows. You need a gnome mold, plaster and labor. A gnome mold is a piece of equipment that costs $1000 and will last exactly one year. After a year, a gnome mold is completely worn out and has no scrap value. With a gnome mold, you can make 500 gnomes per year. For every gnome that you make, you also have to use a total of $7 worth of plaster and labor. In the short run, you can change your employment of plaster and labor as you wish. If you want to produce only 100 gnomes a year with a gnome mold, you spend only $700 a year on plaster and labor, and so on. The number of gnome molds in the industry can not be changed in the short run. To get a newly built one, you have to special-order it from the mold-making factory. The gnome-mold making factory only takes orders on January 1 of any given year, and it takes one whole year from the time a gnome mold is ordered until it is delivered on the next January 1. When a gnome mold is installed in your plant, it is stuck there. To move it would destroy it. Gnome molds are useless for anything other than making garden gnomes.

For many years, the demand function facing the garden gnome industry has been $D(p) = 60,000 - 5,000p$, where $D(p)$ is the total number of garden gnomes sold per year and p is the price. Prices of inputs have been constant for many years and the technology has not changed. Nobody expects any changes in the future and the industry is in long run equilibrium. The interest rate is 10%. When you buy a new gnome mold, you have to pay for it when it is delivered. For simplicity of calculations, we will assume that all of the gnomes that you build during the one year life of the gnome mold are sold at Christmas and that the employees and plaster suppliers are paid only at Christmas for the work they have done during the past year. Also for simplicity of calculations, let us approximate the date of Christmas by December 31.

(a) If you invested $1,000 in the bank on January 1, how much money could you expect to get out of the bank one year later?_____

_____If you received delivery on a gnome making mold on January 1 and paid for it at that time, how much return net of variable costs would you have to have during the year to make it worthwhile to buy the machine?_____Remember that the machine will be worn out and worthless at the end of the year.

(b) Suppose that you have exactly one newly installed gnome mold in your plant, what is your short run marginal cost of production if you produce up to 500 gnomes? _____What is your average variable cost for producing up to 500 gnomes?_____What is the cost in the short run of producing more than 500 gnomes?_____

_____

(c) If you have exactly one newly installed gnome mold, you would produce 500 gnomes if the price of gnomes is above _____dollars. You would produce no gnomes if the price of gnomes is below _____ _____dollars. You would be indifferent between producing any number of gnomes between 0 and 500 if the price of gnomes is _____ _____dollars.

(d) If you could sell as many gnomes as you liked for $10 each and none at a higher price, what rate of return would you make on your $1000 by investing in a gnome making machine?_____Is this higher than the return from putting your money in the bank?_____ _____What is the lowest price for gnomes at which investing in a gnome mold gives the same rate of return as you get from the bank? _____Could the long run equilibrium price be lower than this?_____

(e) At the price you found in the last section, how many gnomes would be demanded each year?_____How many molds would be purchased each year? _____Is this a long run equilibrium price?

_____

23.2 (20) We continue our study of the garden gnome industry. Suppose that initially everything was as described in the previous problem. To the complete surprise of everyone in the industry, on January 1, 1988, the invention of a new kind of plaster was announced. This new plaster made it possible to produce garden gnomes using the same molds, but it reduced the cost of the plaster and labor needed to produce a gnome from $7 to $5 per gnome. Assume that consumers' demand function for gnomes in 1988 was not changed by this news. The announcement came early enough in the day for everybody to change his order for gnome molds to be delivered on January 1, 1989, but of course, the number of molds available to be used in 1988 is already determined from orders made one year ago. The manufacturer of garden gnome molds contracted to sell them for $1000 a year ago, so he can't change the price he charges on delivery.

(a) In 1988, what will be the equilibrium total output of garden gnomes?_

_____What will be the equilibrium price of gar-

den gnomes?_____What rate of return will Deardwarf's cousin, Zwerg, make on his investment in a garden gnome that he ordered

a year ago and for which he paid $1,000._____

(b) Zwerg's neighbor, Munchkin, also makes garden gnomes and he has a gnome mold which is to be delivered on January 1, 1988. Zwerg, who is looking for a way to invest some more money, is considering buying Munchkin's new mold from Munchkin and installing it in his own plant. If the best rate of return that Zwerg can make on alternative investments of additional funds is 10%, how much should he be willing to pay for

Munchkin's new mold?_____

(c) What do you think will happen to the number of garden gnomes ordered for delivery on January 1, 1989? Will it be larger, smaller, or

the same as the number ordered the previous year?_____

_____After the passage of sufficient time, the industry will reach a new long run equilibrium. What will be the new equilibrium price of

gnomes?_____

23.3 (30) On January 1, 1988, there were no changes in technology or demand functions from that in our original description of the industry, but the government astonished the garden gnome industry by introducing a tax on the production of garden gnomes. For every garden gnome produced, the manufacturer must pay a $1 tax. The announcement came early enough in the day so that there was time for gnome producers to change their orders of gnome molds for 1989. Of course the gnome molds to be used in 1988 had been already ordered a year ago. Gnome makers had signed contracts promising to pay $1,000 for each gnome that they ordered and they couldn't back out of these promises.

(a) Recalling from previous problems the number of gnome molds ordered for delivery on January 1, 1988, we see that if gnome makers produce up

to capacity in 1988, they will produce _____ gnomes. Given the demand function, we see that the market price would then have to be

_____

(b) If you have a garden gnome mold, the marginal cost of producing a

garden gnome, including the tax, is _____ Therefore all gnome molds (would) (would not) be used up to capacity in 1988.

(c) In 1988, what will be the total output of garden gnomes? _____

_____ What will be the price of garden gnomes? _____

_____ What rate of return will Deardwarf's cousin Zwerg make on his investment in a garden gnome that he ordered a year ago

and paid $1,000 for at that time? _____

(d) Remember that Zwerg's neighbor, Munchkin, also has a gnome mold which is to be delivered on January 1, 1988. Knowing about the tax makes Munchkin's mold a less attractive investment than it was without the tax, but still Zwerg would buy it if he can get it cheap enough so that he makes a 10% rate of return on his investment. How much should he

be willing to pay for Munchkin's new mold? _____

(e) What do you think will happen to the number of garden gnomes ordered for delivery on January 1, 1989? Will it be larger, smaller, or the

same as the number ordered the previous year? _____

(f) The tax on garden gnomes was left in place for many years and nobody expected any further changes in the tax or in demand or supply conditions. After the passage of sufficient time, the industry reached a new long run

equilibrium. What was the new equilibrium price of gnomes? _____

_____

(g) In the short run, who wound up paying the tax on garden gnomes,

the producers or the consumers? _____ In the long run, did the price of gnomes go up by more, less, or the same amount as the

tax per gnome? _____

(h) Suppose that early in the morning of January 1, 1988, the government had announced that there would be a \$1 tax on garden gnomes, but that the tax would not go into effect until January 1, 1989. Would the producers of garden gnomes necessarily be worse off than if there were no tax? Why or why not?

_____

_____

_____

(i) Is it reasonable to suppose that the government could introduce "surprise" taxes without making firms suspicious that there will be similar "surprises" in the future? Suppose that the introduction of the tax in January, 1988, makes gnome makers suspicious that there will be more taxes introduced in later years. Would this affect equilibrium prices and supplies? How?

_____

_____

_____

23.4 (40) Consider a competitive industry with a large number of firms, all of which have identical cost functions $c(y) = y^2 + 1$ for $y > 0$ and $c(0) = 0$. Suppose that initially the demand curve for this industry is given by $D(p) = 52 - p$. (The output of a firm does not have to be an integer number, but the number of firms does have to be an integer.)

(a) What is the supply curve of an individual firm? $S(p) =$ _____

_____If there are n firms in the industry, what will be the

industry supply curve? _____

(b) What is the smallest price at which the product can be sold? _____

_____

(c) What will be the equilibrium number of firms in the industry? (Hint:

take a guess at what the industry price will be and see if it works.) ____

_____

(d) What will be the equilibrium price? _____What

will be the equilibrium output of each firm? _____

(e) What will be the equilibrium output of the industry? _____

_____

(f) Now suppose that the demand curve shifts to $D(p) = 52.5 - p$. What

will be the equilibrium number of firms? _____(Hint:
can a new firm enter the market and make nonnegative profits?)

(g) What will be the equilibrium price? _____What

will be the equilibrium output of each firm? _____

_____What will be the equilibrium profits of each firm? _____

_____

(h) Now suppose that the demand curve shifts to $D(p) = 53 - p$. What

will be the equilibrium number of firms? _____What

will be the equilibrium price? _____

(i) What will be the equilibrium output of each firm? _____

_____What will be the equilibrium profits of each firm? _____

_____

23.5 (30) In 1990, the town of Ham Harbor had a more-or-less free market
in taxi services. Any respectable firm could provide taxi service as long
as the drivers and cabs satisfied certain safety standards.

Let us suppose that the constant marginal cost per trip of a taxi ride
is \$5, and that the average taxi has a capacity of 20 trips per day. Let the

demand function for taxi rides be given by $D(p) = 1,100 - 20p$, where demand is measured in rides per day, and price is measured in dollars. Assume that the industry is perfectly competitive.

(a) What is the competitive equilibrium price per ride? _____

_____(Hint: In competitive equilibrium, price must equal

marginal cost.) What is the equilibrium number of rides per day? _____

_____How many taxi cabs will there be in equilib-

rium? _____

(b) In 1990 the city council of Ham Harbor created a taxicab licensing board and issued a fixed number of licenses to each of the existing cabs. The board stated that it would continue to adjust the taxi cab fares so that the demand for rides equals the supply of rides, but that they will issue no new licenses in the future. In 1995 costs had not changed, but the demand curve for taxi cab rides had become $D(p) = 1,120 - 20p$. What

was the equilibrium price of a ride in 1995? _____

(c) What was the profit per ride in 1995, neglecting any costs associated

with acquiring a taxicab license? _____What was the

profit per taxicab license per day? _____If the taxi operated every day, what was the profit per taxicab license per year?

_____

(d) If the interest rate was 10% and costs, demand, and the number of licenses were expected to remain constant forever, what would be the

market price of a taxicab license? _____

(e) Suppose that the commission decided in 1995 to issue enough new licenses to reduce the taxicab price per ride to $5. How many licenses

would this take? _____

(f) Assuming that demand in Ham Harbor is not going to grow any more,

how much would a taxicab license be worth at this new fare?_____

_____

(g) How much money would each current taxicab owners be willing to pay

to prevent any new licenses from being issued? _____

_____What is the total amount that all taxicab owners together would

be willing to pay to prevent any new licences from ever being issued?_

_____The total amount that consumers of taxi
rides would be willing to pay to have another taxicab license issued would
be (more than), (less than), (the same as) this amount.

23.6 (20) In this problem, we will determine the equilibrium pattern
of agricultural land use surrounding a city. Think of the city as being
located in the middle of a large featureless plain. The price of wheat at
the market at the center of town is $10 a bushel, and it only costs $5 a
bushel to grow wheat. However, it costs 10 cents a mile to transport a
bushel of wheat to the center of town.

(a) If a farm is located t miles from the center of town, write down a

formula for its profit per bushel of wheat transported to market. _____

_____

(b) Suppose you can grow 1,000 bushels on an acre of land. How much

will an acre of land located t miles from the market rent for? _____

_____

(c) How far away from the market do you have to be for land to be worth

zero? _____

23.7 (10) Consider an industry with three firms. Suppose the firms have
the following supply functions: $S_1(p) = p$, $S_2(p) = p - 2$, and $S_3(p) = 2p$
respectively. On the graph below plot each of the three supply curves,
and the resulting industry supply curve.

Price

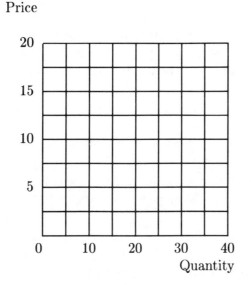

Quantity

(a) If the market demand curve has the form, $D(p) = 10$. What is the

resulting market price?_____Output?_____

_____What is the output level for firm 1 at this price?_____

_____Firm 2?_____Firm 3?_____

_____

23.8 (20) Suppose all firms in a given industry have the same supply
curve given by $S_i(p) = p/2$. Plot and label the four industry supply
curves generated by these firms if there are 1, 2, 3, or 4 firms operating
in the industry.

Price

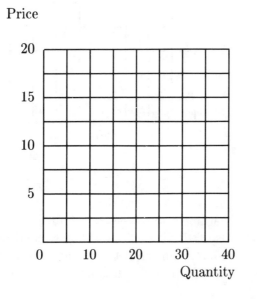

Quantity

(a) If all of the firms had a cost structure such that if the price was below $3 they would be losing money, what would be the equilibrium price and output in the industry if the market demand was equal to $D(p) = 3.5$?

Answer: price =_____, quantity =_____.

How many firms would exist in such a market? _____

(b) What if the identical conditions as above hold except that the market demand was equal to $D(p) = 8 - p$. Now, what would be the equilib-

rium price and output?_____

_____How many firms would operate in such a market?_____

_____

23.9 (30) A number of identical firms operate in a competitive industry. Each firm has a U-shaped average cost curve.

(a) On the diagram below draw a representative firm's average and marginal cost curves using blue ink, and indicate the long run equilibrium level of the market price.

Price

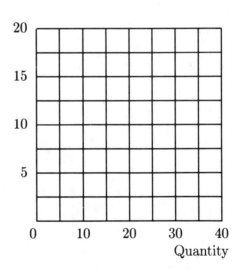

(b) Suppose the government imposes a tax, t, on every unit of output sold by the industry. Use red ink to draw the new conditions on the above graph. After the industry has adjusted to the imposition of the tax, the competitive model would predict the following: the market price would (increase/decrease) by amount _____, there would be (more/the same/fewer) firms operating in the industry, and the output level for each firm operating in the industry would (increase/stay the same/decrease).

(c) What if the government imposes a tax, *l*, on every *firm* in the industry. Draw the new cost conditions on the above graph using black ink. After the industry has adjusted to the imposition of the tax the competitive model would predict the following: the market price would (increase/decrease), there would be (more/the same/fewer) firms operating in the industry, and the output level for each firm operating in the industry would (increase/stay the same/decrease).

23.10 (10) In many communities, a restaurant that sells alcoholic beverages is required to have a license. Suppose that the number of licenses is limited and that they may be easily transferred to other restaurant owners. Suppose that the conditions of this industry closely approximate perfect competition. If a restaurant's revenue is $100,000 a year, and if a liquor license can be leased for a year for $85,000 from an existing

restaurant, what is the average total cost in the industry?_____

_____

23.11 (10) Consider a competitive market involving firms with identical U-shaped average cost curves that is in long run equilibrium. Suppose that the government imposes a lump sum tax on every firm in this industry. A firm can avoid this tax only if it stops production altogether.

(a) How will this tax affect the number of firms in the industry? _____

_____

(b) What will happen to the equilibrium price of the good? _____

_____

(c) When long run equilibrium is re–established, how will each firm's output compare with the initial equilibrium output? _____

_____

Market

24.1 (20) The Miss Manners Refinery in Dry Rock, Oklahoma, converts crude oil into gasoline. It takes 1 barrel of crude oil to produce 1 barrel of gasoline. In addition to the cost of oil there are some other costs involved in refining gasoline. Total costs of producing y barrels of gasoline are described by the cost function $c(y) = y^2/2 + p_o y$, where p_o is the price of a barrel of crude oil.

(a) Express the marginal cost of producing gasoline as a function of p_o

and y. _____

(b) Suppose that the refinery can buy 50 barrels of crude oil for $5 a barrel, but must pay $15 a barrel for any more that it buys beyond 50 barrels.

The marginal cost curve for gasoline will be _____up

to 50 barrels of gasoline and _____thereafter.

(c) Plot Miss Manners' supply curve in the diagram below using blue ink.

Price of Gasoline

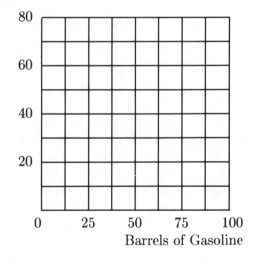

Barrels of Gasoline

(d) Suppose that Miss Manners faces a horizontal demand curve for gasoline at a price of $30 per barrel. Plot this demand curve on the graph

above using red ink. How much gasoline will she supply?_____

(e) If Miss Manners could no longer get the first 50 barrels of crude for $5, but had to pay $15 a barrel for all crude oil, how would her output

change?_____

(f) Now suppose that an entitlement program is introduced that permits refineries to buy one barrel of oil at $5 for each barrel of oil that they

buy for $15. What will Miss Manners' supply curve be now? _____

_____(Assume that it can buy fractions of a barrel in the same manner.) Plot this supply curve on the graph above using black ink. If the demand curve is horizontal at $30 a barrel, how much gasoline

will Miss Manners supply now? _____

24.2 (40) Suppose that a farmer's cost of growing y bushels of corn is given by the cost function $c(y) = y^2/20 + y$.

(a) If the price of corn is $5 a bushel, how much corn will this farmer

grow? _____

(b) What is the farmer's supply curve of corn as a function of the price

of corn? _____

(c) The government now introduces a Payment in Kind (PIK) program. If the farmer decides to grow y bushels of corn, he will get $(40-y)/2$ bushels from the government stockpiles. Write an expression for the farmer's profits as a function of his output and the market price of corn, taking into account the value of payments in kind received.

_____

(d) At the market price p, what will be the farmer's profit maximizing

output of corn? _____Plot a supply curve for corn in the graph below.

Price

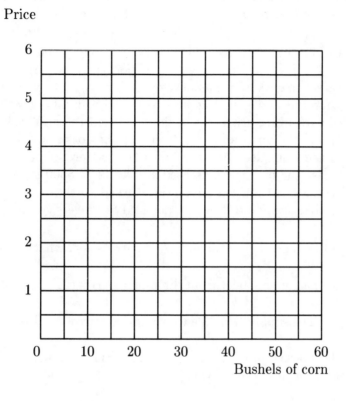

Bushels of corn

(e) If $p = \$2$, how many bushels of corn will he produce? _____

_____How many bushels will he get from the government stockpiles?

_____

(f) If $p = \$5$, how much corn will he supply? _____How many bushels of corn will he get from the government stockpiles, assuming he chooses to be in the PIK program? _____

(g) At any price between $p = \$2$ and $p = \$5$, write a formula for the size of the PIK payment. _____

(h) How much corn will he supply to the market, counting both production and PIK payment, as a function of the market price p? _____

_____

(i) Use red ink to illustrate the total supply curve of corn (including the corn from the PIK payment) in your graph above.

24.3 (40) In order to protect the wild populations of cockatoos, the Australian authorities have outlawed the export of these large parrots. An illegal market in cockatoos has developed. The cost of capturing an Australian cockatoo and shipping him to the U.S. is about $40 per bird. Smuggled parrots are drugged and shipped in suitcases. This is extremely traumatic for the birds and about 50% of the cockatoos shipped die in transit. Each smuggled cockatoo has a 10% chance of being discovered, in which case the bird is confiscated and a fine of $500 is charged. Confiscated cockatoos that are alive are returned to the wild. Confiscated cockatoos that are found dead are donated to university cafeterias.*

(a) When the market price of smuggled parrots is p, what is the expected

return to a parrot-smuggler from shipping a parrot?_____

_____The supply schedule for smuggled parrots will be a horizontal

line at the market price, _____(Hint: At what price does a parrot-smuggler just break even?)

(b) The demand function for smuggled cockatoos in the U.S. is $D(p) = 7200 - 20p$ per year. How many smuggled cockatoos will be sold in the

U.S. per year at the equilibrium price?_____How many cockatoos must be caught in Australia in order that this number of live

birds reaches U.S. buyers?_____

(c) Suppose that the trade in cockatoos is legalized. Suppose that it costs about $40 to capture and ship a cockatoo to the U.S. in a comfortable cage and that the number of deaths in transit by this method is negligible.

What would be the equilibrium price of cockatoos in the U.S.?_____

_____How many cockatoos would be sold in the U.S.?_____

_____How many cockatoos would have to be caught in

Australia for the U.S. market?_____

---

* The story behind this problem is based on actual fact, but the numbers we use are just made up for illustration. It would be very interesting to have some good estimates of the actual demand functions and cost functions.

(d) Suppose that the instead of returning confiscated cockatoos to the wild, the customs authorities sold them in the U. S. market. The profits from smuggling a cockatoo do not change from this policy change. Since the supply curve is horizontal, it must be that the equilibrium price of smuggled cockatoos will have to be the same as the equilibrium price when the confiscated cockatoos were returned to nature. How many live

cockatoos will be sold in the United States in equilibrium? _____

_____How many cockatoos will be permanently removed

from the Australian wild? _____

(e) In the equilibrium with smuggling, how many cockatoos are confiscated alive? (Assume that any cockatoos that are going to die in transit

are already dead by the time the authorities find them.) _____

24.4 (10) The horn of the rhinoceros is prized in Japan and China for its alleged aphrodisiac properties. This has proved to be most unfortunate for the rhinoceroses of East Africa. Although it is illegal to kill rhinoceroses in the game parks of Kenya, the rhinoceros population of these parks has been almost totally depleted by poachers. The price of rhinoceros horns in recent years has risen so high that a poacher can earn half a year's wages by simply killing one rhinoceros. Such high rewards for poaching have made laws against poaching almost impossible to enforce in East Africa. There are also large game parks with rhinoceros populations in South Africa. Since South Africa is much more of a police state than Kenya, game wardens have been able to prevent poaching almost completely. Therefore the rhinoceros population of South Africa has prospered. In a recent program from the television series *Nova*, a South African game warden explained that some rhinoceroses even have to be "harvested" in order to prevent overpopulation of rhinoceroses. "What then," asked the interviewer, "do you do with the horns from the animals that are harvested or that die of natural causes?" The South African game warden proudly explained that since international trade in rhinoceros horns was illegal, South Africa did not contribute to international crime by selling these horns. Instead the horns were either destroyed or stored in a warehouse.

(a) Suppose that all of the rhinoceros horns produced in South Africa are destroyed. Label the axes below and draw world supply and demand curves for rhinoceros horns with blue ink. Label the equilibrium price and quantity.

(b) If South Africa were to sell its rhinoceros horns on the world market,

which of the curves in your diagram would shift and in what direction?___

_____Use red ink to illustrate
the shifted curve or curves. If South Africa were to do this, would world

consumption of rhinoceros horns be increased or decreased? _____

_____Would the world price of rhinoceros horns be

increased or decreased? _____Would the amount of

rhinoceros poaching be increased or decreased?_____

24.5 (20) The sale of rhinoceros horns is not prohibited because of concern about the wicked pleasures of sex-crazed aphrodisiac munchers, but because the supply activity is bad for rhinoceroses. Similarly, the Australian reason for restricting the exportation of cockatoos to the United States is not because having a cockatoo is bad for you. Indeed it is legal for Australians to have cockatoos as pets. The motive for the restriction is simply to protect the wild populations from being over-exploited. In the case of other commodities, it appears that society has no particular interest in restricting the supply activities but wishes to restrict consumption. A good example is illicit drugs. The growing of marijuana, for example, is a simple pastoral activity, which in itself is no more harmful than growing sweet corn or brussels sprouts. It is the consumption of marijuana to which society objects.

Suppose that there is a constant marginal cost of $5 per ounce for growing marijuana and delivering it to buyers. But whenever the marijuana authorities find marijuana growing or in the hands of dealers, they seize the marijuana and fine the supplier. Suppose that the probability that marijuana is seized is .3 and that the fine if you are caught is $10 per ounce.

(a) If the "street price" is p per ounce, what is the expected return to a

dealer from selling an ounce of marijuana? _____What

then would be the equilibrium price of marijuana? _____

_____

(b) Suppose that the demand function for marijuana has the equation
$Q = A - Bp$. If all confiscated marijuana is destroyed, what will be the

equilibrium consumption of marijuana?_____Suppose
that confiscated marijuana is not destroyed but sold on the open market.

What will be the equilibrium consumption of marijuana?_____

_____

(c) The price of marijuana will (increase, decrease, stay the same)?

(d) If there were increasing rather than constant marginal cost in marijuana production, do you think that consumption would be greater if
confiscated marijuana were sold than if it were destroyed? Explain

_____

_____

_____

Chapter 25

NAME_____

Monopoly

Introduction. The profit maximizing output of a monopolist can usually be found by solving for the output at which marginal revenue is equal to marginal cost. Having solved for this output, you find the monopolist's price by plugging the profit maximizing output into the demand function. In general, the marginal revenue function can be found by taking the derivative of the total revenue function with respect to the quantity. But in the special case of linear demand, it is easy to find the marginal revenue curve graphically. With a linear inverse demand curve, $p(y) = a - by$, the marginal revenue curve always takes the form $MR(y) = a - 2by$.

In this section, you will also find some problems about price discrimination. Remember that a price discriminator wants the *marginal revenue* in each market to be equal to the marginal cost of production. Since he produces all of his output in one place, his marginal cost of production is the same for both markets and depends on his *total* output. The trick for solving these problems is to write marginal revenue in each market as a function of quantity sold in that market and to write marginal cost as a function of the sum of quantities sold in the two markets. The profit maximizing conditions then become two equations which you can solve for the two unknown quantities sold in the two markets. Of course if marginal cost is constant, your job is even easier, since all you have to do is find the quantities in each industry for which marginal revenue equals the constant marginal cost.

25.1 (20) Professor Bong has just written the first textbook in Punk Economics. It is called *Up Your Isoquant*. Market research suggests that the demand curve for this book will be $Q = 2,000 - 100p$, where p is its price. It will cost \$1000 to set the book in type. This setup cost is necessary before any copies can be printed. In addition to the setup cost, there is a marginal cost of \$2 per book for every book printed.

(a) Write down the total revenue function $R(Q)$ for Professor Bong's

book. _____

(b) Write down the total cost function $C(Q)$ for producing Professor

Bong's book. _____

(c) Compute the marginal revenue and marginal cost functions. How many copies of the book should be printed in order to maximize Professor

Bong's profits? $MR =$ _____ , $MC =$ _____ , $Q^* =$ _

_____ .

25.2 (10) Peter Morgan sells pigeon pies from a pushcart in Central Park. Morgan is the only supplier of this delicacy in Central Park. His costs are zero due to the abundant supplies of raw materials available in the park.

(a) When he first started his business, the inverse demand curve for pigeon pies was $p(y) = 100 - y$, where the price is measured in cents and y measures the number of pies sold. Use black ink to plot this curve in the graph below. On the same graph, use red ink to plot his marginal revenue curve.

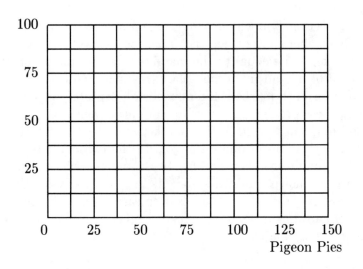

Dollars

(b) What level of output will maximize Peter's profits? _____

_____ What price will Peter charge per pie? _____

(c) After Peter had been in business for several months, he noticed that his demand curve had shifted to $p(y) = 75 - y/2$. Use blue ink to plot this curve in the graph above. Plot his new marginal revenue curve on the same graph with black ink.

(d) What is his profit maximizing output at this new price? _____

_____ What is the new profit maximizing price? _____

25.3 (20) Suppose that the demand function for Japanese cars in the United States is such that annual sales of cars (in thousands of cars) will be $250 - 2P$, where P is the price of Japanese cars in thousands of dollars.

(a) If the supply schedule is horizontal at a price of $5,000 what will be

the equilibrium number of Japanese cars sold in the U.S.? _____

_____thousand. How much money will Americans spend in

total on Japanese cars? _____billion dollars.

(b) Suppose that in response to pressure from American car manufacturers, the United States imposes an import duty on Japanese cars in such a way that for every car exported to the United States the Japanese manufacturers must pay a tax to the U.S. government of $2,000. How many

Japanese automobiles will now be sold in the U.S.? _____

_____thousand. At what price will they be sold? _____

_____thousand dollars.

(c) How much revenue will the U.S. government collect with this tariff?

_____million dollars.

(d) On the graph below, the price paid by American consumers is measured on the vertical axis. Use blue ink to show the demand and supply schedules before the import duty is imposed. After the import duty is imposed, the supply schedule shifts and the demand schedule stays as before. Use red ink to draw the new supply schedule.

Price (thousands)

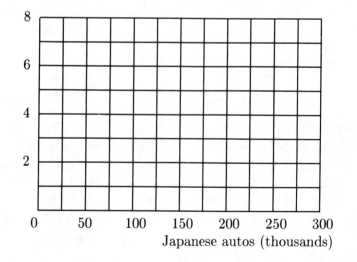

Japanese autos (thousands)

(e) Suppose that instead of imposing an import duty, the U.S. government persuades the Japanese governments to impose "voluntary export restrictions" on their exports of cars to the U.S. Suppose that the Japanese agree to restrain their exports by requiring that every car exported to the United States must have an export license. Suppose further that the Japanese government agrees to issue only 236,000 export licenses and sells these licenses to the Japanese firms. If the Japanese firms know the American demand curve and if they know that only 236,000 Japanese cars will be sold in America, what price will they be able to charge in America

for their cars? _____thousand dollars.

(f) How much will a Japanese firm be willing to pay the Japanese gov-

ernment for an export license? _____thousand dollars. (Hint: Think about what it costs to produce a car and how much it can be sold for if you have an export license.)

(g) How much will be the Japanese government's total revenue from the

sale of export licenses? _____million dollars.

(h) How much money will Americans spend on Japanese cars?_____

_____billion dollars.

(i) Why might the Japanese "voluntarily" submit to export controls?

_____

_____

_____

Calculus **25.4** (40) Danny's Dump Trucks (the only producer of dump trucks) sells its output in both the domestic and the foreign markets. Because of import and export restrictions, there is no possibility that a purchase in one market could be sold in the other market. The demand and marginal revenue curves associated with each market are as follows.

$$P_d = 20,000 - 20Q \quad P_f = 25,000 - 50Q$$
$$MR_d = 20,000 - 40Q \quad MR_f = 25,000 - 100Q$$

Danny's production process exhibits constant returns to scale and he knows from past experience that it takes $1,000,000 to produce 100 trucks.

(a) What is the average cost of producing a truck? _____

_____What is the marginal cost? _____Show the average and marginal cost curves on the graph.

(b) Draw the demand curve for the domestic market in blue ink and the marginal revenue curve for the domestic market in yellow ink. Draw the demand curve for the foreign market in red ink and the marginal revenue curve for the foreign market in black ink.

Dollars (1,000s)

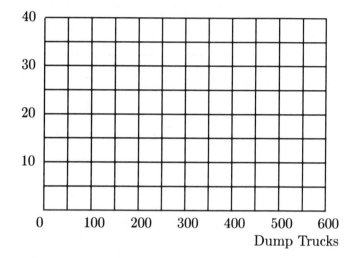

Dump Trucks

(c) If Danny is maximizing his profits, he will sell _____

_____trucks in the domestic market at _____

_____dollars each and _____trucks in the foreign

market at _____dollars each.

(d) What are Danny's total profits? _____

(e) What is the price elasticity of demand in the domestic market? _____

_____What is the price elasticity of demand in the

foreign market? _____What is true about the market

in which the highest price is charged? _____

(f) Suppose the import and export restrictions change so that anybody who buys a dump truck in one market can immediately (and costlessly) resell it in the other. On the graph below, draw the new inverse demand curve (with blue ink) and marginal revenue curve (with black ink) facing Danny.

Dollars (1,000s)

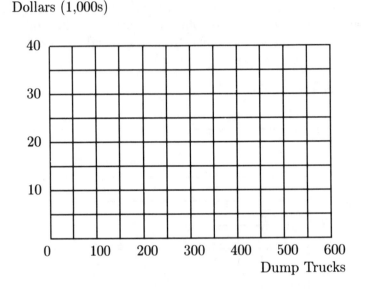

(g) Given that his costs haven't changed, how many dump trucks should

Danny sell? _____What price will he charge? _____

_____How will Danny's profits change now that he

can no longer practice price discrimination? _____

_____

25.5 (20) Ferdinand Sludge has just written a disgusting new book, *Orgy in the Piggery*. His publisher, Graw McSwill estimates that the demand for this book in the U.S. is $Q_1 = 50,000 - 2,000P_1$, where P_1 is the price in America measured in U. S. dollars. The demand for Sludge's opus in England is $Q_2 = 10,000 - 500P_2$, where P_2 is its price in England measured in U.S. dollars. His publisher has a cost function $C(Q) = \$50,000 + \$2Q$, where Q is the total number of copies of *Orgy* that it produces.

(a) If McSwill must charge the same price in both countries, how many

copies should it sell _____and what price should it charge _

_____to maximize its profits, and how much will those

profits be? _____

(b) If McSwill can charge a different price in each country, and wants to

maximize profits, how many copies should it sell in the U.S.? _____

_____What price should it charge in the U.S.? _____

_____How many copies should it sell in England? _____

_____What price should it charge in England? _____How

much will its total profits be? _____

25.6 (10) "Since the monopolist usually sets her output such that price
is greater than marginal cost, all she has to do to increase profits is to sell
one additional unit at a slightly lower price." What is fallacious about
this argument?

_____

_____

_____

25.7 (20) A monopolist has a cost function given by $c(y) = y^2$ and faces
a demand curve given by $P(y) = 120 - y$.

(a) What is his profit maximizing level of output? _____

_____What price will the monopolist charge? _____

_____

(b) If you put a lump sum tax of $100 on this monopolist, what would

his output be? _____

(c) If you wanted to choose a price ceiling for this monopolist so as to
maximize consumer plus producer surplus, what price ceiling should you

choose? _____

(d) How much output will the monopolist produce at this price ceiling?

———————————————

(e) Suppose that you put a specific tax on the monopolist of $20 per unit

output. What would his profit maximizing level of output be? —————

———————————————

25.8 (30) Gargantuan enterprises has a monopoly in the production of antimacassars. Its factory is located in the town of Pantagruel. There is no other industry in Pantagruel and the labor supply equation there is $W = 10 + .1L$, where W is the daily wage and L is the number of person-days of work performed. Antimacassars are produced with a production function, $Q = 10L$, where L is daily labor supply and Q is daily output. The demand curve for antimacassars is $P = 41 - \frac{Q}{1,000}$, where P is the price and Q is the number of sales per day.

(a) Find the profit maximizing output for Gargantuan. —————————

—————————————(Hint: Use the production function to find the labor input requirements for any level of output. Make substitutions so you can write the firm's total costs as a function of its output and then its profit as a function of output. Solve for the profit–maximizing output.)

(b) How much labor does it use? —————————————What is the

wage rate that it pays? —————————————

(c) What is the price of antimacassars? —————————————How

much profit is made? —————————————

25.9 (10) Suppose that a monopolist faces an inverse demand curve given by $p(y) = 13/y$ and has a cost function of $c(y) = y^2$. What is his profit

maximizing level of output? —————————————

25.10 (10) Suppose that a monopolist is able to sell to two different markets: one with a demand curve given by $y_1(p_1) = p_1^{-2}$ and the other with inverse demand curve given by $y_2(p_2) = p_2^{-3}$. He has constant marginal costs of production of 1.

(a) What is the profit maximizing price to charge in market 1? _____

_____

(b) What is the profit maximizing price to charge in market 2? _____

_____

25.11 (20) Suppose that a monopolist faces an inverse demand curve given by $p(y) = 100 - 2y$, and that he has constant marginal costs of 20.

(a) What is his optimal level of output? _____What

price will the monopolist charge? _____

(b) What is the socially optimal price for this firm? _____

_____

(c) What is the socially optimal level of output for this firm? _____

_____

(d) What is the deadweight loss due to the monopolistic behavior of this

firm? _____

(e) Now suppose that this monopolist could operate as a perfectly discriminating monopolist and sell each unit of output at the highest price

it would fetch. The deadweight loss in this case would be _____

_____

25.12 (20) A monopolist has an inverse demand curve given by $p(y) = 12 - y$ and a cost curve given by $c(y) = y^2$.

(a) What will be his profit maximizing level of output _____

(b) Suppose the government decides to put a tax on this monopolist so that for each unit he sells he has to pay the government $2.00. What will

be his output under this form of taxation? _____

(c) Suppose now that the government puts a lump sum tax of $10.00 on

the profits of the monopolist. What will be his output? _____

_____

25.13 (40) In Gomorrah, New Jersey, there is only one newspaper, the
Daily Calumny. The demand for the paper depends on the price and the
amount of scandal reported. The demand function is $Q = 15S^{1/2}P^{-3}$,
where S is the number of column inches of scandal reported in the paper,
Q is the number of issues sold per day, and P is the price. Scandals
are not a scarce commodity in Gomorrah. However it takes resources to
write, edit, and print stories of scandal. The cost of reporting S units of
scandal is $10S$. These costs are independent of the number of papers
sold. In addition it costs money to print and deliver the paper. These
cost $.10 per copy and the cost per unit is independent of the amount
of scandal reported in the paper. Therefore the total cost of printing Q
copies of the paper with S column inches of scandal is $10S + .10Q$

(a) Calculate the price elasticity of demand for the *Daily Calumny.*____

_____Does the price elasticity depend on the number of

scandals reported? _____Is the price elasticity constant over

all prices?_____

(b) Calculate the profit maximizing price._____(Hint: What is
the relation between the profit maximizing price, the marginal cost, and
the price elasticity?) The difference between the profit maximizing price

and the cost of printing and delivering the paper is _____

(c) If the *Daily Calumny* charges the profit maximizing price and prints
100 column inches of scandal, how many copies would it sell? (Round

to the nearest integer) _____Write a general expression for the

number of copies sold as a function of S, $Q(S) =$ _____

(d) Assuming that the paper charges the profit maximizing price, write

an expression for profits as a function of Q and S. _____

_____Using the solution for $Q(S)$ that you found in the last section,
substitute $Q(S)$ for Q to write an expression for profits as a function of
S alone.

(e) If the *Daily Calumny* charges its profit maximizing price, and prints the profit maximizing amount of scandal, how many column inches of

scandal should it print._____How many copies are sold

_____and what is the amount of profit for the Daily

Calumny if it maximizes its profits?_____

25.14 (20) The demand curve facing a monopolist is given by

$$D(p) = \begin{cases} 100/p & \text{for } p \leq 10 \\ 0 & \text{for } p > 10 \end{cases}$$

(a) Plot this demand curve in the graph below.

Price

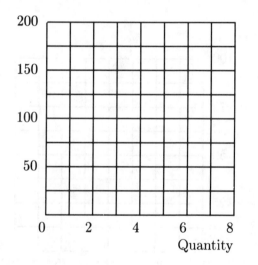

(b) At what price is the (inverse) demand curve discontinuous? _____

_____

(c) Suppose that the monopolist has constant marginal costs of $1 per

unit. What will its profits be if it charges a price of $2?_____

(d) What will its profits be if it charges a price of $5?_____

(e) What price maximizes its profits? _____

(f) What quantity maximizes its profits? _____

25.15 (20) In the graph below, use black ink to draw the inverse demand curve, $p_1(y) = 100 - y$.

(a) If the monopolist has zero costs, where on this curve will it choose to

operate? _____

(b) Now draw another demand curve that passes through the profit maximizing point and is flatter than the original demand curve. Use a red pen to mark the part of this new demand curve on which the monopolist would choose to operate. (Hint: remember the idea of revealed preference?)

(c) The monopolist would have (larger, smaller) profits at the new demand curve than he had at the original demand curve.

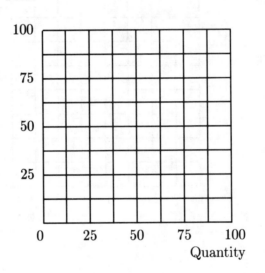

Price

Oligopoly

26.1 (30) Carl and Simon are two rival pumpkin growers who sell their pumpkins at the Farmers' Market in Lake Whichisit, Minnesota. They are the only sellers of pumpkins at the market, where the demand function for pumpkins is $q = 3200 - 1600p$. The total number of pumpkins sold at the market is $q = q_C + q_S$ where q_C is the number that Carl sells and q_S is the number that Simon sells. The cost of producing pumpkins for either farmer is \$.50 per pumpkin no matter how many pumpkins he produces.

(a) The inverse demand function for pumpkins at the Farmers' Market is

$p = a - b(q_C + q_S)$ where $a =$_____and $b =$_____

_____. The marginal cost of producing a pumpkin for

either farmer is _____.

(b) Every spring, each of the farmers decides how many pumpkins to grow. They both know the local demand function and they each know how many pumpkins were sold by the other farmer last year. In fact, each farmer assumes that the other farmer will sell the same number this year as he sold last year. So, for example, if Simon sold 400 pumpkins last year, Carl believes that Simon will sell 400 pumpkins again this year. If Simon sold 400 pumpkins last year, what does Carl think the price of

pumpkins will be if Carl sells 1200 pumpkins this year?_____

_____. If Simon sold q_S^{t-1} pumpkins in year $t-1$, then in the spring of year t, Carl thinks that if he, Carl, sells q_C^t pumpkins this year,

the price of pumpkins this year will be _____.

(c) If Simon sold 400 pumpkins last year, Carl believes that if he sells q_C^t pumpkins this year then the inverse demand function that he faces is $p = 2 - 400/1600 - q_C^t/1600 = 1.75 - q_C^t/1600$. Therefore, if Simon sold 400 pumpkins last year, Carl's marginal revenue this year will be $1.75 - q_C^t/800$. More generally, if Simon sold q_S^{t-1} pumpkins last year, then Carl believes that if he, himself, sells q_C^t pumpkins this year, his

marginal revenue this year will be _____.

(d) Carl believes that Simon will never change the amount of pumpkins that he produces from the amount q_S^{t-1} that he sold last year. Therefore Carl plants enough pumpkins this year so that he can sell the amount that maximizes his profits this year. To maximize this profit, he chooses the output this year that sets his marginal revenue this year equal to his marginal cost. This means that to find Carl's output this year when Simon's output last year was q_S^{t-1}, Carl solves the following equation.

_____.

(e) Carl's Cournot reaction function, $R_C^t(q_S^{t-1})$ is a function that tells us what Carl's profit maximizing output this year would be as a function of Simon's output last year. Use the equation you wrote in the last answer to

find Carl's reaction function, $R_C^t(q_S^{t-1}) = $ _____(Hint: This is a linear expression of the form $a - bq_S^{t-1}$. You have to find the constants a and b.)

(f) Suppose that Simon makes his decisions in the same way that Carl does. Notice that the problem is completely symmetric in the roles played by Carl and Simon. Therefore without even calculating it, we can guess

that Simon's reaction function is $R_S^t(q_C^{t-1}) = $ _____. (Of course, if you don't like to guess, you could work this out by following similar steps to the ones you used to find Carl's reaction function.)

(g) Suppose that in year 1, Carl produced 200 pumpkins and Simon pro-

duced 1000 pumpkins. In year 2, how many would Carl produce?_____

_____How many would Simon produce?_____

_____In year 3, how many would Carl produce? _____

_____How many would Simon produce?_____

_____Use a calculator or pen and paper to work out several more terms in this series. To what level of output does Carl's output

appear to be converging?_____How about Simon's?__

_____

(h) Write down two simultaneous equations that could be solved to find outputs q_S and q_C such that if Carl is producing q_C and Simon is pro-ducing q_S, then they will both want to produce the same amount in the

next period. Hint: Use the reaction functions.

_____

(i) Solve the two equations you wrote down in the last part for an equilibrium output for each farmer. Each farmer, in Cournot equilibrium,

produces _____units of output. The total amount of

pumpkins brought to the Farmers' market in Lake Whichisit is _____

_____. The price of pumpkins in that market is

_____. How much profit does each farmer make?_____

_____

26.2 (30) Suppose that the pumpkin market in Lake Whichisit is as we described it in the last problem except for one detail. Every spring, the snow thaws off of Carl's pumpkin field a week before it thaws off of Simon's. Therefore Carl can plant his pumpkins one week earlier than Simon can. Now Simon lives just down the road from Carl and he can tell by looking at Carl's fields how many pumpkins Carl planted and how many Carl will harvest in the fall. (Suppose also that Carl will sell every pumpkin that he produces.) Therefore, instead of assuming that Carl will sell the same amount of pumpkins that he did last year, Simon sees how many Carl is actually going to sell this year. Simon has this information before he makes his own decision about how many to plant.

(a) If Carl plants enough pumpkins to yield q_C^t this year, then Simon

knows that the profit maximizing amount to produce this year is $q_S^t =$_

_____. Hint: Remember the reaction functions
you found in the last problem.

(b) When Carl plants his pumpkins, he understands how Simon will make his decision. Therefore Carl knows that the amount that Simon will produce this year will be determined by the amount that Carl produces. In particular, if Carl's output is q_C^t , then Simon will produce and sell

_____and the total output of the two producers will be

_____. Therefore Carl knows that if his own output is

q_C, the price of pumpkins in the market will be _____

_____.

(c) In the last part of the problem, you found how the price of pumpkins this year in the Farmers' Market is related to the number of pumpkins that Carl produces this year. Now write an expression for Carl's total revenue in year t as a function of his own output, q_C^t. _____

_____ Write an expression for Carl's marginal revenue in year t as a function of q_C^t. _____

(d) Find the profit maximizing output for Carl. _____

_____ Find the profit maximizing output for Simon. _____

_____ Find the equilibrium price of pumpkins in the Lake Whichisit Farmers' Market. _____ How much profit does Carl make? _____ How much profit does Simon make? _____

_____ An equilibrium of the type we discuss here is known as a _____ equilibrium

(e) If he wanted to, it would be possible for Carl to delay his planting until the same time that Simon planted so that neither of them would know the other's plans for this year when he planted. Would it be in Carl's interest to do this? Explain Hint: What are Carl's profits in the equilibrium above. How do they compare with his profits in Cournot equilibrium.

_____

_____

_____

26.3 (30) Suppose that Carl and Simon sign a marketing agreement. They decide to determine their total output jointly and to each produce the same number of pumpkins. To maximize their joint profits, how many pumpkins should they produce in total? _____ How much does each one of them produce _____ . How much profits does each one of them make?_____

26.4 (30) The inverse market demand curve for bean sprouts is given by $P(Y) = 100 - 2Y$, and the total cost function for any firm in the industry is given by $TC(y) = 4y$.

(a) The marginal cost for any firm in the industry is equal to _____

_____The change in price for a one unit increase in

output is equal to _____

(b) If the bean sprout industry were perfectly competitive, the industry

output would be _____, and the industry price would be ____

_____.

(c) Suppose two Cournot firms operate in the market. The reaction function for Firm 1 would be _____(Reminder: Unlike the example in your textbook, the marginal cost is not zero here.) The reaction function of Firm 2 will be _____If the firms were operating at the Cournot equilibrium point, industry output would be

_____, each firm would produce _____

_____, and the market price would be _____

(d) For the Cournot case draw the two reaction curves and indicate the equilibrium point on the graph below.

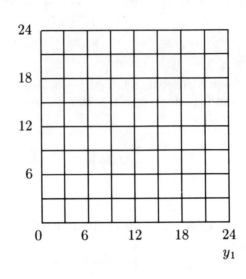

(e) If the two firms decided to collude, industry output would be _____

_____and the market price would equal _____

_____.

(f) Suppose both of the colluding firms are producing equal amounts of output. If one of the colluding firms assumes that the other firm would not react to a change in industry output, what incentive is there for the

firm to increase its output by one unit?_____What is the incentive if the smaller firm is producing only 2 units of the total

industry production?_____

(g) Suppose one firm acts as a Stackelberg leader and the other firm behaves as a follower. The maximization problem for the leader can be written as:

Solving this problem results in the leader producing an output of

_____, and the follower producing _____

_____This implies an industry output of _____

_____and price of _____

26.5 (30) Grinch is the sole owner of a mineral water spring that costlessly burbles forth as much mineral water as Grinch cares to bottle. It costs Grinch $1 per gallon bottle to bottle this water. The inverse demand curve for Grinch's mineral water is $p = \$10 - .10q$, where p is the price per gallon and q is the number of gallons sold.

(a) Write down an expression for profits as a function of q, $\Pi(q) = $ ___

_____Find the profit maximizing choice of q for

Grinch _____

(b) What price does Grinch get per gallon of mineral water if he produces

the profit maximizing quantity? _____How much profit

does he make?_____

(c) Suppose, now, that Grinch's neighbor, Grubb finds a mineral spring that produces mineral water that is just as good Grinch's water, but it costs Grubb $3 a bottle to get his water out of the ground and bottle it. Total market demand for mineral water remains as before. Suppose that Grinch and Grubb each believe that the other's quantity decision is independent of his own.

(d) What is the Cournot equilibrium output for Grubb? _____

(e) What is the price in the Cournot equilibrium? _____

26.6 (40) Albatross Airlines has a monopoly on air travel between Peoria and Dubuque. If Albatross makes one trip in each direction per day, the demand schedule for round trips is $q = 160 - 2p$, where q is the number of passengers per day. (Assume that nobody makes one-way trips.) There is an "overhead" fixed cost of $2,000 per day which is necessary to fly the airplane regardless of the number of passengers. In addition, there is a marginal cost of $10 per passenger. Thus, total daily costs are $\$2,000 + 10q$ if the plane flies at all.

(a) On the graph below, sketch and label the marginal revenue curve, and the average and marginal cost curves.

MR, MC

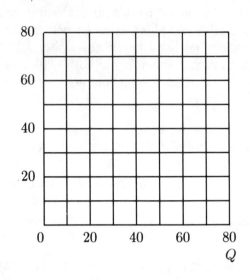

(b) Calculate the profit maximizing price and quantity and total daily

profits for Albatross Airlines. $p =$_____, $q =$_____,

$\pi =$_____.

(c) If the interest rate is 10% per year, how much would someone be willing to pay to own Albatross Airlines' monopoly on the Dubuque-Peoria route. (Assuming that demand and cost conditions remain unchanged

forever.)_____

(d) If another firm with the same costs as Albatross Airlines were to enter the Dubuque-Peoria market and if the industry then became a Cournot

duopoly, would the new entrant make a profit? _____

(e) Suppose that the throbbing night life in Peoria and Dubuque becomes widely known and in consequence the population of both places doubles. As a result, the demand for airplane trips between the two places doubles to become $q = 320 - 4p$. Suppose that the original airplane had a capacity of 80 passengers. If AA must stick with this single plane and if no other airline enters the market, what price should it charge to maximize its

output and how much profit would it make? $p =$_____, $\pi =$__

_____.

(f) Let us assume that the overhead costs per plane are constant regardless of the number of planes. If AA added a second plane with the same costs

and capacity as the first plane, what price would it charge _____

_____, how many tickets would it sell _____

_____and how much would its profits be?_____If AA could prevent entry by another competitor, would it choose to add a

second plane?_____

(g) Suppose that AA stuck with one plane and another firm entered the market with a plane of its own. If the second firm has the same cost function as the first and if the two firms act as Cournot oligopolists, what

will be the price, _____quantities, _____

_____and profits _____?

26.7 (20) Consider an industry with the following structure. There are 50 firms that behave in a competitive manner and have identical cost functions given by $c(y) = y^2/2$. There is one monopolist that has 0 marginal costs. The demand curve for the product is given by

$$D(p) = 1000 - 50p.$$

(a) What is the supply curve of one of the competitive firms? _____

_____

(b) What is the total supply from the competitive sector? _____

_____

(c) If the monopolist sets a price p, how much output will he sell? _____

_____

(d) What is the monopolist's profit maximizing output? _____

_____

(e) What is the monopolist's profit maximizing price? _____

_____

(f) How much will the competitive sector provide at this price? _____

_____

(g) What will be the total amount of output sold in this industry? _____

_____

26.8 (30) Consider a market with one large firm and many small firms. The supply curve of the small firms taken together is:

$$S(p) = 100 + p.$$

The demand curve for the product is:

$$D(p) = 200 - p.$$

The cost function for the one large firm is:

$$c(y) = 25y.$$

Suppose that the large firm is forced to operate at a zero level of output.

(a) What will be the equilibrium price? _____What

will be the equilibrium quantity? _____

Suppose now that the large firm attempts to exploit its market power and set a profit maximizing price. In order to model this we assume that customers always go first to the competitive firms and buy as much as they are able to and then go to the monopolist. In this situation,

(b) What will be the equilibrium price? _____

(c) What will be the equilibrium quantity supplied by the monopolist?

_____

(d) What will be the equilibrium quantity supplied by the competitive

firms _____

(e) What will be the large firm's profits? _____

Finally suppose the large firm could force the competitive firms out of the business and behave as a real monopolist.

(f) What will be the equilibrium price? _____What

will be the equilibrium quantity? _____

(g) What will be the large firm's profits? _____

Calculus **26.9** (30) In a remote area of the American Midwest before the railroads arrived, cast iron cookstoves were much desired, but people lived far apart, roads were poor, and heavy stoves were expensive to transport. Stoves could be shipped by river boat to the town of Bouncing Springs, Missouri. Ben Kinmore was the only stove dealer in Bouncing Springs. He could buy as many stoves as he wished for $20 each, delivered to his store. The only farmers that traded with Bouncing Springs lived along a road that ran east and west through town. Along that road, there was one farm every mile and the cost of hauling a stove was $1 per mile. There were no other stove dealers on the road in either direction. The owners of every farm along the road had a reservation price of $120 for a cast iron cookstove. That is, any of them would be willing to pay up to $120 to have a stove rather than to not have one. Nobody had use for more than one stove. Ben Kinmore charged a base price of $p for stoves and added to the price the cost of delivery. For example, if the base price of stoves was $40 and you lived 45 miles west of Bouncing Springs, you would have to pay $85 to get a stove, $40 base price plus a hauling charge of $45. Since the reservation price of every farmer was $120, it follows that if the base price were $40, any farmer who lived within 80 miles of Bouncing Springs would be willing to pay $40 plus the price of delivery to have a cookstove. Therefore at a base price of $40, Ben could sell 80 cookstoves to the farmers living west of him. Similarly, if his base price is $40, he could sell 80 cookstoves to the farmers living within 80 miles to his east, for a total of 160 cookstoves.

(a) If Ben set a base price of $p for cookstoves where $p < 120$, and if he charged $1 a mile for delivering them, what would be the total number

of cookstoves he could sell? _____

_____(Remember to count the ones he could sell to his east as well as to his west.) Assume that Ben has no other costs than buying the stoves and delivering them. Then Ben would make a profit of $p - 20$ per stove. Write Ben's total profit as a function of the base price, p, that he

charges _____

(b) Ben's profit maximizing base price is _____. (Hint: You just wrote profits as a function of prices. Now differentiate this expression for profits with respect to p.) Ben's most distant customer

would be located at a distance of _____miles from him.

Ben would sell _____cookstoves and make a total profit

of _____

(c) Suppose that instead of setting a single base price and making all buyers pay for the cost of transportation, Ben offers free delivery of cookstoves. He sets a price $\$p$ and promises to deliver for free to any farmer who lives within $p-20$ miles of him. (He won't deliver to anyone who lives further than that, because it then costs him more than $\$p$ to buy a stove and deliver it). If he is going to price in this way, how high should he set p.

_____How many cookstoves would Ben deliver?_____

_____How much would his total revenue be? _____

_____How much would his total costs be (including

the cost of deliveries and the cost of buying the stoves.)_____

_____(Hint: What is the average distance that he has to haul

a cookstove?) How much profit would he make?_____

_____Can you explain why it is more profitable for Ben to use this pricing scheme where he pays the cost of delivery himself rather than the scheme where the farmers pay for their own deliveries?

_____

_____

_____

Calculus **26.10** (30) Perhaps you wondered what Ben Kinmore, who lives off in the woods quietly collecting his monopoly profits, is doing in this chapter on oligopoly. Well, unfortunately for Ben, before he got around to selling any stoves, the railroad built a track to the town of Deep Furrow, just 40 miles down the road, west of Bouncing Springs. The storekeeper in Deep

Furrow, Huey Sunshine, was also able to get cookstoves delivered by train to his store for $20 each. Huey and Ben were the only stove dealers on the road. Let us concentrate our attention on how they would compete for the customers who lived between them. We can do this, because Ben is able to charge different base prices for the cookstoves he ships east from the prices he charges for the cookstoves he ships west. So is Huey.

Suppose that Ben sets a base price, p_B, for stoves he sends west and adds a charge of $1 per mile for delivery. Suppose that Huey sets a base price, p_H, for stoves he sends east and adds a charge of $1 per mile for delivery. Farmers who live between Ben and Huey would buy from the seller who is willing to deliver most cheaply to them (so long as the delivered price does not exceed $120). If Ben's base price is p_B and Huey's base price is p_H, somebody who lives x miles west of Ben would have to pay a total of $p_B + x$ to have a stove delivered from Ben and $p_H + (40 - x)$ to have a stove delivered by Huey.

(a) If Ben's base price is p_B and Huey's is p_H, write down an equation that could be solved for the distance x^* to the west of Bouncing Springs that

Ben's market extends. _____ If Ben's base price is p_B

and Huey's is p_H, then Ben will sell _____ cookstoves

and Huey will sell _____ cookstoves.

(b) Recalling that Ben makes a profit of $p_B - 20$ on every cookstove that he sells, Ben's profits can be expressed as the following function of p_B

and p_H. _____

(c) Suppose that Ben thinks that Huey's price will stay at p_H, no matter what price Ben chooses, what choice of p_B would maximize Ben's

profits? _____ Hint: Set the derivative of Ben's profits with respect to his price equal to zero. Suppose that Huey thinks that Ben's price will stay at p_B, no matter what price Huey chooses,

what choice of p_H would maximize Huey's profits? _____

_____ Hint: From the symmetry of the problem and the answer to the last question, it should be easy to see the answer.

(d) Can you find a base price for Ben and a base price for Huey such that each is a profit maximizing choice given what the other guy is doing? Hint: Find prices p_B and p_H that simultaneously solve the last two

equations. _____ How many cookstoves does Ben sell

to farmers living west of him?_____How much prof-

its does he make on these sales?_____

(e) Suppose that Ben and Huey decided to compete for the customers who live between them by price discriminating. Suppose that Ben offers to deliver a stove to a farmer who lives x miles west of him for a price equal to the maximum of Ben's total cost of delivering a stove to that farmer and Huey's total cost of delivering to the same farmer less 1 penny. Suppose that Huey offers to deliver a stove to a farmer who lives x miles west of Ben for a price equal to the maximum of Huey's own total cost of delivering to this farmer and Ben's total cost of delivering to him less a penny. For example, if a farmer lives 10 miles west of Ben, Ben's total cost of delivering to him is $30, $20 to get the stove and $10 for hauling it 10 miles west. Huey's total cost of delivering it to him is $50, $20 to get the stove and $30 to haul it 30 miles east. Ben will charge the maximum of his own cost, which is $20, and Huey's cost less a penny, which is $49.99.

The maximum of these two numbers is _____. Huey will charge the maximum of his own total cost of delivering to this farmer, which is $50, and Ben's cost less a penny, which is $19.99. Therefore Huey

will charge _____to deliver to this farmer. This farmer

will buy from _____, whose price to him is cheaper by one penny. When the two merchants have this pricing policy, all farmers

who live within _____miles of Ben will buy from Ben

and all farmers who live within _____miles of Huey will buy from Huey. A farmer who lives x miles west of Ben and buys

from Ben must pay _____dollars to have a cookstove delivered to him. A farmer who lives x miles east of Huey and buys from

Huey must pay _____for delivery of a stove. On the graph below, use blue ink to graph the cost to Ben of delivering to a farmer who lives x miles west of him. Use red ink to graph the total cost to Huey of delivering a cookstove to a farmer who lives x miles west of Ben. Use pencil to mark the lowest price available to a farmer as a function of how far west he lives from Ben.

Dollars

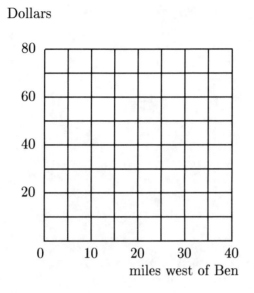

miles west of Ben

(f) With the pricing policies you just graphed, which farmers get stoves delivered most cheaply, those who live closest to the merchants or those

who live midway between them?_____On the graph you made, shade in the area representing each merchant's profits. How

much profits does each merchant make?_____If Ben and Huey are pricing in this way, is there any way for either of them to increase his profits by changing the price he charges to some farmers?

_____

Chapter 27
Game Theory

27.1 (25) Maynard's Cross is a trendy bistro that specializes in carpaccio, and other uncooked substances. Most people who come to Maynard's come to see and be seen by other people of the kind who come to Maynard's. There is however, a hard core of 10 customers per evening who come for the carpaccio and don't care how many other people come. The number of additional customers who appear at Maynard's depends on how many people they expect to see. In particular, if people expect that the number of customers at Maynard's in an evening will be X, then the number of people who actually come to Maynard's is $Y = 10 + .75X$. In equilibrium, it must be true that the number of people who actually attend the restaurant is equal to the number who are expected to attend.

(a) What two simultaneous equations must one solve to find the equilibrium attendance at Maynard's.

(b) What is the equilibrium nightly attendance? _____

(c) On the axes below, draw the lines that represents each of two equations you mentioned in part (a). Label the equilibrium attendance level.

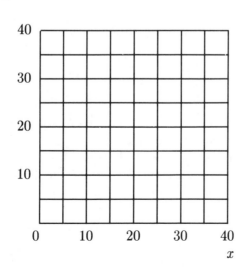

(d) Suppose that one additional carpaccio enthusiast moves to the area. Like the other 10, he eats at Maynard's every night no matter how many others eat there. Write down the new equations determining attendance at Maynard's and solve for the new equilibrium number of customers.

(e) Use a different color ink to draw a new line representing the equation that changed. How many additional customers did the new steady

customer attract? _____

(f) Suppose that everyone bases expectations about tonight's attendance on last night's attendance and that last night's attendance is public knowledge. Then $X_t = Y_{t-1}$, where X_t is expected attendance on day t and Y_{t_1} is actual attendance on day $t - 1$. At any time t, $Y_t = 10 + 3/4X_t$. Suppose that on the first night that Maynard's is open, attendance is 20.

What will be attendance on the second night? _____

(g) What will be the attendance on the third night? _____

_____

(h) Attendance will tend toward some limiting value. What is it? _____

_____

27.2 (20) Yogi's Bar and Grill is frequented by unsociable types who hate crowds. If Yogi's regular customers expect that the crowd at Yogi's will be X, then the number of people who show up at Yogi's, Y, will be the larger of the two numbers, $120 - 2X$ and 0. Thus $Y = \max\{120 - 2X, 0\}$.

(a) Solve for equilibrium attendance at Yogi's. Draw a diagram depicting equilibrium on the axes below.

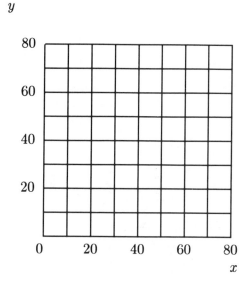

(b) Suppose that people expect the number of customers on any given night to be the same as the previous night's attendance. Suppose that 50 customers show up at Yogi's on the first day of business. How many will

show up on the second day? _____the third day? _____

_____the fourth day? _____the

fifth day? _____the ninety-ninth day? _____

_____the hundredth day? _____

(c) What would you say is wrong with this model if at least some of Yogi's customers have memory spans of more than a day or two?

_____

_____

_____

27.3 (20) Consider the following game matrix.

A game matrix.

		Player B	
		Left	Right
Player A	Top	a, b	c, d
	Bottom	e, f	g, h

(a) If (top, left) is a dominant strategy equilibrium, then we know that

$a >$ _____, $b >$ _____, _____ $> g$, and ___

_____ $> h$.

(b) If (top, left) is a Nash equilibrium, then which of the above inequalities

must be satisfied? _____

(c) If (top, left) is a dominant strategy equilibrium must it be a Nash

equilibrium? _____Why?

_____

27.4 (25) This problem is based on an example developed by the biologist,
John Maynard Smith, to illustrate the uses of game theory in the theory
of evolution. Males of a certain species frequently come into conflict with
other males over the opportunity to mate with females. If a male runs
into a situation of conflict, he has two alternative "strategies." A male
can play "Hawk" in which case he will fight the other male until he either
wins or is badly hurt. Or he can play "Dove," in which case he makes
a display of bravery but retreats if his opponent starts to fight. If an
animal plays Hawk and meets another male who is playing Hawk, they
both are seriously injured in battle. If he is playing Hawk and meets an
animal who is playing Dove, the Hawk gets to mate with the female and
the Dove slinks off to celibate contemplation. If an animal is playing Dove
and meets another Dove, they both strut around for awhile. Eventually
the female either chooses one of them or gets bored and wanders off. The
expected payoffs to each of two males in a single encounter depend on
which strategy each adopts. These payoffs are depicted in the box below.

The Hawk-Dove game.

		Animal B	
		Hawk	Dove
Animal A	Hawk	−5, −5	10, 0
	Bottom	0, 10	4, 4

(a) Now while wandering through the forest, a male will encounter many conflict situations of this type. Suppose that he can not tell in advance whether another animal which he meets will behave like a Hawk or like a Dove. The payoff to adopting either strategy oneself depends on the proportion of the other guys that are Hawks and the proportion that are Doves. For example, suppose all of the other males in the forest act like Doves. Any male that acted like a Hawk would find that his rival

always retreated and would therefore enjoy a payoff of _____

_____on every encounter. If a male acted like a Dove when all other males acted like Doves, he would receive an average payoff of

_____

(b) If strategies which are more profitable tend to be chosen over strategies that are less profitable, explain why there cannot be an equilibrium in which all males act like Doves.

_____

_____

_____

(c) If all the other males acted like Hawks, then a male who adopted the Hawk strategy would be sure to encounter another Hawk and would get a

payoff of _____If instead, this male adopted the Dove strategy, he would again be sure to encounter a Hawk, but his payoff

would be _____

(d) Explain why there could not be an equilibrium where all of the animals acted like Hawks.

_____

_____

_____

(e) Since there is not an equilibrium in which everybody chooses the same strategy, we might ask whether there might be an equilibrium in which some fraction of the males chose the Hawk strategy and the rest chose the Dove strategy. Suppose that the fraction of a large male population that chooses the Hawk strategy is p. Then if one acts like a Hawk, the fraction of one's encounters in which he meets another Hawk is about p and the fraction of one's encounters in which he meets a Dove is about $1 - p$. Therefore the average payoff to being a Hawk when the fraction of Hawks in the population is $p \times (-5) + (1 - p) \times 10 = 10 - 15p$. Similarly, if one acts like a Dove, the probability of meeting a Hawk is about p and the probability of meeting another Dove is about $(1 - p)$. Therefore the average payoff to being a Dove when the proportion of Hawks in the

population is p will be _____

(f) Write an equation that states that when the proportion of the population that acts like Hawks is p, the payoff to Hawks is the same as the

payoffs to Doves. _____

(g) Solve this equation for the value of p such that at this value Hawks do

exactly as well as Doves. This requires that $p =$_____

(h) On the axes below, use blue ink to graph the average payoff to the strategy Dove when the proportion of the male population who are Hawks is p. Use red ink to graph the average payoff to the strategy, Hawk, when the proportion of the male population who are Hawks is p. Label the equilibrium proportion in your diagram by E.

Payoff

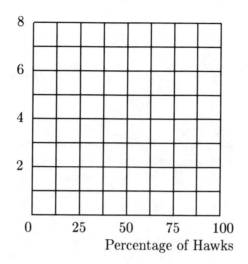

Percentage of Hawks

(i) If the proportion of Hawks is slightly greater than E, which strategy does better? _____ If the proportion of Hawks is slightly less than E, which strategy does better? _____

_____ If the more profitable strategy tends to be adopted more frequently in future plays, then if the strategy proportions are out of equilibrium, will changes tend to move the proportions back towards equilibrium or further away from equilibrium? _____

27.5 (15) Evangeline and Gabriel met at a freshman mixer. They want desperately to meet each other again, but they forgot to exchange names or phone numbers when they met the first time. There are two possible strategies available for each of them. These are Go to the Big Party or Stay Home and Study. They will surely meet if they both go to the party and they will surely not otherwise. The payoff to meeting is 1,000 for each of them. The payoff to not meeting is zero for both of them. The payoffs are described by the matrix below.

Close Encounters of the Second Kind

		Gabriel	
		Go To Party	Stay Home
Evangeline	Go To Party	1000, 1000	0, 0
	Stay Home	0, 0	0, 0

(a) Find all of the dominant strategy equilibria for this game._____

_____

(b) Find all of the pure Nash equilibria for this game._____

_____

(c) Of the pure Nash equilibria that you found, do any of them seem to be "more reasonable" than others? Why or why not?

_____

_____

_____

(d) Let us change the game a little bit. Evangeline and Gabriel are still desperate to find each other. But now there are two parties that they might go to. There is a little party at which they would be sure to meet if they both went there and a huge party where they might never see each other. The expected payoff to each of them is 1,000 if they both go to the little party. Since there is only a 50-50 chance that they would find each other at the huge party, the expected payoff to each of them is only 500. If they go to different parties, the payoff to both of them is zero. The payoff matrix for this game is:

More Close Encounters

| | | Gabriel | |
		Little Party	Big Party
Evangeline	Little Party	1000, 1000	0, 0
	Big Party	0, 0	500, 500

(e) Does this game have a dominant strategy equilibrium?_____

_____What are the two Nash equilibria in pure strategies?

_____

(f) One of the Nash equilibria is Pareto superior to the other. Suppose that each person thought that there was some slight chance that the other would go to the little party. Would that be enough to convince them both

to attend the little party?_____Can you think of any reason why the Pareto superior equilibrium might emerge if both players understand the game matrix, and both know that the other understands it, and each knows that the other knows that he or she understands the game matrix.

_____

_____

_____

27.6 (10) This is a famous game, know to game theorists as "The Battle of the Sexes." The story goes like this. Two people, let us call them Roger and Michelle, although they greatly enjoy each others' company, have very different tastes in entertainment. Roger's tastes run to ladies' mud wrestling, while Michelle prefers the Italian opera. They are planning their entertainment activities for next Saturday night. For each of them, there are two possible actions, go to the wrestling match or go to the opera. Roger would be happiest if both of them went to see mud wrestling. His second choice would be for both of them to go to the opera. Michelle would prefer if both went to the opera. Her second choice would be that they both went to see the mud wrestling. They both think that the worst outcomes would be that they don't agree on where to go. If this happens, they both stay home and sulk.

Battle of the Sexes

		Michelle	
		Wrestling	Opera
Roger	Wrestling	2, 1	0, 0
	Opera	0, 0	1, 2

(a) Is this a zero sum game?_____Does this game have

a dominant strategy equilibrium?_____

(b) Find two Nash equilibria in pure strategies for this game?_____

_____

(c) Find a Nash equilibrium in mixed strategies

_____

27.7 This is another famous two-person game, known to game theorists as "Chicken." Two teenagers in souped up cars drive towards each other at great speed. The first one to swerve out of the road is "chicken." The best thing that can happen to you is that the other guy swerves and you don't. Then you are the hero and the other guy is the chicken. If you both swerve, you are both chickens. If neither swerves, you both end up in the hospital. A payoff matrix for a chicken-type game is the following.

Chicken

		Leroy	
		Swerve	Don't Swerve
Joe Bob	Swerve	1, 1	1, 2
	Don't Swerve	2, 1	0, 0

(a) Does this game have a dominant strategy?_____

_____Does it have any Nash equilibria in pure strategies?_____

_____

(b) Find a Nash equilibrium in mixed strategies for this game._____

_____

27.8 (15) I propose the following game: I flip a coin and while it is in the air you call either heads or tails. If you call the coin correctly, you get to keep the coin. Suppose that the coin always lands on heads, what is the

best strategy for you to pursue? _____

_____

(a) Suppose that the coin is unbalanced and lands on heads 80% of the time and tails 20% of the time. Now what is your best strategy? _____

_____

(b) What if the coin lands 50% of the time on heads and 50% on tails? What is your best strategy? _____

(c) Now, suppose that I am able to choose the type (i.e., the probability that the coin will land on heads) of coin that I will toss, and that you will know my choice. What type of coin should I choose to minimize my losses? _____

(d) What is the Nash mixed strategy equilibrium for this game? (It may help to recognize that a lot of symmetry exists in the game.)

27.9 (20) Ned and Ruth love to play "Hide and Seek." It is a simple game, but it continues to amuse. It goes like this. Ruth hides upstairs or downstairs. Ned can either look upstairs or downstairs but not in both places. If he finds Ruth, Ned gets 1 scoop of ice cream and Ruth gets none. If he does not find Ruth, Ruth gets 1 scoop of ice cream and Ned gets none. Fill in the payoffs in the matrix below.

Hide and Seek

		Ruth	
		upstairs	downstairs
Ned	upstairs		
	downstairs		

(a) Is this a zero sum game? _____What are the Nash equilibria in pure strategies?

_____

(b) Can you find a Nash equilibrium in mixed strategies for this game?

_____

(c) After years of playing this game, Ned and Ruth thought of a way to liven it up a little. Now if Ned finds Ruth upstairs, he gets 2 scoops of ice cream but if he finds her downstairs, he gets 1 scoop. If Ned finds Ruth, she gets no ice cream but if he doesn't find her she gets 1 scoop. Fill in the payoffs in the graph below.

Advanced Hide and Seek

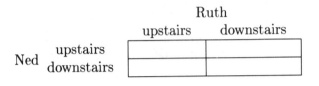

	Ruth	
	upstairs	downstairs
Ned upstairs		
Ned downstairs		

(d) Are there any Nash equilibria in pure strategies? _____

_____ Is there a Nash equilibrium in mixed strategies? _____

27.10 (60) Economic ideas and equilibrium analysis have many fascinating applications in biology. Popular discussions of natural selection and biological "fitness" often take it for granted that animal traits are selected for the "benefit of the species." Modern thinking in biology emphasizes that individuals (or strictly speaking, genes) are the unit of selection. A mutant gene that induces an animal to behave in such a way as to help the species at the expense of the individuals that carry that gene will soon be eliminated, no matter how beneficial that behavior is to the species.

A good illustration is a paper in the *Journal of Theoretical Biology,* 1979, by Brockmann, Grafen, and Dawkins called "Evolutionarily Stable Nesting Strategy in a Digger Wasp." They maintain that natural selection results in behavioral strategies that maximize an individual animal's expected rate of reproduction over the course of its lifetime. According to the authors, "Time is the currency which an animal spends. "

Females of the digger wasp *Sphex ichneumoneus* nest in underground burrows. Some of these wasps dig their own burrows. After she has dug her burrow, a wasp goes out to the fields and hunts katydids. These she stores in her burrow to be used as food for her offspring when they hatch. When she has accumulated several katydids, she lays a single egg in the burrow, closes off the food chamber, and starts the process over again. But digging burrows and catching katydids is time-consuming. An alternative strategy for a female wasp is to sneak into somebody else's burrow while she is out hunting katydids. This happens frequently in digger wasp colonies. A wasp will enter a burrow that has been dug by another wasp and partially stocked with katydids. The invader will start catching katydids, herself, to add to the stock. When the founder and the invader finally meet, they fight. The loser of the fight goes away and never comes back. The winner gets to lay her egg in the nest.

Since some wasps dig their own burrows and some invade burrows begun by others, it is likely that we are observing a biological equilibrium in which each strategy is as effective a way for a wasp to use its time for producing offspring as the other. If one strategy were more effective than the other, then we would expect that a gene that led wasps to behave in the more effective way would prosper at the expense of genes that led them to behave in a less effective way.

We now consider some possible descriptions of equilibrium. These are similar in spirit, but not in detail, to alternatives posed by the authors of the original paper.

Suppose the average nesting episode takes 5 days for a wasp that digs its own burrow and tries to stock it with katydids. Suppose that the average nesting episode takes only 4 days for invaders. Suppose that when they meet, half of the time the founder of the nest wins the fight and half of the time the invader wins. Let D be the number of wasps that dig their own burrows and let I be the number of wasps that invade the burrows of others. The fraction of the digging wasps that are invaded will be about $\frac{5}{4}\frac{I}{D}$. (Assume for the time being that $\frac{5}{4}\frac{I}{D} < 1$.) Half of the diggers who are invaded will win their fight and get to keep their burrows. The fraction of digging wasps who lose their burrows to other wasps is then $\frac{1}{2}\frac{5}{4}\frac{I}{D} = \frac{5}{8}\frac{I}{D}$ Assume also that all of the wasps who are not invaded by other wasps will successfully stock their burrows and lay their eggs.

(a) Then the fraction of the digging wasps who do not lose their burrows

is just _____

Therefore over a period of 40 days, a wasp who dug her own burrow every time would have 8 nesting episodes. Her expected number of

successes would be _____

(b) In 40 days, a wasp who chose to invade every time she had a chance would have time for 10 invasions. Assuming that she is successful on the

average half the time, her expected number of successes would be _____

_____Write an equation that expresses the condition that wasps who always dig their own burrows do exactly as well as wasps who always invade burrows dug by others.

(c) The equation you have just written should contain the expression $\frac{I}{D}$. Solve for the numerical value of $\frac{I}{D}$ that just equates the expected number

of successes for diggers and invaders. The answer is _____

_____

(d) Just when you may have thought you were getting somewhere, we come upon a snag. The problem is that the equilibrium we have found doesn't appear to be stable. To see this, let us draw a diagram. On the axes below, use blue ink to graph the expected number of successes in a 40-day period for wasps that dig their own burrows every time where the number of successes is a function of $\frac{I}{D}$. Use black ink to graph the expected number of successes in a 40-day period for invaders. Notice that this number is the same for all values of $\frac{I}{D}$. Label the point where these two lines cross and notice that this is equilibrium. Just to the right of the crossing, where $\frac{I}{D}$ is just a little bit bigger than the equilibrium

value, which line is higher, the blue or the black? _____

_____At this level of $\frac{I}{D}$, which is the more effective strategy for any

individual wasp? _____Suppose that if one strategy is more effective than the other, the proportion of wasps adopting the more effective one increases. If, after being in equilibrium, the population got joggled just a little to the right of equilibrium, would the proportions of diggers and invaders return toward equilibrium or move further away?

_____

(e) The authors of the study cited above noticed this likely instability and cast around for possible changes in the model that would lead to stability. They observed that an invading wasp does help to stock the burrow with katydids. This may save the founder some time. If founders win their battles often enough and get enough help with katydids from

invaders, it might be that the expected number of eggs that a founder gets
to lay is an increasing rather than a decreasing function of the number
of invaders. On the axes below, show an equilibrium in which digging
one's own burrow is an increasingly effective strategy as $\frac{I}{D}$ increases and
in which the payoff to invading is constant over all ratios of $\frac{I}{D}$. Is this

equilibrium stable? _____

(f) Explain.

_____

_____

_____

(g) The authors of the study investigated whether the average number
of successful nestings per season for a digger was higher or lower if the
digger was invaded more often. The answer turned out to be "lower".
Therefore the story told in the last section, though it might be interesting
for some species that share nests, does not apply to digger wasps. The
authors proposed a more elaborate explanation involving burrows that
were abandoned because of invasions by ants and centipedes. Rather than
pursue that explanation in detail, we will consider a simplified version.
So far, while the payoff to the diggers has depended on $\frac{I}{D}$, the return to
invaders has been independent of this ratio. But suppose invaders have
to spend time searching for a likely burrow to invade. The more invaders
there are relative to diggers, the longer it will take an invader to find
a promising burrow. Furthermore, if there are many invaders relative
to diggers, it becomes probable that more than one invader will enter
some burrows and the invaders may have to compete among themselves

as well as with the original occupant. We can expect, then, that the payoff to invading will also be less profitable as the ratio of diggers to invaders increases. Suppose that a wasp who always chooses to invade other burrows succeeds in producing $\frac{3D}{I}$ viable eggs per 40-day period and that a wasp who always digs her own burrow succeeds in producing $8(1 - \frac{.5I}{D})$ viable eggs per 40-day period. Denote the ratio $\frac{I}{D}$ by x. Write an equation in terms of x that states the condition that wasps who dig their own burrows, will on the average do just as well as wasps who invade

burrows dug by others. _____

(h) Solve this equation for x. This should be a quadratic equation with

two solutions for x. The solutions are _____ and ____

_____

(i) On the axes below, graph the average payoff to diggers and the average payoff to invaders as a function of x. (Hint: One of these lines will be a hyperbola, and the other one will be a straight line.)

(j) in the graph you have just drawn, the lines cross twice, representing two possible equilibrium situations where diggers are just as well off as invaders. Label the equilibrium with the smaller ratio, x, of invaders to diggers with the label A and label the other equilibrium B. If x is just

slightly bigger than A, which kind of wasp does better?_____

_____

(k) If x is just slightly smaller than A, which kind of wasp does better? Assuming that the kind of wasp that is doing better reproduces more than the kind that is doing worse, is there a tendency to move back to

equilibrium after a small deviation from A? _____

(l) If x is just slightly bigger than B, which kind of wasp does better?___

_____

(m) If x is just slightly smaller than B, which kind of wasp does better?

_____

(n) Again assuming that the kind of wasp that is doing better reproduces more than the kind that is doing worse, is there a tendency to move back

to equilibrium after a small deviation from B?_____

Chapter 28

Exchange

28.1 (20) Mutt and Jeff are going to trade corned beef and cabbage. Mutt has 4 pounds of cabbage and no beef, and Jeff has 4 pounds of beef and no cabbage. Mutt is indifferent between corned beef and cabbage. Jeff always consumes corned beef and cabbage in fixed proportions of 1:1.

(a) Illustrate the endowment in the following Edgeworth box. Use blue ink to draw some indifference curves for each person in the Edgeworth box. Use red ink to show the locus of Pareto efficient allocations.

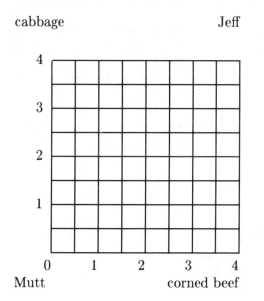

(b) If Mutt and Jeff were to trade using a competitive market, what would be the equilibrium ratio of the price of corned beef to the price of

cabbage? _____What would be the equilibrium con-

sumption bundle for Jeff?_____

28.2 (5) Consider a pure exchange economy with two consumers and two goods. At some given Pareto efficient allocation it is known that both consumers are consuming both goods and that consumer A has a marginal rate of substitution between the two goods of 2. What is consumer B's

marginal rate of substitution between these two goods? _____

28.3 (20) Suppose that Mutt and Jeff have 4 cups of milk and 4 cups of juice to divide between themselves. Each has the same utility function given by $u(m,j) = \max\{m,j\}$, where m is the amount of milk and j is the amount of juice that each has. That is, each of them cares only about the larger of the two amounts of liquid that he has and is indifferent to the liquid of which he has the smaller amount.

(a) Sketch an Edgeworth box for Mutt and Jeff. Use blue ink to show a couple of indifference curves for each. Use red ink to show the locus of Pareto optimal allocations. (Hint: Look for boundary solutions.)

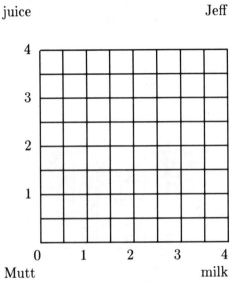

28.4 (20) Al has a utility function given by $u_A(x_A^1, x_A^2) = \min\{x_A^1, x_A^2\}$, and Bob has a utility function given by $u_B(x_B^1, x_B^2) = x_B^1 + x_B^2$. Al initially has 10 units of good 1 and none of good 2. Bob initially has 10 units of good 2 and none of good 1.

(a) In the Edgeworth box below, illustrate a few of each person's indifference curves and the endowment. Mark the endowment with the letter W.

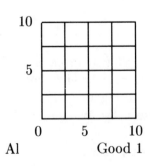

(b) In the same diagram, use a red pencil to draw in the competitive equilibrium budget line. What is p_2/p_1 in equilibrium? _____

_____

28.5 (20) Remember Tommy Twit from Chapter 3? Tommy is happiest when he has 8 cookies and 4 glasses of milk per day and his indifference curves are concentric circles centered around (8,4). Tommy's mother, Mrs. Twit, has strong views on nutrition. She believes that too much of anything is as bad as too little. She believes that the perfect diet for Tommy would be 8 glasses of milk and 2 cookies per day. In her view, a diet is healthier the smaller is the sum of the absolute values of the differences between the amounts of each food consumed and the ideal amounts. For example, if Tommy eats 6 cookies and drinks 6 glasses of milk, Mrs. Twit believes that he has 4 too many cookies and 2 too few glasses of milk, so the sum of the absolute values of the differences from her ideal amounts is 6. On the axes below, plot some other combinations of milk and cookies that Mrs. Twit thinks are no better or worse for Tommy than (6,6).

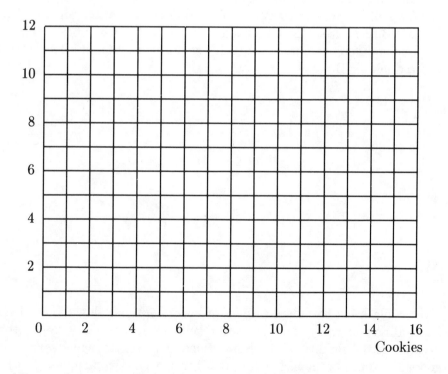

Milk

On the same graph you used for Tommy's indifference curves, use blue ink to draw an indifference curve representing the locus of consumption combinations that Mrs. Twit thinks are exactly as healthy for Tommy as 7 cookies and 8 glasses of milk. Also draw her indifference curve representing consumptions that she thinks are exactly as good for Tommy as 8 cookies and 4 glasses of milk. Use red ink to sketch Tommy's indifference curve running through all combinations that he thinks are exactly as good as 7 cookies and 8 glasses of milk.

(a) On the graph, shade in the area consisting of combinations of cookies and milk that both Tommy and his mother agree are better than 7 cookies and 8 glasses of milk where "better" for Mrs. Twit means she thinks it is healthier, and "better" for Tommy means he likes it better.

(b) Use black ink to sketch the locus of combinations of cookies and milk that have the property that it is impossible to change the combination in such a way as to make Tommy like it better without his mother thinking the change is bad for Tommy. Label the endpoints of this locus A and B.

28.6 (20) Consider a small exchange economy with two consumers, Astrid and Birger, and two commodities, herring and cheese. Astrid's initial endowment is 4 units of herring and 1 unit of cheese. Birger's initial endowment has no herring and 7 units of cheese. Astrid's utility function is $U(H_A, C_A) = H_A C_A$. Birger is a more inflexible person. His utility function is $U(H_B, C_B) = \min\{H_B, C_B\}$. (Here H_A and C_A are the amounts of herring and cheese for Astrid and H_B and C_B are amounts of herring and cheese for Birger.)

(a) Draw an Edgeworth box, showing the initial allocation, and sketching in a few indifference curves. Measure Astrid's consumption from the lower left and Birger's from the upper right. In your Edgeworth box, draw two different indifference curves for each person, using blue ink for Astrid's and red ink for Birger's.

(b) Use black ink to show the locus of Pareto optimal allocations. (Hint: Since Birger is kinky, calculus won't help much here. But notice that because of the rigidity of the proportions in which he demands the two goods, it would be inefficient to give Birger a positive amount of either good if he had less than that amount of the other good. What does that tell you about where the Pareto efficient locus has to be?)

28.7 (30) Dean Foster Z. Interface and Professor J. Fetid Nightsoil exchange bromides and platitudes. Dean Interface's utility function is

$$U_I(B_I, P_I) = B_I + 2\sqrt{P_I}.$$

Professor Nightsoil's utility function is

$$U_N(B_N, P_N) = B_N + 4\sqrt{P_N}.$$

Dean Interface's initial endowment is 6 bromides and 2 platitudes. Professor Nightsoil's initial endowment is 8 platitudes and 4 bromides.

(a) Label the initial endowment E in the following Edgeworth box.

Platitudes

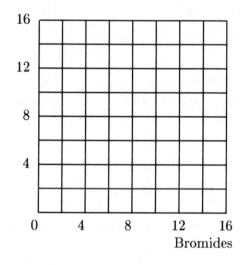

Bromides

(b) If Dean Interface consumes P_I platitudes and B_I bromides, his marginal rate of substitution will be _____. If Professor Nightsoil consumes P_N platitudes and B_N bromides, his marginal rate of substitution will be _____.

(c) On the contract curve, Dean Interface's marginal rate of substitution equals Professor Nightsoil's. Write an equation that states this condition.

_____This equation is especially simple because each person's marginal rate of substitution depends only on his consumption of platitudes and not on his consumption of bromides.

(d) From this equation we see that $P_I/P_N =$ _____at all points on the contract curve. This gives us one equation in the two unknowns P_I and P_N.

(e) But we also know that along the contract curve it must be that $P_I +$

$P_N =$ _____, since the total consumption of platitudes must equal the total endowment of platitudes.

(f) Solving these two equations in two unknowns, we find that everywhere on the contract curve, P_I and P_N are constant and equal to _____

_____and _____.

(g) Therefore the contract curve is a (vertical) (horizontal) (diagonal) line in the Edgeworth box.

(h) Dean Interface has thick gray penciled indifference curves. Professor Nightsoil has red indifference curves. Draw a few of these in the Edgeworth box you made. Use blue ink to show the locus of Pareto optimal points.

(i) Find the competitive equilibrium prices and quantities. You know what the prices have to be at competitive equilibrium because you know what the marginal rates of substitution have to be at every Pareto optimum. _____

28.8 (35) A little exchange economy contains just two consumers, named Ken and Barbie, and two commodities, quiche and wine. Ken's initial endowment is 3 units of quiche and 2 units of wine. Barbie's initial endowment is 1 unit of quiche and 6 units of wine. Ken and Barbie have identical utility functions. We write Ken's utility function as, $U(Q_K, W_K) = Q_K W_K$ and Barbie's utility function as $U(Q_B, C_B) = Q_B W_B$, where Q_K and W_K are the amounts of quiche and wine for Ken and Q_B and W_B are amounts of quiche and wine for Barbie.

(a) Draw an Edgeworth box below, to illustrate this situation. Put wine on the horizontal axis and quiche on the vertical axis. Measure goods for Ken from the lower left corner of the box and goods for Barbie from the upper right corner of the box. (Be sure that you make the length of the box equal to the total supply of wine and the height equal to the total supply of quiche.) Locate the initial allocation in your box and label it W. On the sides of the box, label the quantities of quiche and wine for each of the two consumers in the initial endowment.

(b) Use blue ink to draw an indifference curve for Ken that shows allocations in which her utility is 4. Use red ink to draw an indifference curve for Barbie that shows allocations in which his utility is 6.

(c) Write an expression for each person's marginal rate of substitution between quiche and wine as a function of that person's consumption of

each good. For Ken, _____ For Barbie, _____

_____

(d) At a Pareto optimal allocation in which each person gets some of each good, what must be true of the two people's marginal rates of substitution?

_____

_____

(e) Write an equation that states this condition in terms of the consumptions of each good by each person. On your graph, show the locus of points that are Pareto efficient. (Hint: If two people must each consume two goods in the same proportions as each other, and if together they must consume twice as much wine as quiche, what must those proportions be?)

_____

_____

(f) Is the allocation where Ken gets 3 quiches and 6 containers of wine

Pareto efficient?_____

(g) Calculate each person's marginal rate of substitution at this point.

The MRS for Ken is _____and the MRS for Barbie is

_____

(h) Show that in this example, Ken's marginal rate of substitution between quiche and wine is equal to 2 at all Pareto optimal allocations.

_____

_____

_____

(i) What must be the relative prices of quiche and wine at a competitive

equilibrium? _____

(j) We know that a competitive equilibrium must be Pareto optimal and that in competitive equilibrium, each person's marginal rate of substitution between quiche and wine must be equal to the ratio of the price of quiche to the price of wine. Since demand and supply depend only on *relative* prices, there is a competitive equilibrium in which the price of

wine is 1 and the price of quiche is _____

(k) What must be Ken's consumption bundle in competitive equilibrium?_

_____How about Barbie's consumption bundle?_

_____(Hint: You found competitive equilibrium prices above. You know Ken's initial endowment and you know the equilibrium prices. In equilibrium Ken's income will be the value of her endowment at competitive prices. Knowing her income and the prices, you can compute her demand in competitive equilibrium. Having solved for Ken's consumption and knowing that total consumption by Ken and Barbie equals the sum of their endowments, it should be easy to find Barbie's consumption.)

(l) On the Edgeworth box for Ken and Barbie, draw in the competitive equilibrium allocation and draw Ken's competitive budget line (with black ink).

28.9 (50) This problem combines equilibrium analysis with some of the things you learned in the chapter on intertemporal choice.

On the planet Drongo, there is just one commodity, cake, and two time periods. There are two kinds of creatures, "old" and "young." Old creatures have an income of I units of cake in period 1 and no income in period 2. Young creatures have no income in period 1 and an income of I^* in period 2. There are N_1 old creatures and N_2 young creatures. The consumption bundles of interest to creatures are pairs (c_1, c_2), where c_1 is cake in period 1 and c_2 is cake in period 2. All creatures, old and young, have identical utility functions, representing preferences over cake in the +two periods. This utility function is $U(c_1, c_2) = c_1^a c_2^{1-a}$, where a is a number such that $0 \leq a \leq 1$.

(a) If current cake is taken to be the *numeraire*, (that is, its price is set at 1), write an expression for the present value of a consumption bundle

(c_1, c_2). _____ Write down the present value of income

for old creatures _____ for young creatures_____

_____ The budget line for any creature is determined by the condition that the present value of its consumption bundle equals the present value of its income. Write down this budget equation for old

creatures _____ for young creatures_____

_____.

(b) If the interest rate is r, write down an expression for an old creature's

demand for cake in period 1 _____ and in period 2 ____

_____ Write an expression for a young creature's

demand for cake in period 1 _____, in period 2_____

_____. (Hint: remember that if someone has a budget line $p_1 c_1 + p_2 c_2 = W$ and a utility function of the form proposed above, then that individual's demand function for good 1 is $c_1 = aw/p$ and demand for good 2 is $c_2 = (1 - a)w/p$.) If the interest rate is zero, how

much cake would a young creature choose in each period? _____

_____ For what value of a would it choose the same amount in

each period if the interest rate is zero?_____ If $a = .55$, what would r have to be in order that young creatures would want to consume the same amount in each period.

(c) The total supply of cake in period 1 equals the total cake earnings of all old creatures, since young people earn no cake in this period. There are N_1 old creatures and each earns I units of cake, so this total is $N_1 I$. Similarly, the total supply of cake in period 2 equals the total amount

earned by young creatures. This amount is _____

(d) At the equilibrium interest rate, the total demand of creatures for period 1 cake must equal total supply of period 1 cake, and similarly the demand for period 2 cake must equal supply. If the interest rate is r,

then the demand for period 1 cake by each old creature is _____

_____and the demand for period 1 cake by each young

creature is _____Since there are N_1 old creatures and N_2 young creatures, the total demand for period 1 cake at interest rate r

is _____.

(e) Using the results of the last section, write an equation that sets the demand for period 1 cake equal to the supply. Write a general expression for the equilibrium value of r, given N_1, N_2 I_1, and I_2.

_____

Solve this equation for the special case when $N_1 = N_2$ and $I_1 = I_2$ and $a = 11/21$.

(f) In the special case at the end of the last section, show that the interest rate that equalizes supply and demand for period 1 cake will also equalize supply and demand for period 2 cake.

_____

_____

_____

(g) Why does this happen?

_____

_____

_____

Production

29.1 (30) Tip and Spot finally got into college. Tip has found that he can write term papers at the rate of ten pages per hour and solve workbook problems at the rate of three per hour. Spot on the other hand, can write term papers at the rate of six pages per hour, and solve problems at the rate of two per hour. Like all good students, both Tip and Spot only work six hours per day.

(a) If Tip spends zero hours working on term papers, how many problems can he solve in a day?_____If Tip works two hours on term papers, he can produce _____pages and solve ___ _____workbook problems. If Tip spends six hours working on term papers how many pages can he write?_____

_____

(b) In the graph below draw and label Tip's production possibility curve. Draw Spot's production possibility curve (you might want to use a technique similar to that used for Tip above). If you could hire either Tip or Spot at no charge, which one of them would you employ?_____

_____

Problems

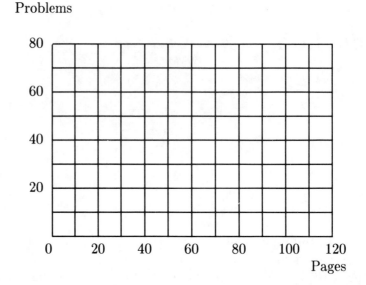

(c) What is Tip's marginal rate of transformation between pages and

problems?_____What is Spot's marginal rate of transformation?_

_____Which of the two has a comparative ad-

vantage in the production of term papers?_____

(d) Tip and Spot decide to work together (gasp!). On the above graph plot their joint production possibility curve. Whenever they need to write

a term paper, (Tip,Spot) always works on the paper until over _____

_____pages are needed, at which time (Tip,Spot) begins to help.

(e) True or False? Since Tip can solve three workbook problems in the time it takes Spot to solve two, Tip should always do the workbook problems. Why?

_____

_____

_____

29.2 Assume a Robinson Crusoe economy. For each of the following situations give either graphical or verbal explanation of the economics involved.

(a) An economy with constant returns to scale where the firm makes positive profits is not a competitive equilibrium.

_____

_____

_____

(b) A production function exhibiting increasing returns to scale is incompatable with a competitive equilibrium.

_____

_____

_____

(c) It is possible to have a competitive equilibrium, even though the firm has increasing returns to scale over some small initial range of production. (Hint: draw a graph that illustrates the possibility.)

(d) (20) Assuming a standard production function (see for example the one depicted in Figure 29.4), for any given competitive equilibrium: too high a wage rate will result in an excess supply of labor, and too low a wage will result in an excess demand for labor.

(e) It is possible to have a competitive equilibrium even with a non-concave production function.

29.3 (30) Recall our friends the Mungoites of Chapter 2. They have a strange two-currency system consisting of Blue Money and Red Money. Originally, there were two prices for everything, a blue money price and a red money price. The blue currency prices are 1 bcu per unit of ambrosia and 1 bcu per unit of bubblegum. The red currency prices are 2 rcu's per unit of ambrosia and 4 rcu's per unit of bubblegum.

(a) Harold has a blue income of 9 and a red income of 24. If he has to pay in *both* currencies for any purchase, draw his budget set in the graph below. (Hint: you answered this question a few months ago.)

Bubblegum

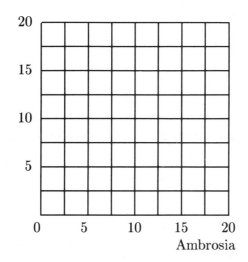

(b) The Free Choice party campaigns on a platform that Mungoites should be allowed to purchase goods at *either* the blue money price or the red money price, whichever they prefer. We want to construct Harold's budget set if this reform is instituted. To begin with, how much bubblegum could Harold consume if he spent all of his blue money and his red money

on bubblegum? _____

(c) How much ambrosia could he consume if he spent all of his blue money

and all of his red money on abrosia? _____

(d) If Harold were spending all of his money of both colors on bubblegum and he decided to purchase a little bit of ambrosia, which currency would

he use?_____

(e) How much ambrosia could he buy before he ran out of that color

money? _____

(f) What would be the slope of this budget line before he ran out of that

kind of money? _____

(g) If Harold were spending all of his money of both colors on ambrosia and he decided to purchase a little bit of bubblegum, which currency

would he use?_____

(h) How much bubblegum could he buy before he ran out of that color

money? _____

(i) What would be the slope of this budget line before he ran out of that

kind of money? _____

(j) Use your answers to the above questions to draw Harold's budget set if he could purchase bubblegum and ambrosia using either currency in the above graph.

Chapter 30

Welfare

30.1 (20) One possible method of determining a social preference relation is the *Borda count* also known as rank order voting. Each voter is asked to rank all of the alternatives. If there are 10 alternatives, you give your first choice a 10, your second choice a 9, and so on. The individual scores for each alternative are then added over all individuals. The total score for an alternative is called its Borda count. The social preference relation is defined so that x is "socially at least as good as" y if x has at least as high a Borda count as y. Suppose that there is only a finite number of alternatives to choose from and that every individual has complete, reflexive, and transitive preferences. For the time being, let us also suppose that individuals are never indifferent between any two different alternatives but always prefer one to the other.

(a) Is the social preference ordering defined in this way complete?_____

_____, reflexive?_____, transitive?__

_____

(b) If everyone prefers x to y, will the Borda count rank x as socially preferred to y? Explain your answer.

_____

_____

_____

(c) Suppose that there are two voters and three candidates, x, y, and z. Suppose that Voter 1 ranks the candidates, x first, z second, and y third. Suppose that Voter 2 ranks the candidates, y first, x second, and z third.

What is the Borda count for x?_____, for y?_____

_____, for z?_____Now suppose that

it is discovered that candidate z once lifted a beagle by the ears. Voter 1, who has rather large ears himself, is appalled and changes his ranking to x first, y second, z third. Voter 2, who picks up his own children by the ears, is favorably impressed and changes his ranking to y first, z second,

x third. Now what is the Borda count for x?_____, for

y?_____, for z?_____

(d) Does the social preference relation defined by the Borda count have the property that social preferences between x and y depend only on how people rank x versus y and not on how they rank other alternatives. Explain.

_____

_____

_____

30.2 (10) Another possible way to make a social ordering is to put the names of all of the alternatives in a hat, draw the names out at random one at a time, and number them by the order in which they are drawn. The proposed social ranking will then be x is "socially preferred to" y if x is drawn before y. Which of the Arrow axioms are satisfied and which are violated by this ranking?

_____

_____

_____

30.3 (20) Suppose the utility possibility frontier for two individuals is given by $U_A + 2U_B = 100$. On the graph below plot the utility frontier.

U_B

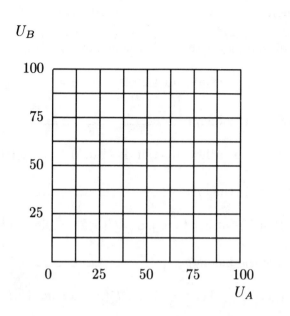

(a) Assume that we want to maximize social welfare. If we have a Nietzschian social welfare function, $W(U_A, U_B) = \max\{U_A, U_B\}$, the maximum will have U_A equal to _____and U_B equal to

_____

(b) If instead we use a Rawlsian criterion, $W(U_A, U_B) = \min\{U_A, U_B\}$,

then the social welfare function is maximized where U_A equals _____

_____and U_B equals _____

(c) Suppose that social welfare is given by $W(U_A, U_B) = U_A^{0.5} U_B^{0.5}$. In

this case, social welfare is maximized where U_A equals _____

_____and U_B is _____. (Hint: you might want to think about the similarities between this maximization problem and the consumer's maximization problem with a Cobb-Douglas utility function.)

(d) Show the three social maxima on the above graph. Use black ink to draw a Nietzschian isowelfare line through the Nietzschian maximum. Use red ink to draw a Rawlsian isowelfare line through the Rawlsian maximum. Use blue ink to draw a Cobb-Douglas isowelfare line through the Cobb-Douglas maximum.

30.4 (20) A parent has two children named A and B and she loves both of them equally. She has a total of \$1,000 to give to them.

(a) The parent's utility function is $U(a, b) = \sqrt{a} + \sqrt{b}$, where a is the amount of money she gives to A and b is the amount of money she gives

to B. How will she choose to divide the money? _____

(b) Suppose that her utility function is $U(a, b) = -\frac{1}{a} - \frac{1}{b}$. How will she

choose to divide the money? _____

(c) Suppose that her utility function is $U(a, b) = \log a + \log b$. How will

she choose to divide the money? _____

(d) Suppose that her utility function is $U(a, b) = \min\{a, b\}$. How will she

choose to divide the money? _____

(e) Suppose that her utility function is $U(a, b) = \max\{a, b\}$. How will she

choose to divide the money? _____

(Hint: In the above three cases, we notice that the parent's problem is to maximize $U(a, b)$ subject to the constraint that $a + b = 1,000$. This is just like the consumer problems we studied earlier. It must be that the parent sets her marginal rate of substitution between a and b equal to one since it costs the same to give money to each child.)

(f) Suppose that her utility function is $U(a, b) = a^2 + b^2$. How will

she choose to divide the money equally between her children._____

_____Explain why she doesn't set her marginal rate of substitution equal to 1 in this case.

_____

_____

_____

30.5 (20) In the previous problem, suppose that A is a much more efficient shopper than B so that A is able to get twice as much consumption goods as B can for every dollar that he spends. Let a be the amount of consumption goods that A gets and b the amount that B gets. We will measure consumption goods so that one unit of consumption goods costs \$1 for A and \$2 for B. Thus the parent's budget constraint is $a + 2b = 1000$.

(a) If the mother's utility function is $U(a, b) = a^2 + b^2$, which child will

get more money?_____Which child will get to consume

more?_____

(b) If the mother's utility function is $U(a, b) = \log a + \log b$, which child will

get more money?_____Which child will get to consume

more?_____

(c) If the mother's utility function is $U(a, b) = -\frac{1}{a} - \frac{1}{b}$, which child will

get more money?_____Which child will get to consume

more?_____

(d) If the mother's utility function is $U(a, b) = \max\{a, b\}$, which child will

get more money?_____Which child will get to consume

more?_____

(e) If the mother's utility function is $U(a, b) = \min\{a, b\}$, which child will

get more money?_____Which child will get to consume

more?_____

30.6 Calc (20) Norton and Ralph have a utility possibility frontier which is given by the following equation, $U_R + U_N^2 = 100$ (where R and N signify Ralph and Norton respectively).

(a) If we set Norton's utility to zero, what is the highest possible utility

Ralph can achieve? _____If we set Ralph's utility to

zero, what is the best Norton can do? _____

(b) Plot the utility possibility frontier on the graph below (put Ralph's utility on the vertical axis).

Ralph's utility

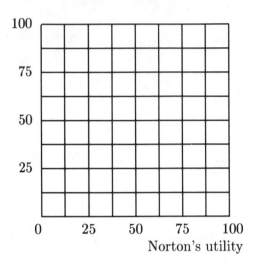

Norton's utility

(c) Derive an equation for the slope of the above utility possibility curve.___

(d) Both Ralph and Norton believe that the ideal allocation is given by maximizing an appropriate social welfare function. Ralph thinks that $U_R = 75, U_N = 5$ is the best distribution of welfare, and presents the maximization solution to a weighted-sum-of-the-utilities social welfare function which confirms this observation. What was Ralph's social welfare function? (Hint: what is the slope of Ralph's social welfare function.)

(e) Norton, on the other hand, believes that $U_R = 19, U_N = 9$ is the best distribution. What is the social welfare function Norton presents?

30.7 (20) Roger and Gordon have identical utility functions, $U(x, y) = x^2 + y^2$. There are 10 units of x and 10 units of y to be divided between them. Roger has blue indifference curves. Gordon has red ones.

(a) Draw an Edgeworth box showing some of their indifference curves and mark the Pareto optimal allocations with black ink. (Hint: Notice that the indifference curves are nonconvex.)

(b) What are the fair allocations in this case? _____

30.8 (20) Paul and David consume apples and oranges. Paul's utility function is $U_P(A_P, O_P) = 2A_P + O_P$ and David's utility function is $U_D(A, O) = A_D + 2O_D$, where A_P and A_D are apple consumption for Paul and David and O_P and O_D are orange consumption for Paul and David. There are a total of 12 apples and 12 oranges to divide between Paul and David. Paul has blue indifference curves. David has red ones. Draw an Edgeworth box showing some of their indifference curves. Mark the Pareto optimal allocations on your graph.

(a) Write one inequality that says that Paul likes his own bundle as well as he likes David's and write another inequality that says that David likes his own bundle as well as he likes Paul's.

_____

_____

(b) Use the fact that at feasible allocations, $A_P + A_D = 12$ and $O_P + O_D = 12$ to eliminate A_D and O_D from the first of these equations. Write the resulting inequality involving only the variables A_P and O_P. Now in your Edgeworth box, use blue ink to shade in all of the allocations such that Paul prefers his own allocation to David's.

(c) Use a procedure similar to that you used above to find the allocations where David prefers his own bundle to Paul's. Describe these points with an inequality and shade them in on your diagram with red ink.

_____

(d) On your Edgeworth box, mark the fair allocations.

30.9 (30) Romeo loves Juliet and Juliet loves Romeo. Besides love, they consume only one good, spaghetti. Romeo likes spaghetti, but he also likes Juliet to be happy and he knows that spaghetti makes her happy. Juliet likes spaghetti, but she also likes Romeo to be happy and she knows that spaghetti makes Romeo happy. Romeo's utility function is $U_R(S_R, S_J) = S_R^a S_J^{1-a}$ and Juliet's utility function is $U_J(S_J, S_R) = S_J^a S_R^{1-a}$, where S_J and S_R are the amount of spaghetti for Romeo and the amount of spaghetti for Juliet respectively. There is a total of 24 units of spaghetti to be divided between Romeo and Juliet.

(a) Suppose that $a = 2/3$. If Romeo got to allocate the 24 units of spaghetti exactly as he wanted to, how much would he give himself?_____

_____How much would he give Juliet?_____

_____(Hint: Notice that this problem is formally just like the choice problem for a consumer with a Cobb-Douglas utility function choosing between two goods with a budget constraint. What is the budget constraint?)

(b) If Juliet got to allocate the spaghetti exactly as she wanted to, how much would she take for herself? _____How much would she give Romeo?_____

(c) What are the Pareto optimal allocations? (Hint: An allocation will not be Pareto optimal if both persons' utility will be increased by a gift from one to the other.)

_____

(d) When we had to allocate two goods between two people, we drew an Edgeworth box with indifference curves in it. When we have just one good to allocate between two people, all we need is an "Edgeworth line" and instead of indifference curves, we will just have indifference dots. Draw an Edgeworth line below. Let the distance from left to right denote spaghetti for Romeo and the distance from right to left denote spaghetti for Juliet.

_____

(e) On the Edgeworth line you drew above, show Romeo's favorite point and Juliet's favorite point.

(f) Suppose that $a = 1/3$. If Romeo got to allocate the spaghetti, how much would he choose for himself? _____If Juliet got to allocate the spaghetti, how much would she choose for herself? _____

_____Draw an Edgeworth line below showing the two people's favorite points and the Pareto optimal points.

(g) When $a = 1/3$, at the Pareto optimal allocations what do Romeo and Juliet disagree about?

_____

_____

_____

30.10 (20) Hatfield and McCoy hate each other but love corn whiskey. Because they hate for each other to be happy, each wants the other to have less whiskey. Hatfield's utility function is $U_H(W_H, W_M) = W_H - W_M^2$ and McCoy's utility function is $U_M(W_M, W_H) = W_M - W_H^2$, where W_M is McCoy's daily whiskey consumption and W_H is Hatfield's daily whiskey consumption (both measured in quarts.) There are 4 quarts of whiskey to be allocated.

(a) If McCoy got to allocate all of the whiskey, how would he allocate it?

_____If Hatfield got to allocate all of the whiskey, how

would he allocate it? _____

(b) If each of them gets 2 quarts of whiskey, what will the utility of each

of them be?_____If a bear spilled 2 quarts of their
whiskey and they divided the remaining 2 quarts equally between them,

what would the utility of each of them be?_____If it is
possible to throw away some of the whiskey, is it Pareto optimal for them

each to consume 2 quarts of whiskey?_____

(c) If it is possible to throw away some whiskey and they must consume

equal amounts of whiskey, how much should they throw away? _____

_____

Chapter 31

Externalities

31.1 (20) Horsehead, Massachusetts, is a picturesque village on a bay which is inhabited by the delectable crustacean, *homarus americanus*, also known as the lobster. Horsehead issues permits to trap these creatures, and is trying to determine how many permits to issue. The economics of the situation are this:

1. It costs $2,000 dollars a month to operate a lobstering boat.
2. If there are x boats operating in Horsehead Bay, the total revenue from the lobster catch per month will be $f(x) = 10x - x^2$, measured in thousands of dollars.

(a) In the graph below, plot the average product, $AP(x) = f(x)/x$, and the marginal product $MP(x) = 10 - 2x$ curves. In the same graph plot the line indicating the cost of operating a boat.

AP,MP

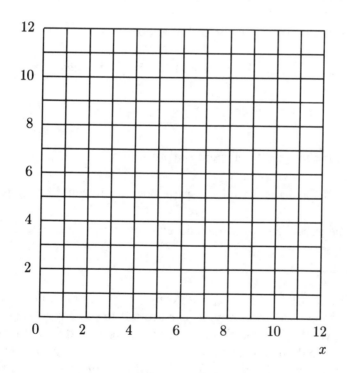

(b) If the permits are free of charge, how many boats will trap lobsters in Horsehead, Massachussets? (Hint: How many boats must enter before there are zero profits?) _____

(c) What number of boats maximizes total profits? _____

_____

(d) If Horsehead, Massachusetts, wants to restrict the number of boats to the number that maximizes total profits, what fee should it charge for

the monthly lobstering permit?_____

31.2 (20) Suppose that a honey farm is located next to an apple orchard, and each acts as a competitive firm. Let the amount of apples produced be measured by A and the amount of honey produced be measured by H. The cost functions of the two firms are given by: $c_H(H) = H^2/100$ and $c_A(A) = A^2/100 - H$. The price of honey is \$2 and the price of apples is \$3. If the firms each operate independently, the equilibrium amount

of honey produced will be _____and the equilibrium

amount of apples produced will be _____

(a) Suppose that the honey and apple firms merged. What would be

the profit maximizing output of honey for the combined firm?_____

_____What would be the profit maximizing amount of

apples? _____

(b) What is the socially efficient output of honey?_____

_____If the firms stayed separate, how much would honey production

have to be subsidized to induce an efficient supply? _____

_____

31.3 (20) In El Carburetor, California, population 1,001, there is not much to do except to drive your car around town. Everybody in town is just like everybody else. While everybody likes to drive, the citizens all complain about the congestion, noise, and pollution caused by traffic. A typical citizen's utility function is $U(m, d, t) = m + 16d - d^2 - 6t/1,000$, where m is the citizen's consumption of Big Macs, d is the number of hours per day that he, himself, drives and t is the total amount of driving (measured in person hours per day) done by all of the other citizens of El Carburetor. Each individual can afford 10 Big Macs. To keep our calculations simple, suppose it costs nothing to drive a car.

(a) If an individual can choose how many hours per day he wants to drive and if he believes that the amount of driving he does won't affect the amount that others drive, how many hours per day will he choose

to drive? _____(Hint: What value of d maximizes $U(m, d, t)$.)

(b) If everybody chooses his best d, then what is the total amount, t,

of driving by other persons? _____(Hint: If everyone drives d hours, then each citizen will find that the total driving by others is $1,000d$.)

(c) What will be the utility of each individual? _____

(d) Suppose that everybody drives 6 hours a day, what will be the utility

level of a typical citizen of El Carburetor?_____

(e) Suppose that the citizens decided to pass a law restricting the total number of hours that any one is allowed to drive. What amount of driving should everyone be allowed if the objective is to maximize the utility of

the typical citizen. _____(Hint: Rewrite the utility function, substituting $1,000d$ for t, and maximize with respect to d.)

(f) Could the same objective be achieved with a tax on driving? _____

_____

(g) If so, how much would the tax have to be per hour of driving? (Hint: This price would have to equal an individual's marginal rate of substitution between driving and Big Macs when he is driving the "right" amount.)

31.4 (30) Tom and Jerry are roommates. Tom likes raucous music, while Jerry likes peace and quiet. Every week, Tom and Jerry each get two dozen chocolate chip cookies sent from home. Draw an Edgeworth box depicting the possible allocations of cookies and hours of music played in their room. On the vertical axis put hours of music. On the horizontal axis, measure cookies for Tom from left to right and cookies for Jerry from right to left. (Notice that both must get the same amount of music, while they can get different amounts of cookies.)

(a) Suppose the dorm's policy is that you must have your roommate's permission to play music. If this is the case, label the initial endowment points in the above diagram. Draw the highest indifference curves Tom and Jerry can possibly achieve without any trade. Shade in all of the allocations that would make both roommates better off than their initial endowments. If trade was allowed, indicate the potential final allocations.

(b) Now suppose the dorm's policy is "rock-n-roll is good for the soul," and thus you don't require your roommate's permission to play music. Complete the steps described above for this new case.

(c) Under the policy of getting your roommate's permission to play music, what is the highest level of utility Jerry can achieve if he is an astute trader? _____What is the highest level Tom can achieve if he is a shrewd trader? _____Under the rock-n-roll policy what are the two utility levels? _____

(d) Which dorm policy would Tom prefer?_____Which policy does Jerry prefer?_____Could it ever happen that this was not the case?_____

(e) Suppose Jerry is indifferent to the amount of music Tom plays (this may be due to a profound hearing loss caused by listening to loud music while in high school). In the diagram below draw the new Edgeworth diagram.

(f) In the above diagram label the following: (1) the endowment point if you need your roommate's permission, (2) the endowment point if you don't need your roommate's permission, (3) the potential endowments which would make both roommates better off under each set of property rights, and (4) the pareto optimal trades under each set of property rights.

(g) Which property right distribution does Tom prefer? _____

_____Which one does Jerry prefer?

_____. What is the intuition behind these results?

_____

_____

_____

31.5 (20) The cottagers on the shores of Lake Invidious are an unsavoury bunch. There are 100 of them and they live in a circle around the lake. Each cottager has two neighbors, one on his right and one on his left. There is only one commodity and they all consume it on their front lawns in full view of their two neighbors. Each cottager likes to consume the commodity, but is very envious of consumption by the neighbor on his left. Curiously, nobody cares what the neighbor on his right is doing. In fact every consumer has a utility function $U(c, l) = c - l^2$, where c is his own consumption and l is consumption by his neighbor on the left. Suppose that each consumer owns 1 unit of the consumption good and consumes it.

(a) Calculate his utility level._____

(b) Suppose that each consumer consumes only 3/4 of a unit. Will all individuals be better off or worse off? _____

(c) What is the best possible consumption if all are to consume the same amount? _____

(d) Suppose that everybody around the lake is consuming 1 unit, can any two people make themselves both better off either by redistributing consumption between them or by throwing something away?_____

_____

(e) How about a group of three people?_____

(f) How large is the smallest group that could cooperate to benefit all of its members?_____

Public Goods

32.1 (20) Bob and Ray are two hungry economics majors who are sharing an apartment for the year. In a flea market they spot a 25 year old sofa that would look great in their living room.

Bob's utility function for money and sofas is $u_B(S, M_B) = (1+S)M_B$ and Ray's utility function for money and sofas is $u_R(S, M_R) = (2+S)M_R$. In these expressions M_B and M_R are the amounts of money that Bob and Ray have to spend on other goods, $S = 0$ when the sofa is not available, and $S = 1$ when the sofa is available. Bob has W_B dollars to spend, and Ray has W_R dollars.

(a) What is Bob's reservation price for the sofa?_____

(b) What is Ray's reservation price for the sofa?_____

(c) If the sofa costs $10, shade in the combinations of (W_B, W_R) for which buying the sofa is a Pareto improvement over not having it.

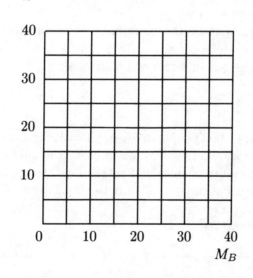

32.2 (10) Cowflop, Wisconsin, has 1,000 people. Every year they have a fireworks show on the fourth of July. The citizens are interested in only two things — drinking milk and watching fireworks. Fireworks cost 1 gallon of milk per unit. People in Cowflop are all pretty much the same.

In fact, they have identical utility functions. The utility function of each citizen i is $U_i(x_i, y) = x_i + \sqrt{y}/20$, where x_i is the number of gallons of milk per year consumed by citizen i and y is the number of units of fireworks exploded in the town's Fourth of July extravaganza. (Private use of fireworks is outlawed)

(a) Solve for each citizen's marginal rate of substitution between fireworks

and milk. _____

(b) Find the Pareto optimal amount of fireworks for Cowflop. _____

_____

32.3 (30) Muskrat, Ontario, has 1,000 people. Citizens of Muskrat consume only one private good, Labatt's ale. There is one public good, the town skating rink. Although they may differ in other respects, inhabitants have the same utility function. This function is $U_i(X_i, Y) = X_i - 100/Y$, where X_i is the number of bottles of Labatt's consumed by citizen i and Y is the size of the town skating rink, measured in square meters. The price of Labatt's ale is \$1 per bottle and the price of the skating rink is \$10 per square meter. Everyone who lives in Muskrat has an income of \$1,000 per year.

(a) Write down an expression for the marginal rate of substitution between skating rink and Labatt's ale for a typical citizen. _____

_____What is the marginal cost of an extra square meter of

skating rink (measured in terms of Labatt's ale.)?_____

_____

(b) Since there are 1,000 people in town, all with the same marginal rate of substitution, you should now be able to write an equation that states the condition that the sum of marginal rates of substitution equals marginal cost. Write this equation and solve it for the Pareto efficient amount of Y.

_____

_____

_____

(c) Suppose that everyone in town pays an equal share of the cost of the skating rink. Total expenditure by the town on its skating rink will be $10Y$. Then the tax bill paid by an individual citizen to pay for the skating rink is $\$10Y/1,000 = \$Y/100$. Every year the citizens of Muskrat vote on how big the skating rink should be. Citizens realize that they will have to pay their share of the cost of the skating rink. Knowing this, a citizen realizes that if the size of the skating rink is Y, then the amount

of Labatt's ale that he will be able to afford is _____

(d) Therefore we can write a voter's budget constraint as $X_i + Y/100 = 1,000$. In order to decide how big a skating rink to vote for, a voter simply solves for the combination of X_i and Y that maximizes his utility subject to his or her budget constraint and votes for that amount of Y. How

much Y is that in our example? _____

(e) If the town supplies a skating rink that is the size demanded by the voters will it be larger than, smaller than, or the same size as the Pareto

optimal rink? _____

(f) Suppose that the Ontario cultural commission decides to promote Canadian culture by subsidizing local skating rinks. The provincial government will pay 50% of the cost of skating rinks in all towns. The costs of this subsidy will be shared by all citizens of the province of Ontario. There are hundreds of towns like Muskrat in Ontario. It is true that to pay for this subsidy, taxes paid to the provincial government will have to be increased. But there are hundreds of towns from which this tax is collected, so that the effect of an increase in expenditures in Muskrat on the taxes its citizens have to pay to the state can be safely neglected. Now, approximately how large a skating rink would citizens of Muskrat

vote for. _____(Hint: Rewrite the budget constraint for individuals observing that local taxes will be only half as large as before and the cost of increasing the size of the rink only half as much as before. Then solve for the utility maximizing combination.)

(g) Does this subsidy promote economic efficiency?_____

_____

32.4 (20) Ten people have dinner together at an expensive restaurant and agree that the total bill will be divided equally among them.

(a) What is the additional cost to any one of them of ordering an appetizer that costs $20.

_____

(b) Explain why this may be an inefficient system.

_____

_____

_____

32.5 (20) Bonnie and Clyde are business partners. Whenever they work, they have to work together. Their only source of income is profit from their partnership. Their total profits per year are $50H$, where H is the number of hours that they work per year. Since they must work together, they both must work the same number of hours. Bonnie's utility function is $U_B(C_B, H) = C_B - .02H^2$ and Clyde's utility function is $U_C(C_C, H) = C_C - .005H^2$, where C_B and C_C are the annual amounts of money spent on consumption for Bonnie and for Clyde and where H is the number of hours that they both work.

(a) If the number of hours that they both work is H, what is Bonnie's marginal rate of substitution between private and public goods (that is, the ratio of her marginal utility of public goods to her marginal utility

of private goods.)?_____What about Clyde's? _____

_____

(b) Write an expression for the sum of their marginal rates of substitution._

_____

(c) What is the marginal cost in terms of public good of reducing their

work effort by one unit?_____

(d) Write an equation that can be solved for the Pareto optimal number of hours for Bonnie and Clyde to work.

_____

(e) Now solve this equation for the Pareto optimal H_____

_____(Hint: This model is formally the same as a model with one public good H and one private good, income.)

32.6 (20) Lucy and Melvin share an apartment. They spend some of their income on private goods like food and clothing that they consume separately and some of their income on public goods like the refrigerator, the household heating, and the rent which they share. Lucy's utility function is $2X_L + Y$ and Melvin's utility function is $X_M Y$, where X_L and X_M are the amounts of money spent on private goods for Lucy and for Melvin and where Y is the amount of money that they spend on public goods. Lucy and Melvin have a total of $8,000 per year between them to spend on private goods for each of them and on public goods.

(a) What is Lucy's marginal rate of substitution between private and

public goods?_____What is Melvin's?_____

_____

(b) Write an expression for the efficiency condition for provision of the

Pareto efficient quantity of the public good._____

(c) Suppose that Melvin and Lucy each spend $2,000 on private goods for themselves and they spend the remaining $4,000 on public goods. Is

this a Pareto efficient outcome?_____

(d) Give an example of another Pareto optimal outcome in which Melvin gets more than $2,000 and Lucy gets less than $2,000 worth of private goods.

_____

Give an example of another Pareto optimum in which Lucy gets more than $2,000.

_____

(e) Describe the set of Pareto optimal allocations.

_____

_____

_____

(f) The Pareto optima that treat Lucy better and Melvin worse will have (more of, less of, the same amount of) public good as the Pareto optimum that treats them equally.

32.7 (20) On the planet Jumpo there are two goods, aerobics lessons and bread. The citizens all have Cobb-Douglas utility functions of the form $U_i(A_i, B_i) = A_i^{1/2} B_i^{1/2}$, where A_i and B_i are i's consumptions of aerobics lessons and bread. Although tastes are all the same, there are two different income groups, the rich and the poor. Each rich creature on Jumpo has an income of 100 and every poor creature has an income of 50 fondas (the currency unit on Jumpo). There are two million poor creatures and one million rich creatures on Jumpo. Bread is sold in the usual way, but aerobics lessons are provided by the state despite the fact that they are private goods. The state gives the same amount of aerobics lessons to every creature on Jumpo. The price of bread is 1 fonda per loaf. The cost to the state of aerobics lessons is 2 fondas per lesson. This cost of the state-provided lessons is paid for by taxes collected from the citizens of Jumpo. The government has no other expenses than providing aerobics lessons and collects no more or less taxes than the amount needed to pay for them. Jumpo is a democracy and the amount of aerobics to be supplied will be determined by majority vote.

(a) Suppose that the cost of the aerobics lessons provided by the state is paid for by making every creature on Jumpo pay an equal amount of taxes. On planets, such as Jumpo, where every creature has exactly one head, such a tax is known as a "head tax". If every citizen of Jumpo gets

20 lessons, how much will be total government expenditures on lessons?_

_____How much taxes will every citizen have to

pay._____If 20 lessons are given, how much will a rich

creature have left to spend on bread after it has paid its taxes?_____

_____How much will a poor creature have left to spend

on bread after it has paid its taxes?_____

(b) More generally, when everybody pays the same amount of taxes, if x lessons are provided by the government to each creature, the total cost

to the government is _____times x and the taxes that

one creature has to pay is _____times x.

(c) Since aerobics lessons are going to be publically provided with everybody getting the same amount and nobody able to get more lessons from another source, each creature faces a choice problem that is formally the same as that faced by a consumer, i, who is trying to maximize a Cobb-Douglas utility function subject to the budget constraint $2A + B = I$, where I is its income. Explain why this is the case.

_____

_____

_____

(d) Suppose that the aerobics lessons are paid for by a head tax and all lessons are provided by the government in equal amounts to everyone.

How many lessons would the rich people prefer to have supplied?_____

_____How many would the poor people prefer to

have supplied?_____(Hint: In each case you just have to solve for the Cobb-Douglas demand with an appropriate budget.)

(e) If the outcome is determined by majority rule, how many aerobics

lessons will be provided? _____How much bread will

the rich get?_____How much bread will the poor get?_

_____

(f) Suppose that aerobics lessons are "privatized" so that no lessons are supplied publically and no taxes are collected. Every creature is allowed to buy as many lessons as it likes and as much bread as it likes. Suppose that the price of bread stays at 1 fonda per unit and the price of lessons stays

at 2 fondas per unit. How many aerobics lessons will the rich get?_____

_____How many will the poor get?_____

_____How much bread will the rich get?_____

_____How much bread will the poor get?_____

(g) Suppose that aerobics lessons remain publically supplied but are paid for by a proportional income tax. The tax rate will be determined so that tax revenue pays for the lessons. Suppose that if A aerobics lessons are offered to each creature on Jumpo, the tax bill for a rich person will be $3A$ fondas and the tax bill for a poor person will be $1.5A$ fondas. If any number, A, of lessons are given each creature, show that with this tax scheme the total tax revenue collected will be equal to the total cost of A lessons.

_____

_____

_____

(h) With the proportional income tax scheme discussed above, what budget constraint would a rich person consider in deciding how many aerobics

lessons to vote for?_____What is the relevant budget

constraint for a poor creature?_____With these tax

rates, how many aerobics lessons per creature would the rich favor?_____

_____How many would the poor favor?_____

_____What quantity of aerobics lessons per capita would

be chosen under majority rule?_____How much bread

would the rich get?_____How much bread would the

poor get?_____

(i) Calculate the utility of a rich creature under a head tax_____

_____under privatization_____under

a proportional income tax._____(Hint: In each case, solve for the consumption of bread and the consumption of aerobics lessons that a rich person gets and plug these into the utility function.)

Now calculate the utility of each poor creature under the head tax_____

_____, privatization_____, and under the proportional income tax_____. (Express these utilities as square roots rather than calculating out the roots.)

(j) Is privatization Pareto superior to the head tax?_____

_____Is a proportional income tax Pareto superior to the head tax?

_____Is privatization Pareto superior to the proportional income tax? Explain this last answer

_____

_____

_____

ANSWERS

1 The Market

1.2a. Top row: 18, 18, 18, 18, 25, 25, 25, 25. Bottom row: 15, 15, 15, 15, 18, 15, 18, 18.

1.2b. Nothing.

1.4a. E, who is willing to pay only $10 for an apartment would sublet to F, who is willing to pay $18.

1.4b. $18

1.4c. A, B, C, D, F

1.4d. It's the same.

2 The Budget Set

2.2a. $10x_1 + 5x_2 = 40$.

2.2b. 4.

2.2c. 8.

2.2e. $20x_1 + 5x_2 = 40$

2.2f. 2 units.

2.2g. $20x_1 + 5x_2 = 60$.

2.2i. 2; 4.

2.4k. 1.

2.4l. 11.

2.4m. Given the budget constraint you could obtain 5.5 units of each good, which would make you better off.

2.6a. $20W + 80T + 50M = 400$.

2.6c. $20W + 50M = 320$.

2.8a. 0.

2.8b. 5.

2.8c. $6C - 2G = 0$ or equivalently, $6C = 2G$.

2.10a. He can buy $5000/500 = 10$ ads. Each ad is read by 1,000 MBA's and by 300 lawyers. Therefore the number of readings by MBA's is $10 \cdot 1,000 = 10,000$ and the number of readings by lawyers is $10 \cdot 300 = 3,000$.

2.10b. 6,000; 5,000.

2.10c. 8,000; 4,000.

2.10d. No. $M + 2L = 16,000$. 2.

3 Preferences

3.2a. Negative.

3.8a. Goldilocks.

3.8b. Grubs.

3.8c. Grubs verses Goldilocks, then Honey verses the winner.

3.8d. They are not transitive.

3.10a. No.

3.10b. Yes.

3.10c. 15.

3.10d. 2 cheeseburgers for 1 Coke.

4 Utility

4.2a. 12.

4.2b. No.

4.2c. Quasilinear preferences.

4.4a. $u(X,Y) = X + 2Y$, or a monotonic transformation of this.

4.4b. $u(X,Y) = X + Y$, or a monotonic transformation.

4.4c. $u(X,Y) = 2X + 4Y$ would be one example. Any other monotonic transformation would do.

4.4d. An example is the following. Shirley would prefer two 16 ounce cans and no 8 ounce cans to three 8 ounce cans and no 16 ounce cans. Lorraine would prefer three 8 ounce cans and no 16 ounce cans to two 16 ounce cans. Of course there are many other possible examples.

4.6c. Yes.

4.6d. Yes.

4.6e. There is no difference between their indifference curves.

4.6f. Their utility functions only differ by a monotonic transformation.

4.8b. 12.

5 Choice

5.2d. 1 unit of X and 9 units of Y.

5.2e. 1 unit of X and 14 units of Y.

5.4a. Less than 2.

5.4c. No.

5.6b. 60 degrees, $100.

5.6c. $80.

5.6d. $70.

5.6g. August and December.

5.6h. 2.

5.6i. 3.

5.6j. 2 and 3.

5.8a. $(80, 8)$.

6 Demand

6.2a. 8 curds.

6.2b. 16 whey.

6.4b. 5 units.

6.6a. MRS $= -2y/3x$.

6.6b. $-1/3$.

6.6c. $p_x/p_y = 5/20 = 2y/3x$.

6.6d. $5x + 20y = 1,000$.

6.6e.

$$10x + 40y = 2,000$$

$$15x - 40y = 0,$$

therefore, adding the two equations yields

$$25x = 2,000,$$

or $x = 80$, which implies $y = 30$.

6.8a. MRS $= -2(y+2)/3(x+1)$

6.8b. $x_d = 1/5P_x(2I - 3P_x + 4P_y)$, and $y_d = 1/5P_y(3I - 4P_y + 3P_x)$.

6.10a. a/b, $a/2c$, a/d

6.10b. $b/a = 1/2$; $c/2a = 1/2$; $d/a = 1/2$.

6.10c. $a = m/5p_a$, $b = m/5p_b$, $c = 2m/5p_c$, and $d = m/5p_d$.

6.12a. Ale is a substitute for cakes. An increase in the price of ale reduces demand for cakes.

6.12b. $q_c = 120 - 30p_c$

6.12d. $p_c = 4 - q_c/30$, \$3

7 Revealed Preference

7.2a. Bob is better off. He can afford Pierre's bundle and would still have income left to buy more bread or wine.

7.2b. 7.5 units of wine and no bread is one example. This is a bundle that Pierre can afford but does not choose. If Pierre and Bob had the same preferences, we would have a violation of the weak axiom of revealed preference because each can afford, but rejects the other person's bundle.

7.4a.

$$p_h \frac{m}{q_h + q_d} + p_d \frac{m}{q_h + q_d} \leq m.$$

7.4b.

$$q_h \frac{m}{p_h + p_d} + q_d \frac{m}{p_h + p_d} \leq m.$$

7.4c. Only when $p_h + p_d = q_h + q_d$.

7.4d. No.

7.4e. Yes.

7.6b. 60 degrees.

7.6c. 40 degrees.

7.8a. 300; 150.

7.8c. Coupon; you can get more food even when other expenditure is constant.

8 Slutsky Equation

8.2a. 30

8.2b. 35

8.2c. \$75

8.2d. E, C

8.2e. F, C, E, F.

8.2f. An inferior good.

8.4e. All income effect.

9 Buy and Sell

9.6c. $.2m_1 + .1m_2 = 200$, $m_1 + m_2 = 1500$, 1,000

9.6d. 833.33, no, yes

9.6e. \$50; 1,000

9.6f. 833.33; none; -166.66

10 Labor Supply

10.2'. $wL + 50$.

10.2a. 4,500.

10.2b. 5,000.

10.2c. 0.

10.4a. $I + 10R = 1,680$.

10.4c. More.

11 Intertemporal Choice

11.2a. $x/(1.1)^2 = 100 + 55/1.1$ or $x = 181.5$

11.4a. $c_1 + c_2/(1 + r) = m_1 + m_2/(1 + r)$.

11.4b. $1;1/(1 + r);m_1 + m_2/(1 + r)$.

11.4c. $c_1 = .2m_1 + .2m_2/(1 + r)$.

11.4d. $c_2 = .8(1 + r)m_1 + .8m_2$.

11.4e. Decrease; Increase; Increase.

11.6b. Better off.

11.6c. Can't tell.

11.8a. 100; 150; 75.

11.8b. 80.

11.8c. -25%; 25%.

11.10'. She will remain a borrower, and be better off after the change.

11.12a. $c_1 + c_2/(1 + r) = (1 - t)[m_1 + m_2/(1 + r)]$.

11.12b. $c_1 + c_2/(1 + (1 - t)r) = (1 - t)[m_1 + m_2/(1 + (1 - t)r)]$.

11.12c. If he saves X, he will have $c_1 = (1 - t)(m_1 - X)$ left to consume. Solving for X gives: $X = m_1 - c_1/(1 - t)$.

11.12d. $c_1 + c_2/(1 + r) = (1 - t)[m_1 + m_2/(1 + r)]$.

12 Asset Markets

12.2a. The present value of \$50,000 a year for 20 years will be less than a million dollars, since sums of money delivered later will be worth less than if they were delivered now.

12.2b. \$10.

12.2c. \$500,000.

12.2d. \$0.15.

12.2e. \$1.50.

12.2f. \$8.50.

12.2g. $8.50 \times 50,000 = \$425,000$.

12.4a. It has cost $.02x$.

12.4b. The equation is $.02x = 100$.

12.4c. \$5,000.

12.4d. No.

12.6a. Brown should buy municipal bonds.

12.6b. Black should buy ordinary bonds.

12.6c. 0, \$250

12.6d. \$30,000, \$250

12.6e. It would reduce it to zero.

12.6f. They will have to pay 10%.

12.6g. The price of the old bonds will fall until their yield equals 10%.

12.8a. The price of guano delivered to the field must be the present value of \$30. This is $\$27.27 = 30/1.1$.

12.8b. $30/(1.1)^{10} = 11.57$

13 Uncertainty

13.2a. 0, \$20,000, 70.71, 100

13.2b. 122.5, 100, take.

13.2c. \$30,000.

13.2c. The equation is $100 = \frac{1}{2}\sqrt{x}$. The answer is $x = 40,000$.

13.2d. 40,000.

13.2e. 40,000.

13.2f. \$6,715.73

13.4c. The slope is -2.

13.4e. The price is 2.

13.6'. $u = \frac{1}{2}\ln c_r + \frac{1}{2}\ln c_r$.

13.6a. Morgan's utility function is just the natural log of Sam's, so the answer is yes.

13.6b. He will consume 17.5 on the sunny days and 35 on the rainy days. This is the same as Sam's consumption.

13.8a. \$300, \$150.

13.8c. 250, 200.

14 Asset Markets with Uncertainty

14.2a. $r_x = 30x + 10(1 - x)$.

14.2b. $\sigma_x = 10x$.

14.2c. The budget line is $r_x = 2\sigma_x + 10$.

14.2e. Since the utility function has the perfect complements form, the optimal solution must involve setting $r_x = 30 - 2\sigma_x$. The budget line requires that $2\sigma_x + 10 = r_x$. Solving these two equations in two unknowns yields $r_x = 20$ and $\sigma_x = 5$.

14.2g. Using the answer to part (a), we want to find an x that solves $20 = r_x = 30x + 10(1 - x)$. The answer is $x = .5$.

14.4a. The expected return is 10%. The standard deviation is $\frac{1}{2}\%$.

14.4b. The expected return is 10%. The standard deviation of the return is zero percent.

14.4c. He should choose the second pasture since it has the same expected return and lower risk.

15 Consumer's Surplus

15.2a. The utility level under the perfect complements utility function is 4.

15.2b. The money metric utility level is minimum amount of income which will make the consumer as well off as at $(4, 4)$. Given the form of the preferences, we know that regardless of the prices, the consumer will purchase the bundle $(4, 4)$ to achieve utility level 4, therefore the money metric utility level is $4 \times 2 + 4 \times 2 = 16$.

15.2c. If the prices change to $(2, 3)$ then the money metric utility is $4 \times 2 + 4 \times 3 = 20$.

15.2d. The utility level of bundle $(5, 8)$ is 5.

15.2e. Given the form of the preferences, we know that the consumer will always choose to buy an equal number of goods when maximizing her utility for a given set of prices, and therefore will buy bundle $(5, 5)$ to achieve utility level 5. The cost of such a bundle, and consequently the level of money metric utility is $20 and $25 under prices of $(2, 2)$ and $(2, 3)$ respectively.

15.4a. In this case, the willingness to pay is the area under the demand curve between $0 \leq b \leq 10$, which is equal to $\frac{1}{2}(20 \times 10)$ (the upper triangle) plus 10×10 (the lower rectangle), or $200. His consumer's surplus is equal to the area of the upper triangle, or alternatively his total benefit minus the cost, which is $200 - 10 \times 10 = 200 - 100 = 100$.

15.4b. At a price of $10 we have seen that Mr. Flintstone has a consumer's surplus of $100. At a price of $14, Mr. Flintstone will demand 8 burgers, yielding a net consumer's surplus of $\frac{1}{2}(16 \times 8) = 64$. The change in consumer's surplus is therefore $-$36. Another way of calculating this is to think about the change in consumer's surplus, that is Mr. Flintstone will, due to the higher price, lose $4 \times 8 = 32$ on the 8 units he will still purchase, and will lose $1/2(4 \times 2) = 4$ of consumer surplus on the 2 units he quit consuming. Thus, the change in his consumer's surplus is $-$36.

15.6a. $15.

15.6b. She does 10 hours of ringing. This is as bad as loosing $20 of income.

15.6c. She does 0 ringing. This is as bad as losing $30 of income.

15.8a. The Consumer would need $m(p_1^t, p_2^t, x_1^s, x_2^s)$.

15.8b. $I = m(p_1^t, p_2^t, x_1^s, x_2^s)/e^s$.

15.8c. It would cost him $p_1^t x_1^s + p_2^t x_2^s$.

15.8d. Less than or equal to.

15.8e. Greater than or equal to.

15.10a. $p = 1 - x$, $x = 1 - p$

15.10b. $1 - p$, $m - p(1 - p)$

15.10c. $u = m + (1 - p)^2/2$

15.10d. The equation is $\frac{(1-p)^2}{2} + m = x - x^2/2 + y$.

15.10e. Just solve the equation given in the last part for m.

15.10f. $(1/2, 11/4)$, $(0, 3)$

15.10g. $1/8$, equivalent

15.10h. $1/8$, compensating, same

15.10i. $1/8$

16 Market

16.2a. $p(q) = 5 - q/2$ if $q < 10$. There is no non-negative price that would get buyers to buy more than 10.

16.2b. $p(q) = 10,000/q^2$

16.2c. $p(q) = 20^{.5}q^{-.5}$

16.2d. $p(q) = (10 - \ln q)/4$

16.4a. $1.

16.4b. $(m - p + 1)2 = m + 1$, $p = (m + 1)/2$

16.6a. $P = 5$

16.6b. $Q = 5$

16.8a. $2p/(p + 1)$

16.8b. At $p = 1$.

16.8c. $R(p) = pq = p/(p+1)^2$. Differentiating and solving gives $p = 1$.

17 Supply and Demand

17.2a. 25 and 175.

17.2b. 40, 190 and 10.

17.2c. The price should be 30.

17.2d. The deadweight loss is $\$225 = 15 \times 30/2$.

17.4a. The equilibrium price is $10.

17.4b. The equilibrium quantity is 10.

17.4c. The demanders pay $20, the suppliers receive 5 and the quantity supplied is 5.

17.6a. The equations are $200 - 4P_S - 2P_L = 100$ and $200 - 3P_L - P_S = 150$.

17.6b. $P_S = 20$, $P_L = 10$.

17.6d. $P_S = 23$, $P_S = 9$.

17.8a. It would rise by about 2% a year.

17.8b. $(400, 400)$.

17.8c. 1.5 percent; 2 percent.

17.8d. It would double if demand didn't change.

17.8e. Since the demand has elasticity of -1, the revenue would stay the same.

17.8f. They would recover to their old levels.

17.10a. The quantity is 3, the price is 9.

17.10b. Solve $18 - 3Q_D = 6 + Q_S - 2$.

17.10c. The quantity is 3.5.

17.10d. The equilibrium supply price is 9.5.

17.10e. It is 7.5.

17.10f. The percent change is $-1.5/9 \approx -17\%$.

17.10g. It will go down by about 8 percent.

17.12a. 20.

17.12b. The long-term demand is 20, the short-term demand is 80.

17.12c. The new supply is 80 units.

17.12d. The equation is $200 - 6p = 80$. The solution is $p = 20$.

17.12e. It will remain constant at $30.

18 Technology

18.2a. 1, remains constant, 1, remains constant, -1, constant.

18.2b. 1, remains constant, 3, remains constant, $-1/3$, constant.

18.4a. $\frac{1}{2}x_1^{-1/2}x_2^{3/2}$

18.4b. Decreases.

18.4c. $3/2x_1^{1/2}x_2^{1/2}$, increases.

18.4d. Increases.

18.4e. $-x_2/3x_1$

18.4f. Increasing.

18.6a. $H = 16 - 4G/5$.

18.8'. $f(tx_1, tx_2, tx_3) = A(tx_1)^a(tx_2)^b(tx_3)^c\ t^{a+b+c}f(x_1, x_2, x_3)$, which implies increasing returns to scale since $a + b + c > 1$.

18.8a. When $a + b + c < 1$. When $a + b + c = 1$.

19 Profit Maximization

19.2'. No, it is not possible. Suppose a firm is earning positive profits at some level of input. By doubling the amount of inputs it can more than double its profits. But then it couldn't be profit maximizing in the first place.

19.4a. 200; 400.

19.4b. 300, 300.

19.4c. An infinite number of apples, and 250 jugs of cider.

19.4e. 200, 0, 1000.

19.6a. $\pi = 400\sqrt{x} - 50x$.

19.6b. It will use 16 units of the input and produce 16 units of the output.

19.6c. Its output and input remain at 16.

19.6d. $\pi = .50 \times (400\sqrt{x} - 50x)$. The profit maximizing amount of output doesn't change.

19.8'. No, it could not produce this combination. If it could, then it would have made more profits by choosing that combination than what it actually did when the price of oil was $40.

20 Cost Functions

20.2b. Constant.

20.2c. 10 units, 5 units

20.2d. It can *only* produce 10 units of output by using the bundle $(10, 5)$, so this is the cheapest way. It will cost $15.

20.2e. $c(w_1, w_2, 10) = 10w_1 + 5w_2$.

20.2f. $(w_1 + w_2/2)y$.

20.4a. 1 hour.

20.4b. 1/2 hour.

20.4c. It would be cheaper to talk.

20.4d. $c(w_1, w_2, h) = \min\{\frac{w_1}{2}, w_2\}h$.

20.4e. $t(w_1, w_2, h) = h$ if $w_2 < w_1/2$ and 0 otherwise

20.4f. $f(w_1, w_2, h) = h/2$ if $w_2 > w_1/2$ and 0 otherwise. (If $w_2 = w_1/2$ then a variety of possibilities result).

20.6a. Decreasing.

20.6b. 100 units; $100w$.

20.6c. y^2, y^2w

20.6d. yw

20.8'. 1/3.

20.10b. Decreasing returns to scale.

20.10c. Use $(16,8)$ which costs $24

20.10d. Use $(25,12.5)$, $37.50

20.10e. $3y^2/2$

20.10f. $(w_1 + w_2/2)y^2$

20.12a. $9,980

20.12b. $c(1, 1, y) = y^2 - 20$.

21 Cost Curves

21.2'. $2s^2$, 10, $2s$, $10/s$, $2s + 10/s$, and $4s$.

21.4a. $MC = \frac{y}{100}$, $AC = \frac{200}{y} + \frac{y}{200}$, $y = 200$, $AC = 2$.

21.4b. $MC = y/250$, $AC = (500/y) + y/500$, 500, 2.

21.4c. $MC = y/500$, $AC = (1,000/y) + y/1,000$, 1,000, 2

21.6a. $Q^{4/3}$.

21.6b. $2Q^{4/3} + 100$.

21.6c. $\frac{8}{3}Q^{1/3}$

21.6d. $2Q^{1/3} + 100/Q$.

21.8'. $y^* = 2$

21.8a. $y^* = 0$

21.10'. $6.

22 Firm Supply

22.2'. $14.

22.4a. $y\bar{c}$, infinite, 0, any amount.

22.4b. The equilibrium price would be $\bar{c}$. The amount of output produced by each firm can not be determined.

22.6a. $2y$, $y + 10/y$.

22.6b. $\sqrt{10}$, $\sqrt{10}$

22.6c. $2\sqrt{10}$, $\sqrt{10}$

22.8a. 8.

22.8b. 8 hours.

22.8c. $p - 1$.

22.8d. $6.

22.8e. $S(p) = 8$ for $p > 6$, 0 otherwise.

23 Industry Supply

23.2a. 14,000; $9.20; 110%

23.2b. $1,909

23.2c. larger; $7.20.

23.4a. $S(p) = p/2$, $Y = np/2$

23.4b. $p^* = 2$

23.4c. Guess at $p^* = 2$. This gives $D(p) = 52 - 2 = n2/2$, which says $n^* = 50$

23.4d. $p^* = 2$, $y^* = 1$

23.4e. $Y^* = 50$

23.4f. Suppose that a new firm did enter in. Then there would be 51 firms, so that the demand equals supply equation would be: $52.5 - p = 51p/2$. Solving gives $p^* = 105/53$. This is less than 2, so the industry cannot support a new firm. The equilibrium number of firms is still $n^* = 50$.

23.4g. Solve $52.5 - p = 50p/2$ to get $p^* = 2.02$ $y^* = 1.01$ Around .02.

23.4h. $n = 51$ $p = 2$

23.4i. $y = 1$ zero

23.6a. profit per bushel $= 5 - .10t$

23.6b. rent $= 5000 - 100t$

23.6c. 50 miles

23.8a. $3.50; 3.5, 2.

23.8b. $3.20; 4.8; 3.

23.10'. $15,000.

24 Market

24.2a. 40 bushels.

24.2b. $y = 10p - 10$.

24.2c. $py - c(y) + p(40 - y)/2 = py - y^2/20 - y + p(40 - y)/2$.

24.2d. $S(p) = 5p - 10$

24.2e. At this price he produces zero output, so he receives the maximum PIK payment of 20.

24.2f. At this price he will want to supply 15 bushels of corn, so he will get a PIK payment of $12.50.

24.2g. His supply curve is $S(p) = 5p - 10$, and his payment is $(40 - y)/2$. Thus the number of bushels he will supply in total is $25 - 2.5p$.

24.2h. Sum the supply curve and the PIK payment to get $TS(p) = 2.5p + 15$.

24.4b. Supply curve to right; increased; decreased; decreased.

25 Monopoly

25.2b. He will sell 50 pies at 50 cents a pie.

25.2d. He should sell 75 pies at 37.5 cents per pie.

25.4a. $10,000; $10,000

25.4c. 250; $15,000; 150; $17,500

25.4d. $2,375,000.

25.4e. -3; -2.33; less elastic.

25.4g. 400; $15,714; decrease by $89,400.

25.6'. In order to sell one additional unit at a lower price, the monopolist must lower her price on all of the units she is currently selling (unless we assume price discrimination). This lowering of the price may nullify the profits from the additional sale.

25.8a. 10,000

25.8b. 1,000; $110

25.8c. $31; $200,000.

25.10a. $2.

25.10b. 3/2

25.12a. 3

25.12b. 2.5

25.12c. 3

25.14b. $p = 10$

25.14c. $50

25.14d. $80

25.14e. 10

25.14f. 10

26 Oligopoly

26.2a. $1200 - q_C^t/2$

26.2b. $1200 - q_C^t/2$, $1200 + q_C^t/2$ $1.25 - q_C^t/3200$

26.2c. $1.25 - q_C^t/1600$

26.2d. 1200, 600, $7/8, $450, $225, Stackleberg

26.2e. No. Carl's profits in Stackleberg equilibrium are larger than in Cournot equilibrium. So if the output when neither knows the other's output this year until after planting time is a Cournot equilibrium, Carl will want Simon to know his output.

26.4a. 4, −2.

26.4b. 48, $4.

26.4c. $y_1 = 24 - y_2/2$; $y_2 = 24 - y_1/2$; 32; 16; $36

26.4e. 24, $52

26.4f. An increase in profits of $35 $(13(51 - 4) - 12(52 - 4))$, and $45 $(3(51 - 4) - 2(52 - 4))$.

26.4g.
$$\max_{y_1}(100 - 2(y_1 + 24 - y_1/2))y_1 - 4y_1$$

24, 12, 36, $28.

26.6b. $p = 45$, $q = 70$, $\pi = \$450$ per day.

26.6c. About $1.6 million.

26.6d. No; losses would be about $900 per day.

26.6e. 60; 2,000

26.6f. $45; 140; $900; No.

26.6g. $100/3; 280/3; $1600/9

26.8a. 50; 150

26.8b. $37.50

26.8c. 25

26.8d. 137.5

26.8e. $937.50

26.8f. 225/2; 175/2

26.8g. $(175/2)^2$

26.10a. $p_B + x^* = p_H + (40 - x^*)$ $20 + (p_H - p_B)/2$ $20 + (p_B - p_H)/2$

26.10b. $(20 + (p_H - p_B)/2)(p_B - 20)$

26.10c. $p_B = 20 + p_H/2$, $p_H = 20 + p_B/2$

26.10d. $p_B = p_H = 40$, 20, $400

26.10e. $49.99, $50.00, Ben, 20, 20, $60 - x$, $60 - x$

26.10f. Those who live midway between them. $400, No.

27 Game Theory

27.2b. 20; 80; 0; 120; 0; 120.

27.2c. Customers would notice that last night's attendance is not a good predictor of tonight's attendance. In fact, if the cycle were to persist, they would notice that attendance is low on odd numbered days and high on even numbered days. Noticing this, they would tend to come on odd numbered days.

27.4a. 10; 4

27.4b. If you know that you are playing opposite a Dove, then the payoff from playing a Hawk will dominate the payoff from playing a Dove. Therefore, everyone playing a Dove is not a Nash equilibrium.

27.4c. −5; 0

27.4d. If everyone plays Hawk, it would be profitable to play Dove.

27.4e. $p \times 0 + (1 - p) \times 4$

27.4f. $4 - 4p = 10 - 15p$

27.4g. 6/11

27.4i. D; H; closer together.

27.6b. No; No; Both go to the opera. Both go to the mud wrestling.

27.6c. Roger chooses wresting with probability 2/3; Michelle choose wrestling with probability 1/3.

27.8'. Always call heads.

27.8a. Always call heads.

27.8b. It doesn't matter—you can either always call heads, always call tails, or randomize your calls, since the expected value will be the same in any of these cases.

27.8c. I should choose a fair coin (probability of landing on heads equal to 50%).

27.8d. The mixed strategy Nash equilibrium for this game is for me to choose a fair coin, and for you to choose to randomize your calls with 50% heads and 50% tails. Suppose I choose a coin which lands more than 50% of the time on heads. Then it would benefit you to always call heads. Now suppose you always call heads. Then it would benefit me to switch to a coin which always produced tails. Similar arguments can be made if the initial coin is more likely to land on tails. The only situation where there is no incentive for either of us to change our choices is when we both randomize 50:50.

27.10a. $1 - \frac{5}{8}\frac{I}{D}$

27.10a. $8 - 5\frac{I}{D}$

27.10b. 5; $8 - 5\frac{I}{D} = 5$

27.10c. $\frac{3}{5}$

27.10d. black; invade; further away

27.10e. stable

27.10g. $\frac{3}{x} = 8 - 5x$

27.10h. 1; 3/5

27.10j. Invaders

27.10k. Diggers

27.10l. Diggers

27.10m. Invaders

27.10n. Yes.

28 Exchange

28.2'. 2

28.4b. $p_2/p_1 = 1$

28.8c. $W_K/Q_K, W_B/Q_B$

28.8d. They must be equal.

28.8e. $W_B/Q_B = W_K/Q_K$

28.8f. Yes.

28.8g. 2 for each.

29 Production

29.2a. If the firm is making positive profits under constant returns to scale, then the profit maximizing firm can increase its profits by expanding output. However, this implies that it must have additional labor, but since the amount of labor is finite, the firm will demand more labor than is forthcoming, and thus there will be excess demand in the labor market.

29.2b. In order to increase its profits the firm can always produce more output (a vertical shift in the isoprofit line). However, in order to produce more output the firm must use more labor, but since labor is finite, the demand for labor by the firm will exceed the supply.

29.2c. Graphical

29.2d. Graphical.

29.2e. Graphical.

30 Welfare

30.2'. The Pareto rule is violated: even if everyone prefers x to y, the social ranking will depend on the order in which they are drawn.

30.4a. $a = b = \$500$

30.4b. $a = b = \$500$

30.4c. $a = b = \$500$

30.4d. $a = b = \$500$

30.4e. $a = \$1,000$, $b = 0$, or vice versa

30.4f. She gives everything to one of the children; this is a corner solution. Her preferences are not convex, her indifference curves are quarter circles.

30.6a. 100; 10

30.6c. $\frac{dU_R}{dU_N} = -2U_N$.

30.6d. $W = U_R + 10U_N$.

30.6e. $W = U_R + 18U_N$.

30.8a. $2A_P + O_P \geq 2A_D + O_D A_D + 2O_D \geq A_P + 2O_P$

30.8b. $2A_P + O_P \geq 18$

30.10a. $W_M = 4$, $W_H = 4$

30.10b. $_2$; 0; no

30.10c. 3 quarts.

31 Externalities

31.2'. 100; 150

31.2a. 150, 150

31.2b. 150; $1 per unit

31.4d. Rock-n-roll, roommate's permission, this is always the case if preferences are convex.

31.4g. Tom would probably prefer the rock-n-roll distribution; however, it is possible that he achieves the same utility under the permission distribution. Jerry would probably be better off if music isn't allowed, although, it is again the case that he could be indifferent to the final allocation under rock-n-roll. The basic intuition is that since Jerry is indifferent to the level of music, he can never be induced to trade some of his food for a reduction in the level of music. Even when Tom does not have the property rights, he may be able to convince Jerry to allow the full amount of music, given that Jerry doesn't care about it. In this case Tom is as well off as in the case of being given full music rights. However, even though Jerry is indifferent, when he has the property rights, he may use them to achieve additional food in exchange for allowing some more music (which Jerry doesn't even care about!).

32 Public Goods

32.6a. $1/2\ X_M/Y$

32.6b. $1/2 + X_M/Y = 1$

32.6d. One example would be Melvin $2500 Lucy $500 Y=$5,000

32.6d. Lucy $5,000 Melvin $1,000 $Y = \$2,000$

32.6e. The allocations that satisfy the two equations $X_M/Y = 1/2$ and $X_L + X_M + Y = \$8,000$.